More Praise for Do Me Twice

"Sonsyrea Tate has shared mile marker thoughts along the way to wholeness. In her new provocative book, Tate challenges religion and relationships. She clears the way to revolutionary, radical forgiveness, but most of all, she forces us to rethink ideas we have taken for granted. Her journey may not be yours, her conclusions may not be your own, but her words and thoughts are well worth your deepest contemplation. It is clear that she is not a woman to be ignored!"

—BISHOP T.D. JAKES, SR.

"Sonsyrea Tate's autobiographical book is a powerful and poignant story of dignity, grace and struggle. Don't miss it!"

—CORNEL WEST, Princeton University on
Little X: Growing up in the Nation of Islam

"This book is Sonsyrea Tate's triumphant shout testifying to a life filled with grace and courage. It is a testimony for anyone who has to fashion her *own* life from the legacy of burdens and encouragement handed down by parents, by culture, by religion and by society. In other words, this is a story about becoming fully human and living life out loud—on your own terms."

—PATRICE GAINES, auth

Do Me Twice

My Life After Islam

A MEMOIR

Do Me Twice

My Life After Islam

A MEMOIR

Sonsyrea Tate

SBI

STREBOR BOOKS

NEW YORK LONDON TORONTO SYDNEY

Strebor Books
P.O. Box 6505
Largo, MD 20792
http://www.streborbooks.com

This book is a work of nonfiction. Some of the names have been changed to protect the privacy of certain individuals.

ISBN-13 978-1-59309-122-4
ISBN-10   1-59309-122-2
LCCN 2007923861

First Strebor Books trade paperback edition August 2007

Cover design: Atria Books
Cover photo: Allison Pasek

10   9   8   7   6   5   4   3   2   1

Manufactured in the United States of America

For information regarding special discounts for bulk purchases, please contact Simon & Schuster Special Sales at 1-800-456-6798 or business@simonandschuster.com

Dedication

This book is dedicated to my wonderful family, who showed me love and taught me patience, perseverance, forgiveness, and faith. It is dedicated to my ancestors, those who passed on before me— Uncle Edward, Uncle Hussein, and my baby brother Halim.

I dedicate this book to my parents, Joseph (Yusef) and Meauvelle (Munira) Tate, for allowing me to appreciate and pursue one of my God-given talents—writing, and showing by example that the talent itself is the reward and that God's grace is sufficient to meet all our needs; and to my siblings—my sisters, Sakinah Tate Mayes, Takiyah Tate, Abena Tate, and Malaika Tate Scott, with whom I grew to appreciate womanness over womanhood; and my brothers, Darren, Furard, Atif, and Hakim, from whom I learned to love men in all their complexities. It is dedicated to my nieces and nephews, Darren, Keyona, Anejel, Eamoni, Anzion, my special angel from God, Janeesa, Zahara, Kiamsha, and Simone.

It also is dedicated to my grandparents, Clifford and Irene Thomas, and Willie Tate; to my aunts and uncles, especially Vernelda Taylor-Harris, Brenda Fuller, Julia Clyburn, Carolyn Drake, Wallace Tate, William Fuller, Sharrief Tate, Avon Tate, Nashid Sadiq, Greg Fuller, Michael Fuller, Tony Fuller, and Kenny Fuller. And to my multitude of cousins, especially Tracie Queen and her siblings I grew up with—Asiyah Sabour, Halima Sabour, Buhira Sabour and Luqman Sabour, and Beyete Tate and Shaheed Tate. Also to my childhood friends LaShawn Fortes and Cynthia Copeland.

And to my wonderful husband, Mike Montgomery, and his parents.

Acknowledgments

I thank God, Most Gracious, Most Merciful, Master of the Day of Judgment, My Provider and My All in All for all the wonderful people present in my life and for those who paved the way for me. I am thankful for Langston Hughes and Mark Twain and August Wilson for their fine example crafting rich dialogue from everyday conversations, and thankful for Zora Neale Hurston and Oprah Winfrey and Marita Golden for showing how bold and trailblazing women can be. I am thankful for Congresswoman Eleanor Holmes Norton, Denise Rolark Barnes, and Aisha Karimah for giving me faith and confidence in understanding and using our power as women without imitating men. And thankful for so many sages along the way—E. Ethelbert Miller, Judege Hassan El-Amin, Imam Yusef Saleem, and Yvonne Lamb. I also am thankful for Patrice Gaines who has been a very special angel in many ways lighting and guiding my literary career. I also thank God for a few newspaper editors who made incredible impressions on my work— Vanessa Gallman, Debbie Simmons, Adrienne Washington, Richard "Dick" Bayer, and Francis Hopkins.

I thank my close friends, who remained encouraging in ways big and small—Warner Coleman, Joseph Burgess, Avis Matthews Davis,

Jackie Woody Brown, Dorothy Bailey, Faye Powell, Teresa Reeder Wiggins, Lolita Rhodes Cusic, and Avis Thomas Lester.

I also am thankful for professors, Dr. Cornel West and Aminah McCloud, whose powerful endorsements of my first book provided necessary confidence for me to continue writing.

I thank God, too, for the vision, courage and fortitude of Zane, who blazed her own trail and invited me and others to do the same. I am thankful also for her sister, Charmaine, whose efforts made this book possible.

To My Literary Ancestors:

My writing hero is not Khalil Gibran, although I love his succinct, very insightful poems that read like wisdom of the ages. I love that he was writing for me a hundred years before I was born, leaving me insights I could use at fourteen years old when arguing for my mother to stop beating us with her belt. "Your children are not your own," he wrote. "They are the sons and daughters of Life's longing for itself. You may give them your love but not your thoughts. They have their own thoughts…" I used that as it became clear that my values would differ from my mother's. She valued family; I valued freedom. "You may house their bodies, but not their souls. For their souls dwell in the house of tomorrow, which you may not visit, not even in your dreams." I thank Gibran, though he is not my highest hero.

My writing hero is not Judy Blume, although her book *Are You There God, It's Me Margaret* offered me companionship when I thought no one else understood how it felt to be alone at thirteen years old.

My hero is not Maya Angelou, either, although I learned several of her powerful poems by heart and offered them to my younger sisters to do the same. "You may write me down in history, with your bitter, twisted lies. You may trod me in the very dirt, but still, like dust, I'll rise."

My hero is not Nikki Giovanni, although her poem "Ego Trippin'" still inspires me way deep down inside. "I designed a pyramid so tough that a star that only glows every one hundred years falls into the center giving divine perfect light. I am bad."

My greatest hero is Zora Neale Hurston, but not just because she preserved important history and culture in her tales of progressive women, and not just because her stories celebrate our African-American history and culture. She's my highest hero because of a line in one of her books, which proved more instructional than all my years in schools. She said, "Two things everybody's got to do fo' theysef. Everybody got to live they own life; and everybody got to get to know God for theysef."

I thank God for each of these literary ancestors' presence in my life.

Introduction

Watching daily news accounts of the war in Iraq—U.S. soldiers shot, burned, chopped to pieces and dragged through the streets—I am reminded of when, as an African-American Muslim child I had been taught to despise America. Islam was the fastest-growing religion in the United States through the 1990s, with most of the growth a result of African Americans converting to the Arab-born religion. I was a part of the first wave of new American Muslims back in the 1970s. The second wave of conversions in the 1990s did not surprise me.

I was three years old when I was first taught in my Muslim school—Muhammad's University of Islam in Washington, D.C.—that America is one of the most wicked and vile nations on earth, one that would someday be destroyed. I was nine when my Muslim school closed down and I entered a public school but was told at home to reject the morning Pledge of Allegiance. I would not stand, place my hand over my heart, and pledge allegiance to the flag of the United States of America. I sat out the Pledge of Allegiance every morning and tried to explain to some of my sixth-grade African-American classmates why they should reject it, too.

As a young woman, I took a writing workshop, and the instructor prompted us by saying, "The story I must tell in order to be transformed is…" I wrote straight from the heart: The story I must tell in order to be transformed is the story of my coming out—out of Islam, out of my parents' house, out of traditional choices, out of conventional thinking—in a way, out of my mind.

I need to tell why, after twenty years of Muslim girl training, I married the Muslim man next door but quickly divorced him after marital rape and his infidelity proved too much for even me, who had been trained to be a stereotypical domesticated little Muslim woman. Free from the marriage, I rolled over men one after the other for some time, and three men in one week did not strike me as being nasty, unhealthy, stupid or any of the things my friends said they were because sex was just something to do to express myself now. Sex for me was no more than stress relief at the end of a long day working in a job I'd dreamed of as a newspaper reporter.

I need to tell how the marital rape freed me from believing my sex organs were God's greatest gift to me, and my greatest gift to the world. I need to tell how I found my humanity. Finding my humanity—serious joy and serious pain—I felt freer to pursue greater passions.

This is a story I need to tell as much as the world suddenly needs to know more about Muslim women behind the veil. People need to know how real and humane individuals who happen to have been born into Islam really are. I was raised as a Muslim girl in the African-American community, but mine really is a universal coming-of-age story.

I began questioning Islam by the time I was twelve, and by twenty-one I was sure Islam was not for me. My transformation out of Islam coincided with my coming of age as an African-American woman, and the story of that transition is a story I feel compelled to share.

This is a story about me as a young woman struggling with a wealth of ideas from my parents' Islam and my grandparents' Christianity—that contradicted each other and wore me out.

There was a time when the world had three main religions, but each nation had mainly two—the one that was dominant and a group of all the others that were discredited or killed. But that time is gone. In those days, people died early from physical sickness, but I need to tell why I died an early spiritual death from too many convictions. I no longer wholeheartedly believed in any religion by the time I was sixteen.

I need to tell my grandmothers that I was not some weak-willed, misguided dupe laid to waste by every man I slept with but didn't marry. That I enjoyed sex, yes I did, and I gave as good as I got and, well, times have changed.

I need to tell of my freedom, my choices—whether to choose my brainchild (a college degree) or my breast child (a heartfelt desire to pursue career) over my biological one, although my Muslim upbringing dictated I should marry young and strive to have ten babies to go to paradise.

I want to tell of my choice to marry into a family of journalists or authors or politicos rather than a traditional family of parents and children. Tell that I did not need to grow up and make a family because I could grow up and begin discovering the one I already had, the one I only thought I knew.

I need to tell the story that shows I'm no forsaken sinner because I turned from Islam. Thank God in America, so-called apostates aren't executed or imprisoned as they are in some Muslim countries. But for years I was afraid Allah would reach down from heaven and strike me dead for leaving Islam. The Quran repeats, "Woe to those who reject faith. We have a hell fire set for them." I want to tell how I came to know that faith and religious doctrines are not one and the same.

I need to tell of my father, raised in the Nation of Islam from the time he was six, who struggled to reconcile his Muslim self with his African-American self and ended up on drugs for the better part of his life. Daddy started out serving as a proud Fruit of Islam "young soldier" in the Nation of Islam and ended up blowing his saxophone on a street corner for a penny, a quarter, a dollar, or ten. So many of the brothers ended up on drugs. So many were left for dead—emotionally and psychologically void of belief in anything much.

I must tell how I finally found peace with some of the Islamic values so deeply instilled in my personality that I could not shake. I found practical uses for some of the skills I learned in Muslim girl training. I grew up to understand some of the rationale behind what seemed like silly superstitious practices. And I finally felt free enough to accept any, some, or none of it.

I tap into discussion groups in cyberspace—debates between Muslims and Christians—among converts out of Islam. I am not surprised at the nastiness of some of the discussions. I have been that bitter, that defensive, that defenseless myself. I log out of the groups with having typed nary a word.

In recent years I have met individuals who grew up Muslim and remained so because the religion worked for them. No surprise there. Though I wonder if some of them simply were too afraid to take a different course. Surprisingly, I also have met Arab-born individuals who were raised Muslim but turned Atheist, intellectualizing their way out of religion altogether. I have thought their thoughts, lived their life, too, for a while.

When the world as I knew it, the Nation of Islam that was my life, crumbled after the death of Elijah Muhammad in 1975, I was only nine, but it was the death of my innocence in many ways.

This is a story I must tell.

As American soldiers toppled the statue of Saddam Hussein, even as Iraqis cheered in the streets, I cringed for the people. Life as they knew it was over, their future uncertain. I wept, especially for the young whose foundation was rocked harder than the ground on which they stood. For the next ten, twenty or thirty years they might be torn between the religion and values of their past and the dubious western culture and values set before them.

Here is the story of my life after Islam. It is a story of cultures clashing—my Islamic upbringing clashing with opportunities I was entitled to as a young African-American, and both of these cultures clashing with my urban ghetto life.

Chapter One
An Abortion of Faith

Ron had been in and out of juvenile detention centers and jail since he was fourteen. The last time he was in, charged with attempted robbery and attempted murder, he converted to Islam and changed his name to Dawud. Of course I didn't know the extent of his lawlessness, nor did I know about the twenty-years-to-life sentence hovering over him when I embraced him.

Ron considered himself my life coach or street teacher in some ways. Yes, he was my first sex partner. His stepfather told him I looked like an uptight little girl and he needed to turn me out. He did that promptly, and I made him marry me shortly after by guilt-tripping him. That wasn't hard to do. He had been in and out of prison already, in and out of court. It's not hard to manipulate the guilt of a man who already feels guilty.

I felt guilty, too, for having sex outside the honored institution of marriage. I knew I wasn't going to stop sneaking around to be with him, screwing him in his mother's car or in their basement because after I got used to it, it got kinda good. I insisted we get married to make the sex legal.

Funny how the guilt from the back of your mind springs forth into actions to punish you and whoever is involved. Ron didn't even have a job when I insisted we get married. Sure, I knew he felt bad about not having a job, not having money to buy me things. I knew because he got teary-eyed and ended up yelling at me when I complained about the cheap card and plastic rose he bought me for our first Valentine's Day. That was the February before we got married in May. We were sitting in the back of his mother's car, him presenting his cheap-ass present to me, and I couldn't hide my disgust.

"This is all?" I said. No yelling or screaming on my part, but my words seemed to cut into him just the same.

"You think I don't want to be able to get you something nice?"

He shoved the back of the car seat, snarled at me, and moved away.

"What ya'll back there fussing about?" his mother said, looking up in her rearview mirror. "Ya'll always fussing, like two old married people. Ya'll might as well go on and get married the way ya'll act."

"I'm just saying, you knew Valentine's Day was coming up. You could've saved up for something," I said, still feeling mousy-like, not realizing the bite in my soft-spoken words.

We rode the rest of the way home in silence and when his mother pulled into her parking space in the lot between our houses, I hopped out and headed for my door.

"Ray-Ray. You just gon' leave?" he said.

"Yeah. I'm tired," I said. What I meant was, *your ass is tired*.

"You're not even gon' take your card?"

"Oh. I forgot."

His mother shook her head.

"Ya'll gon' end up married," she said.

"Sonsyrea! You need to get in here in a hurry," my mother yelled from where she was standing at the back door.

I figured I was in for lecture number 999 because she had already complained about me spending too much time with that young man next door and what was I doing in his mother's car and if he wanted to make proper intentions on me, then he needed to have a talk with my father. I was in no mood for Ma's fantasy world right about now.

"I'm coming," I yelled back to her. "I'll get my folder from you tomorrow," I said to Ron, loud enough for him to know I was speaking for my mother's ears and so he wouldn't hand me his Valentine's gift, which I would have to explain.

The next time his mother picked both of us up from school, she asked me why I was keeping our relationship a secret from my mother.

"If you're ashamed of my son, then he needs to find somebody else to be with," she said. "My son is a good man, and he's gon' take real good care of you one day."

"I'm not supposed to have a boyfriend. So, I can't tell my mother," I explained, slumping in the backseat, Ron sitting up front.

"What you mean you can't have a boyfriend? Shit. Ain't this 'bout your second or third year in college? I heard of being strict, but goddamn. They gotta let you grow up at some time," she said.

"Ma, she don't need to hear all that. She don't like talking about it," Ron said.

"Well shit, ya'll better do something. What you think, you just gon' keep sneaking around? You know they say whatever is done in the dark gon' come out in the light."

That's what I liked about Ms. Bates. She was real. She knew I was sexually active and wasn't nothing wrong with it. I was just a girl growing into my womanhood.

"That's that Mooslem stuff, ain't it?" she continued. "That's why I couldn't be no Mooslem. I mean, some of that stuff is all right, but people got to be who they are. What you 'posed to do, stay a virgin all your life?"

"Until you're married," I mumbled.

"Well, goddamn. What if ya'll ain't ready to get married? My son don't need to be trying to get married right now. Let him finish school and get a job. Shit. You ain't but, what? How old are you, Ray-Ray?"

"Eighteen."

"Well, shit, you too young to be thinking 'bout getting married."

She just went on and on and most of what she said danced around my head without me even hearing it. At least two of her daughters were unwed teenage mothers. So much for her logic. But she sort of made sense in a way. Why should I get married just to have sex when neither one of us really could afford to live up to the roles of husband and wife. Neither one of us could take care of a baby if we had one. My Muslim community insisted young people get married to avoid the sin of sex. Just get married and Allah would make a way. Birth control also was prohibited. So, just get married to avoid the hell fire your raging hormones could cause, and go on and have the babies, having faith that Allah would provide.

None of this shit made any sense, but guilt is a powerful motivator. Guilt and sex together can lead you right into a hell of your own making.

"We're going to have to get married because I ain't goin' to hell for you or nobody," I told Ron one afternoon when we were riding the bus home from campus together.

"That's what you really want to do?" he said. "You know I can't even buy you a ring right now."

"I think we should. Just do it so we won't be sinnin'. If it doesn't work out, we can always get a divorce."

"So, you want to tell your moms and pops we gettin' married?"

"Yeah. I guess I better figure out the best way, though. I don't want to go through all that stuff my mother wants to do, bringing the families together and all that La-La Land stuff."

It was a Friday, so I decided to call my grandparents and tell them I was spending the night at my parents' house so they wouldn't expect me home at a decent hour. I told my mother I was spending the night at my girlfriend's. Instead, I crept around to Ron's house and tapped on the back door to his basement and we made serious love—until we were rudely interrupted.

"Ron, Ma said…Oh! Aw! Ray-Ray?!"

We had started dancing and ended up grinding against the wall until my blouse was up and his pants were down and, whoa, we were making serious love against the wall when his sister rudely interrupted us. I ran to hide under the covers on his bed.

"Won't you knock!" Ron yelled. "Didn't you see my door closed?!"

"Ma told me to come ask you if you was getting up to wash her car in the morning."

"Tell Ma I'll be up there in a little while."

I knew it was only a matter of time before his big-mouth sister began spreading my business around the neighborhood. Innocent little Ray-Ray wasn't so innocent after all and she had seen me screwing her brother with her own eyes. Weeks passed and the wild girls from down the street rolled their eyes at me like, *I know she can't do him like I could.*

April came and I ended up with a secret only two of my friends would know, a secret Ron's mother suspected.

"Ray-Ray, you pregnant?" she blurted out one evening when I was sitting on her porch talking to Ron. "My son's been sleeping a lot. I told him he must've gotten you pregnant. You know men get symptoms, too," she said.

"Ma, she would know if she was pregnant. You don't have to be asking her that," he said.

"No, I ain't pregnant," I said.

"You been sleeping a lot?" he asked.

"No."

I think that was the first lie between us. I had been very tired. Come to think of it, my period was late. When I got home, I checked the small calendar I kept in my drawer with my period days marked. I had not been on since the last part of February and it was now April 5. I didn't even feel like I was about to come on, but my breasts felt a little tender to the touch.

That weekend I would buy a home pregnancy test from Peoples Drug store, and that Monday morning I would call a clinic from a phone booth at school and make an appointment to take an official pregnancy test and get an abortion if necessary. I was thinking fast now.

I didn't feel like seeing Ron this Friday evening, so I went straight home to my grandparents after class. I ate the baked chicken, mashed potatoes and green beans left for me on the stove, then headed straight up to my room to hibernate for the rest of the evening. I kept looking in the mirror. I couldn't help it. My face looked the same. I sat on the edge of my bed facing the mirror, just looking at my face. Then the phone rang.

"Did you come on your period yet?" Shawn asked. She was the only one I'd told.

"No," I said. "Not even a spot."

"What are you gon' do?"

"If I'm pregnant, I won't be for long," I said. "My appointment is week after next."

"You would get an abortion?" she asked, shocked.

"I can't stay pregnant."

She offered to go with me, but I told her I wanted to go alone and not make it a big deal. In my mind, I would keep it a small detail. I slipped up and got pregnant, okay. It didn't have to be the end of the world. I'd slipped up several times and had sex with this guy. Were they really slip-ups though? I'd thought he was "taking me," but I kept going back for more, so I must've wanted it. It was all so confusing, the guilt, the pleasure, the shame, and the pleasure. So confusing. No way was I going to bring a baby into this kind of madness.

"You really shouldn't go through that alone, Ray-Ray," Shawn said sympathetically. "That's what friends are for. You don't think Ron will go with you since you don't want me to go?"

"I'm not telling him," I said. "This is my body, my life. I'm just gon' do what I need to do."

"What time is the appointment? I can meet you there and make sure you get a cab afterwards."

"Really. It's no big deal. They said the procedure only takes about ten minutes. You rest for about fifteen minutes, then they send you home. I'm sure I can call a cab from there," I said.

"Let me know if you change your mind," she said.

"I'll be all right," I assured her. "Let me call you later. I'm sleepy."

When I hung up the phone I stood and turned sideways in the mirror, smoothing my blouse down over my stomach.

If I'm pregnant now, I won't be next week, I thought. The home test said positive, but I wanted the doctors to say for sure.

I was glad I had money in the bank thanks to Uncle Hussein, who had told me to put away a little something every time I got paid. I had enough for the abortion if needed. The next week couldn't pass quickly enough, but before I knew it, I was at the clinic. Stupid people out front carried signs against abortions. Signs showing a dead baby in a jar or a mother pointing a gun at her pregnant womb. Stupid people. They were fools, all of them. Crazy, religious nuts blowing stuff way out of proportion.

I was shocked to find the waiting room full and a whole list of women signed up on a list to get the procedure. When I was called the first time, I had to step into the bathroom and pee in a jar. When I was called the second time, I had to step into another room and talk to a counselor. Yes, I knew what I was doing. No, I didn't need anyone's support. No, I wouldn't be burdened with guilt. I didn't care what the father thought. No, I wouldn't need follow-up therapy. Can we just get this little thing over with? The third time my name was called I went into a room where I was handed a white plastic robe to put on after taking off my clothes and showed what gurney to take. Less than thirty minutes later I was done, handed a small cup of apple juice to replenish my blood sugar, and freed to leave.

I didn't feel any different, except I was relieved that I wasn't pregnant anymore.

I decided I could catch a cab at the curb rather than call one and have to wait twenty minutes or so for it to get there. I didn't pay no never mind to the idiots outside the clinic still carrying the signs. When I got home, I was glad my grandparents weren't there so I could slip up to my room and hibernate for the rest of the day. I just wanted to sleep. I was glad it was over. I was exhausted from having worried two whole weeks. I crawled under my sheets.

When the phone rang later that day it was Shawn again.

"Did you go?"

"Yep."

"Well?"

"I was pregnant. But I'm not anymore."

"So, how do you feel?"

"I'm fine."

"Are you sure? I heard…"

"I'm fine. I'm just glad I caught it in time. They said if I had waited any longer it would've cost a lot more to terminate."

When I hung up the phone and lay alone with my thoughts, I was glad that I had not interrupted my own life, which I was trying to improve through study and career planning, but even more glad that I had not brought another life into this madness. What could I teach a little person? That the world is all fucked up and then you die, like Uncle Hussein? He had been the most righteous person I knew but look how he died. I couldn't teach a little person that you do well and live well, that you follow this religion or that religion and you'll be okay. The world was a very fucked-up place, a place I hated and did not understand. No way would I bring somebody else into it.

Abortion was a sin, they say, but I figured the real abortion in my life had occurred long before I slid up on that gurney to let the doctor snatch a fetus out of my womb. The real abortion had occurred when my fledgling faith in a big god with a capital "G" had been snatched from my soul several years before I arrived at the clinic.

It was nobody's fault, per se. Things just happen. You can say my first abortion happened when I was nine and I learned that my Savior, Elijah Muhammad, was dead. I had believed in him, his religion, and his world and it was snatched right out from my heart. Nobody did it, but it was done. No grown-up said, "Let me reach down and shake this child's faith for the next thirty years." Nobody thought that a child so young thought that much about the religion unfolding around her. Nobody noticed a little soul gasping for air, gasping for faith. What do I believe in now? All that stuff we learned was false? Our prophet was false? We had been worshipping a false God? What the hell did that mean, and what do I do now?

The people around me had been too busy to notice that a little girl still showing up to school every day with homework complete had actually died in some way. Where did my God go? And how could he just up and die like that, leaving my world to fall apart?

Then it happened again. My other saviors died, my personal, real-life ones. Daddy got arrested and Uncle Hussein was dying from multiple sclerosis, his body shriveling and shaking beyond his control. My gods had died—been murdered by fate—long before I stretched my body out on a gurney and sacrificed my own flesh and blood.

My parents' Islam and my grandparents' Christianity prohibited abortion, but I didn't believe in their Islam or their Christianity all that much anymore. Neither had saved my uncle from dying a wretched death from multiple sclerosis, and neither had saved my father from getting arrested and whisked away to jail. I felt overwhelmed with too much religion, too many rules, many of which contradicted each other, if you asked me. Jesus said love everybody, but Christians couldn't see clear to loving their own Muslim family. The Quran said honor and obey your parents, but I guess that didn't apply to grown children who threw their parents' Christianity back at them like a dirty rag. It was all too much. Madness.

With the abortion, I was giving myself a new life. And I decided somewhere around that time that my career would be my new religion. Journalism. That was practical. I could follow the rules of reporting and writing and meeting deadlines and see the result in print the next day. That made sense to me.

I didn't feel guilty about aborting a life because I figured God gives women miscarriages often enough and taking it upon myself to end a pregnancy was no different from allowing stress or something else to cause a natural termination. I'd known about my mother's sister-friends' miscarriages, and my mother gave birth to a set of twins born dead. That all seemed so unnatural and out of order at first. Babies aren't supposed to die in the womb or be born dead. So what if I'd made a decision to terminate a pregnancy on my own.

I felt more powerful after the abortion. I had saved a little person from a messed-up life. It would take almost twenty years for me to learn that although I had terminated a pregnancy, I had not ended a life. Twenty years later, my nephews and nieces struggled with the very same chaos and confusion I'd hoped to spare the next generation. The offspring of my generation's spirits—the good and bad in us—would be born anyway. That's when I realized I was not God and could not give life or take it except according to some divine order beyond my control. In the meantime, for now, I enjoyed a sense of power that comes naturally at nineteen years old.

I felt like with the abortion, I had given new life and a stronger purpose to my career. I had decided to shape my life the way I thought it should go, not according to my mother's Muslim plans for me to marry and become a wife and mother to another houseful of kids, and not according to my grandparents' Christian values of maintaining the status quo of a marriage: two kids, a house, a dog, and a car.

I felt powerful mostly, but doubt would creep up on me from time to time. Did I do the right thing? Am I supposed to get married and have kids? I was confused, so I took the birth control pills religiously to avoid another pregnancy. Then, since I wanted to continue seeing Ron and having sex, I decided to do what might be the right thing. If it didn't work out we could change it.

I didn't tell him about the abortion or the pills. This was still my business. My secret. My life. I was thinking of marrying him to make sex legal not because I had any fantasies about us being together happily ever after. I wasn't thinking that far down the road. I loved him now, and needed him now, that's all.

Over the next twenty years, I would think about the abortion from time to time, like when I was a reporter covering abortion marches or anti-abortion marches, and when I was thirty-five and realizing maybe I was never going to get married again or have kids. But I looked back and thanked God that I had the opportunity to choose a different life for myself. I lived in a country where I did not have to maintain traditions and an ancient—if dubious—morality. By the time I was thirty-five, I realized I had helped raise some of my younger siblings from the time they were born and maybe Ma had those babies for me. I had been a surrogate mother to them and maybe that was enough mothering for me.

Chapter Two
A New Life

R on and I were catching the 96 bus from Mary McCloud Bethune Park to the university one day when I mentioned marriage again.

"We should get married so we don't have to keep sneaking around," I said, giggling like a silly girl, but really being serious.

"Whatever my main apple scrapple wants," he said. "We can go right now. You know they marry Muslims at the Islamic Center."

"I didn't mean right now. I'm just saying instead of sneaking around and, you know, we could do it the right way. That's all I'm saying."

"We can go right now and do it. It's no difference between today or next week or next year. Snap. I can't take care of you like I want. I can't really be the man that a man's supposed to be until I get a job, but I don't like to feel like I gotta sneak around to be with you either."

Since we were already on the bus that could take us to the Islamic Center in Washington, D.C., we decided to go there instead of getting off at the subway to go to our classes. Skipping one class wouldn't hurt us, we agreed. It was a Friday, after all, and we were sure a licensed imam would be there because Friday was the Muslim's holy day. We pulled a string to sound the bell for our stop, and the driver let us off a block away from the immaculate building with an Arab-styled dome and Arabic writing around the building. We sat at a waterfall in the courtyard and removed our shoes before going into the prayer room to perform the obligatory two rakats, a prayer ritual customary for anyone arriving at a mosque. I found a veil at the entrance of the mosque and kept it on after prayer as Ron and I walked hand-in-hand into the mosque office to request a marriage service.

"Um, As-Salaam-Alaikum, ahk," Ron said in our Black English. He said "ahk" also was the Arabic word for "brother." We stood at the counter and Ron did all the talking. "Me and this beautiful sister here want to get married—today. Who do we see about that?"

A man who looked Arab, with tan skin, a white turban, and a beard twisted in a style I hadn't seen before, talked to Ron as if I weren't standing there. He asked if we'd brought two witnesses with us. I really didn't like Arab men. Really didn't understand their culture. I'd heard that women in Muslim countries weren't allowed to drive or work outside the home or inherit their father's wealth, and all my encounters with Arab men confirmed their sexist attitudes. But I spoke up when this man asked about two witnesses.

"We can get a couple of witnesses," I said. "What time do you close?"

I asked to use their office phone, and he obliged.

"Dad! I'm so glad I caught you at home! Are you busy?"

Sometimes Dad took off work Friday afternoons so he could go to Jumah prayers at the mosque where he grew up, Muhammad's Mosque on New Jersey Avenue, which once was one of the Nation of Islam temples. Dad said he was on his way to Jumah, so I figured he could do me a quick favor and kill two birds with one stone.

"Well, can you come make Jumah at the Islamic Center so you can be a witness to my wedding afterward? Me and Ron are getting married. We need two witnesses. If you'll come, we'll only need one more."

Dad told me to put Ron on the phone. Dad talked Ron out of getting married that day, but a couple weeks later, Ron and I had gone to the Justice of the Peace and applied for a marriage license.

I talked my parents into allowing us to have a wedding in our home. Ron and I sat down with a Muslim minister one of my uncles recommended, my parents and Ron's mother were witnesses, and we exchanged vows. My sisters and brothers all refused to participate, considering this some silly shit.

I moved in with Ron's family next door, then, a few months later, moved with them into a public housing project that was worse than the one my family lived in.

Ron tried to teach me the wisdom of the streets. We were in the kitchen cooking together one evening, me chopping onions for potato salad, him dusting chicken parts for frying, when he noticed the way I was standing and told me I was standing wrong.

"People watch the way you stand," he said.

Standing there with flour on his hands, the thick scent of fried chicken grease in the air, how could he be thinking about the outside world?

"Huh?"

"You always wanna stand strong, like you can't be knocked down. Like this," he said, spreading his feet apart, locking his knees back, looking like a city cowboy or something.

"Sure-ya-right," I said, laughing.

"I'm serious," he said. "Serious as a heart attack."

He chopped the back of one of my knees and my whole body buckled.

"See? That's a sucka stance. Shows people you weak, like they can come by and easily knock you down, take whatever you got."

"Ron, ain't nobody watching me like that," I said.

"I'm serious, baby. People watch the way you stand, the way you walk, what you do with your feet when you sittin' on the bus. They can tell whether you confident and might fight back or not."

I had heard bits and pieces of this wisdom growing up. Grandma Thomas had insisted I was too old to be walking pigeon-toed when I was twelve or so, and that I should straighten my shoulders and back. At the Temple, girls were taught to walk with our heads high to show we were dignified. Uncle Umar had once watched me walk from his back door and take a long way around the courtyard to avoid some guys lingering around. He'd called me back and told me never to walk in a way that showed I was avoiding somebody.

"People sense fear," he had told me. "Never show fear. People sense it and they'll pounce on you because they know they can." Uncle Umar knew what he was talking about because he had been to war, the Vietnam War, and he was still like a soldier at home as he commanded people to do things in a certain way. Some of the things I thought I was learning from Ron I really already knew, but when you think your world is falling apart, sometimes you forget what you know and somebody has to remind you. It seemed that my world, as I had known it, was falling apart. I had grown up believing that ours was a strong, solid family because my father went to work every day and my mother stayed home and raised us. This seemed idyllic. But the truth was undeniable since Dad's arrest. Everybody in the neighborhood knew we had problems.

I'd learned domestic skills. I could plan a weekly menu, cook a complete meal with a meat, a starch, a vegetable, and a dessert for a whole family. I could manage to keep the house clean by scheduling certain chores on different days of the week. I could create a household budget, knowing I would need to allocate money for soap, deodorant, and other basic necessities.

Some of the things I'd learned growing up could benefit Ron. He'd figured as much when he saw me snapping string beans for dinner one evening on our front porch. Once we got married, I cooked for him and his family, kept the house clean—or at least our room in the house, and budgeted my little bit of money to make sure we kept groceries and bus fare while he wasn't working.

When his family moved into a house in a worse public housing project, a project where families weren't even trying to buy the house, where families had even less hope, I was glad for some of the things I'd learned growing up. We did not have a washing machine and dryer or a big washtub in a basement or a nearby Laundromat, and I did not know how the families in that neighborhood cleaned their clothes. I was not about to buy a laundry cart and take our clothes five blocks away to the main Laundromat. Somebody I knew might see me and know that my life was going down, down, down.

Ron's sisters had boyfriends with cars who took them to the Laundromat, but I wasn't that close to my sisters-in-law to go with them. And I could never know when Ron's mother would come by the house or let him use her car. She'd moved into an apartment with her boyfriend in the suburbs and had the project house just for her half-grown kids to have a place to finish growing up. I lived there with Ron, his younger sisters Kim and her toddler daughter; Saundra, and her five-year-old daughter; and Nee-Nee, who was only sixteen but was allowed to let her boyfriend move in because he had no place else to go. Although Ron's sisters had babies out of wedlock and were not book smart like me, I respected their survival skills. Kim had barely graduated from high school with my help, and Saundra had dropped out, but I saw them as survivors. They had not had a stable home with at least one parent trying to do right. They had not had regular religion, no one making them study in school.

They had raised themselves and each other. Ron had started stealing groceries for them and himself when he was twelve. I thought it was amazing that they survived and did so while somehow still loving life. They laughed a lot with each other. They fought, fist fights that were not allowed between my siblings and me in our house, but when they made up they had some serious good times.

They'd get money from their boyfriends and throw themselves cookouts in the back of the house. We didn't have a yard or a patio, just concrete out back, but they bought a small hibachi, blasted music from a bedroom window, pulled some folding chairs out the house, and had a cookout. I felt like we were having a picnic in hell, and I admired them for managing to do it. If it wasn't for them, I would have stayed depressed; thinking about how far down in life I seemed to be going.

"Ron, go get that stuck-up so-called wife of yours out the bedroom," I would hear Kim say. "Tell her she ain't too good to party with us. Tell her to bring her ass on down and get some chicken."

They'd be eating from paper plates on their laps, a beer on the ground next to the chair, talking loud. Kids running around having a good time, barbecue smoke wafting around us, music blasting, then it would get even better. One of their cousins would come in with a bushel of steamed, salted crabs, and a card table.

"Ron, where that little Mooslem wife of yours?"

Then Ron would holler up to the window.

"Sonsyrea! What you doing? Come on down here, girl."

I'd go down like I just got up from a nap or claiming I'd been studying.

I thought nothing of Ron drinking beer and smoking weed during the day, then leading me in salat before bedtime. I was used to that hypocrisy from home where I used to smell Dad smoking weed with his band in the evenings, after he'd led us in salat throughout the day. I'd hated the hypocrisy, but learned to live with it. I had learned so much growing up, and now I had to put some of it to good use.

I was glad I knew how to wash my laundry by hand with soap powder in the bathtub, wring it out real good and hang it on the clothesline out back. I also was glad I knew how to stretch meals through the week with a big bag of rice. We could have rice and chicken, rice fried with eggs, rice with leftover beef stew, rice with beans. Rice could fill you up. I'd learned that much from Ma. But I found a new staple I liked even better—Oodles of Noodles. I stirred them with boiled eggs and soy sauce for an oriental meal; with cheese and butter and oregano for an Italian-flavored one; or with leftover barbecue chicken for soul food flavor.

I felt pitiful carrying our groceries home, weighed down on both sides by heavy plastic grocery bags with handles. Noodles were light, but cans of tuna fish, corn, string beans, chili beans, and fruit cocktail were heavy. I couldn't stand waiting around for Ron to go with me or trying to coordinate our schedules so we could go together. When I needed to do something, I just did it.

I didn't feel like I was married. I felt like I had a boyfriend—a playmate, a sex partner—and had made it legal.

The sex was better now since my enjoyment was not tempered by guilt. It was better for me, at least. I don't know if Ron enjoyed the thrill of the chase and the taste of me as forbidden fruit better or not. The games we played before marriage made the sex good—but risky.

Before we were married, I'd sneak over to Ron's house for a hug and a kiss, knowing, in the back of my mind, that it might go further. Deluding myself, I went unprepared to prevent a pregnancy or sexually transmitted disease. Another time, Ron wanted some so bad, he handed me a balloon telling me it was a condom and in the darkness of his bedroom basement, in the heat of all our passion, I didn't know the difference. I had too many sensations going on to know the difference between when he was wearing a condom and when he wasn't.

We'd start with a passionate kiss, chasing each other's tongues. He'd push me against a wall and fondle my clitoris. I'd squirm and clutch at his neck until he moved my hands to his pants for me to pull them off his waist. This particular time, we'd started the kissing on his front porch, then he led me by the hand through the front door and quickly down to his room in the dark basement. It smelled like dirty sweat socks and the Egyptian Musk oil Muslim men sold on the streets. I heard music blasting upstairs, so I knew someone was home. In the basement, he led me to the twin-size, fold-away bed he slept on. I could see the dingy beige sheet wasn't fitted, but that didn't matter. He pushed me onto the bed, on my back, and pulled my jeans off before I could say a word. Before I knew it he was on top of me, sticking his hot, juicy tongue in my ear and I melted. He sucked on my neck and pinched my nipples and I felt like a ball of melting wax.

"Ron, we gotta get the condom," I panted.

"I got this, baby. I can pull out."

"We gotta get a condom, please."

"Stop worrying about it, baby. I got you."

His fingers were groping inside my panties as he sucked my nipple and it was all I could do not to lose it.

"Ron, please!"

I began tensing and resisting.

"I can't get pregnant, Ron, we gotta…"

He jumped up, huffing, and stepped over to his dresser drawer. Finding nothing, he said he'd be right back. He pulled his sweatpants on and rushed through the door, then came back telling me he had a condom.

"Look, baby. I told you I got you," he said, touching the rubber to my chin so I could feel that we had protection. I relaxed and went with the flow again.

It was sooooo good. I clawed at his back and moaned as he held down my hips and worked himself in and out of my vagina. He massaged my breasts and I was lost in a world I'd only heard about before. He kissed my face and ears, then my neck, and I was becoming someone I had not discovered before. He kissed my neck again, and I stopped him.

"Don't put no marks on my neck, Ron," I said. My mother used to frown at girls walking around with red passion marks on their necks. She said it was downright disgusting for young girls to have no shame or discretion. He kissed my neck and rubbed his juicy lips up and down it instead of sucking it. Then he was back inside.

"Ummm, you like that," he said. "You trying to make big daddy come, ain't you? Ain't you. You like it, don't you? You want this dick. You know you like it, don't you. You trying to make me come." Then he pulled out and I was still panting and excited and out of my mind. Then he did something I'd never even heard about. He kissed my clit. That sensation was so intense my heart pounded even faster. I could tell he was smiling. Then he was licking and sucking down there and I thought for sure I'd have a heart attack. It was all I could do to grab the sides of the bed to keep my squeals down. He was laughing and I thought my heart would explode. Then he climbed back up to me, kissing me all the way up to my mouth, pushed himself back inside, and pumped until he came. I didn't know whether to laugh or cry. I didn't know what all I was feeling except that it felt extremely good.

"Ron-oh! Ron, you down there! You got some girl down there while you s'posed to be keeping an eye on Anthony," I heard his mother yelling from the top of the stairs. "I wanna see you. Anthony's up here 'bout to burn the damn house down trying to make hisself some hotdogs and you down there fuckin' some little bitch. Ron! Ron! You'll see the next time you wanna use my damn car!"

His mother was home from work earlier than expected. She had a good government job working at the Department of Energy, and her hours usually were predictable. Ron jumped up and pulled his sweatpants back on, no drawers or nothing, and I jumped up to run out the back door. He dashed upstairs and as I was bending over to get my panties, I saw a balloon next to the bed. A little blue balloon he must've gotten out of his little brother's room. Suddenly I was stiff with fear. I was mad that he'd lied to me, but more than anything, I was afraid that I could've gotten pregnant. Still, my fear was no match for the intense pleasure I was still feeling all over my body. I crept out the back door and was surprised that it was almost dark outside.

By the time we got married, I had taken birth control into my own hands. I would not trust him to use condoms. I would faithfully pop my birth control pills each morning, without telling Ron that I was taking them.

Although Ron would not trick me again with a balloon, he would prove to be at least as deceptive as I was about my birth control pills. He lied about spending nights at my grandmother's house with my brother when, I would later learn, he had been out with his girlfriend who let him use her car. He'd come home early in the morning in Karren's beat-up little brown car just in time to give me a ride to school. He claimed he and Karren were just friends, and I believed him.

We had our good times going to the movies, going out to dinner, then skipping out on the bill because he had no job and the money I earned in my stay-in-school job went to buy groceries and bus fare for both of us and our laundry. Growing up, my friends and I used to laugh at college-educated fools, and now I'd become one. I was book smart, but stupid as hell when it came to real-life matters. I was just having fun. I was discovering parts of myself no book could tell me about. Intense joy, intense pain. I felt more alive than ever before.

We got high together some nights, smoking weed.

In school I could have learned about others' lifestyles. I could've read about somebody like Ron. He was more than a ghetto hoodrat; he was an independent, defiant, self-determined man. I could have learned about other cultures by studying books, but I chose this hands-on real-life internship, without realizing what I was choosing. Twenty years later, my younger sisters, having witnessed this brand of foolishness, decided to get traveling passports and visit other cultures and study others' perspectives in books and group discussions rather than opting for the self-appointed sage from the 'hood.

Even if someone had explained to me a thing or two about the merits of formal education and the value of learning abroad, I might not have believed I could afford such experiences. So, I learned some things the hard way.

Chapter Three
My Man Ron

One night, Madonna's song "Like a Virgin" came on and reminded me of my introduction to sex. It was as if Ron had been an angel—a fallen one, perhaps—sent to help ease me out of my sheltered home. Not that it was sheltered for real, but it was sheltered by the denial of the adults who ignored the criminal behavior simmering for years before it exploded. Ron had introduced me to the joys and pains of sexual relations, and his grandmother, wilder than any woman I had ever met, had introduced me to skin flicks.

We stopped by her apartment one evening in the middle of the week and were invited to join her and her boyfriend in the living room. Grandma was drinking Wild Irish Rose, her boyfriend was rolling joints, and they had a porn tape playing in the VCR. Before I could even get over the shock of a grandmother getting high and having a boyfriend instead of a husband, the porn was tripping me out. I was too excited to feel uncomfortable though. This was like going to Disney World or something, it was so far-fetched from what I was used to. It was a fantasy to believe anyone could be so free—free from others' judgments and expectations.

On the large TV screen, nasty-looking Black women had men sucking on their titties and licking their clits two at a time. Double pleasure?

"Baby, have a beer," Ron said.

I shook my head.

"I don't really like the taste," I explained.

"Aw, girl, have a beer. You gotta loosen up."

"Ron, if the girl said she don't like beer, don't try to force it. Damn. The girl know what she like and don't like. Muthafuckas always want somebody to do what they want 'em to do. The girl told you, shit. She said, 'No, I don't like beer...'"

His grandmother was constantly between the kitchen, living room and her bedroom as Ron and her boyfriend enjoyed getting high and laughing with the video playing in the background, the moaning and groaning affecting mostly me. I liked the tape, found it instructional, and inspiring in a way. It wasn't so much a fantasy about having the attention of two men sexually, but the fantasy of being free from conventional convictions. Sex is never just about sex, and that became clear to me, lost in a porn flick. Pleasure and power is what we come in a body to experience, I thought. In the long run, many years later, I would acquire my own stash of porn flicks to enjoy at my leisure.

I knew what I knew about Ron even if I couldn't explain it to any of my girlfriends. They didn't know what I liked about this snaggle-toothed brother, but to me he was rock solid, a survivor. He'd survived the cruddy streets around us, survived the craziness of his mother's home, and had even survived prison. At nineteen, he was just a year older than me, but in real-living terms, by my estimates, he was much older and wiser, too. He thought I was intelligent. I think he liked the idea of going with the only college girl in our neighborhood. He thought I used big words, though I really didn't; they just sounded big to him because I articulated all the syllables and often spoke in complete sentences. Really, I spoke two separate languages. I spoke the King's language when I entered the white and middle-class Black world uptown at a radio station where I worked an internship, but back home on our turf I killed the King's language like everybody else. Language is important to preserving culture, and we were still carving out our culture as African Americans, distinct with our unique values and dialect, based on our unique abilities and needs.

"Good morning. How are you?" was how I greeted people at work.

"Hiyoudoin?" was the greeting at home.

In fact, you could say in some ways, I spoke a third language. Around my house and in the Muslim community, we greeted each other with "As-Salaam-Alaikum" and interspersed Arabic terms into our conversations whenever we could. I hated that, too. Why must I adopt the language of yet another male-dominated, light-skinned imperialistic culture?

"What are your plans for today?"

"Inshallah (If it be Allah's will), I'll get over to the market today. I tried yesterday, but just had too much to do. Mashallah (So be it, Allah knows best)."

"Did you make wudu (wash) for salat (prayer)?"

"Laa (no)."

To tell you the truth, I hated the Arabic phrases even more than I hated standard English. Neither one were mine. My ancestors hadn't helped create English or Arabic. On the one hand, I realized I needed to be able to speak proper English to communicate with English-speaking people anywhere in the country. And, in a way, I was glad I'd learned Arabic prayers, so I could sort of claim I knew another language, and because I liked the idea of being able to pray with Muslims from anywhere in the world in one language. I thought that was a powerful sound. On the other hand, the prideful part of me resented the English and Arab worlds' languages as an imposition on my world.

For some reason, Ron liked using Muslim words as often as he could. Muslims were a model to him as they were to a lot of African Americans, especially men, who identified with the Arabs' independence and fierce resistance to European imperialism. Here was a small nation that had managed to maintain its independence and its wealth whereas our African nations had not. Our African nations had been primed and poisoned by the white man's Christianity, then plundered for everything—diamonds, oil, and humans. But the Arabs held their own. Ron used Arabic terms and ghetto slang. He sounded slick the way he prefaced everything with "bet" or "you know."

Ron was proud to wear a white knit kufi, a small cap Arab Muslim men wear. His favorite outfit was a red, white and blue, nylon Adidas sweatsuit with a white kufi. That should have told me right there he didn't know who the hell he was—a Black boy in the hood, ready for the basketball court; a patriotic American; or a prayerful Muslim. But at least he was trying on identities for size. I hadn't decided what I would be except a reporter. I wore beige or dark blue khakis, burgundy loafers or tan Hush Puppies, and plain shirts most days. I pulled my hair back in a nondescript ponytail. One of my little sisters teased that I was trying to dress like a preppy white girl, but to me I was just wearing a uniform—neutral colors, just clothes to cover my body with no statement of style.

If Ron was an older man looking for a young girl to shape and mold, I would have seemed prime. But I think I was expecting more from him than he from me. I needed him to save my life. Uncle Hussein, one of my main two soldiers since I could remember, was gone. And worse, he had withered away right before my eyes. Now Dad might be going, too. I didn't think a clear thought about it. At no time did I sit and think, "My men are gone, I better get a replacement." Neither did I think, "Now Ron's a strong man. Maybe he can help me survive this world of mine that's crumbling." I didn't think those thoughts clearly. I was just following my convoluted instincts, which told me to simply survive any way I could. School gave me hope. I felt like I could complete the course work and certainly proceed with my career plans. But what I was putting in my head was doing nothing to fill the hole in my heart. If I had a soul that had once been happy, bright and hopeful, it was now black and dusty as ash. The slightest wind could blow me away right about now. This much I knew. But Ron was a rock. He could hold me down. I could hide under him. I couldn't articulate this, but instinctively, I knew it.

My world had crumbled as surely as if a tornado had blown through and leveled everything in it. God wasn't good or merciful. Uncle Hussein's death taught me that. Five salats and fasting during the month of Ramadan were not society's cure-all, or the cure-all for any family living in a society sick with greed, corruption, confusion, condemnation, racism, exploitation, and a host of other germs that sicken people to the core of their character. The world I'd known as a young child was no more. The tidy little household with a mother who stayed home to raise the kids and a dad who went out to work and children who were mostly smart and obedient was no longer a reality. What was real for me now was not the image we had all agreed to project. What was real for me now was that the weed I smelled coming from our basement, the weed I sometimes stole and smoked myself meant we were as ghetto, as pained, as pressed for money and life as our neighbors.

Ron had accepted his reality a long time ago. His whole family had. His mother drove a sporty black Firebird and stepped out of it looking fly as ever in silk dresses and high-heeled shoes. We all knew that some of her finest silks, leathers, and suede had probably been bought from our neighborhood guys who ripped off high-end department stores. This was not shameful to her and her family. It was not shameful to most of us. It was honorable in a way, a form of taking back what the man took from us. It was a different kind of protest. Ron and his family were rebels of a sort. Of course, my mother thought we were different, that we were better, but I figured we were the same in some essential ways. Again, it wasn't a clear thought I had one day. It was something I knew but could not articulate. The similarities were not evident to the naked eye. On the surface, it appeared that I was from a fairly decent family—parents married, living in a clean home, eating balanced meals, studying hard, worshipping together, that sort of thing; and it appeared Ron was a lost cause—his parents split, his father in and out of jail, his five siblings fathered by three different men, most of his sisters barely passing in school.

The reality was, we all endured the same sorry circumstances, living in subsidized housing, looked-down on by middle-class folks. We all struggled each month to come up with enough money for our basic needs, and we all tried to understand and explain to ourselves and others why we were different from the world beyond our little community. My mother said we were better because we knew better and we controlled our circumstances rather than allowing those circumstances to control us. For instance, we knew that being hungry didn't mean you had to steal to eat; it meant you needed to practice fasting during the month of Ramadan so you could survive long periods without food if you had to. In fact, that's one of the reasons Muslims held themselves above others. We believed we could study and master our spiritual selves so we couldn't be defeated by the physical demands and persecutions facing us all. I understood none of this as a young woman. Even after understanding this when I was older, I could appreciate that on some levels I was—and am—as common as anyone, subject to so many things beyond our control.

Ma—and some of the other mothers in the neighborhood, in

fact—believed Ron and I were a mismatch. That we were the classic good-girl-bad-boy disaster. That he could only bring me down. I knew better. I saw past his badness, past the fact that he had been in and out of juvenile jails since he was twelve when he got caught stealing steaks from the grocery store to feed his sisters dinner. He was a survivor. That was what I needed, all that mattered.

The first time we kissed was sloppy. I'd kissed enough boys to know sloppy when it pressed against my lips. I'd kissed Billy at twelve, and after him Vincent, then Carlos, then Darrell, then Elmer. Ron wasn't the worst, but he sure was no Billy.

It was almost the end of summer, one August evening, just a sliver of moon hanging overhead. Ma thought I was around the corner at my girlfriend Chee-Chee's house, but I was right up under Ma's nose on Ron's porch next door. Ma's window was open, so we talked in whispers.

"My main apple scrapple. Bet. What'd you fix for dinner today?" he whispered, grinning up in my face from where he sat next to me in one of the two dining room chairs he'd brought out for us to sit on.

"Why you always ask me that?"

"'Cause, you know, I know you can cook. Not like the rest of these knucklehead girls around here."

"You seem to like these knuckleheads. I be seeing Bunnys coming out your basement in the mornings."

His eyes smiled the sun.

"Bet. You jealous of Bunnys?" he said, licking his lips, the silkiness of his mustache glistening in a way I hadn't noticed before. "Don't be jealous of her. You gon' be my wife. Bet."

"I ain't getting married," I said.

He was still smiling.

"My apple scrapple. You'd make a good wife. Bet. You already know how to cook. You smart. Not like the rest of these knuckleheads. I be seeing you out here hanging up the laundry. Bet. You take care of your little brothers and sisters. You gon' be my main apple scrapple."

"Stop saying that. You sound so corny," I said.

"You think *I'm* corny?" he said.

Mosquitoes flittered around the porch light behind us, and as Ron began stretching his legs out in front of him and pulling his arms back behind him in a full body stretch, I realized our chairs were set too close. I pushed his arm from in front of me and felt the hardness of his muscle.

"Don't be putting your arm up in my face like that," I said. "And why you got on this hot jacket as hot as it is out here?"

He stood up, stepped back a few steps, and leaned on the wall. I smelled bacon wafting from the other house next door and thought it was way too late for breakfast food. I wasn't wearing a watch, but it had been shortly after ten when I slipped out through the basement door around back and breezed around front to Ron's house to sneak a date right up under my mother's nose.

"Bet. Apple scrapple, come over here with me," he said, extending his arms as if I was going to walk right into them.

I went and stood next to him, holding my hands still behind my back, leaning on the wall. A group of girls descended on the courtyard and I figured it was only a matter of time before they noticed us on the porch and blew my cover. If one of them even called my name out loud, my mother would hear and I'd be busted. I envied their freedom. They wore little shorts shorter and tighter than anything I could wear out the house or thin dresses with no slip underneath or designer sweatsuits with the latest tennis shoes, whatever they felt like on any given day. They mostly dressed to be cute, with hair gelled down or hard curled, thick gold chains layering their necks and huge gold earrings like African queens. Some wore braids with extensions swinging across their backs. They were free to talk loud and talk shit.

"Ya'll notice how Peanut was walking coming out of Greg's house today?" one of them said, laughing loudly.

"Yeah. That bitch was walking like he fucked a hole in her head," another added.

"Aw, bitch. You just mad 'cause he ain't fucking you," came a shrieking voice. That was Nellie. I knew her shrill a mile away.

"Fuck that bitch. Fuck Greg, too. Dirty bitch. They just right for each other, if you ask me. Her ass lunchin'. His ass dirty. They just right for each other, if you ask me."

"Girl, come here. You act like I'm gon' bite you or something," Ron said, pulling my arm to pull me in front of him. He cupped my face in his hands.

"I don't want to get you in trouble. Bet."

His breath smelled like Doublemint, and I was suddenly aware of how unprepared I was for a close encounter. Hadn't brushed my teeth since morning. Hadn't thought about it. I tried to back up, but the next thing I knew, he was shoving his huge tongue down my throat. I pushed back, but he grabbed me around my waist and held tight, pressing his tongue way down my throat. I was looking around for an escape, but couldn't see past his sweaty butter-colored skin. It was a yucky sensation—a bright porch light, the smell of bacon, sticky humidity, and now, up close, his Doublemint gum and one of those Muslim oils the brothers sell on the street. I hated those oils.

"What's that smell," I said, managing to push him off a bit.

He held me in a bear hug.

"Bet. Egyptian Musk. You like it?"

"Not really."

He lifted my chin with the curl of his index finger and kissed my lips softly.

"Bet. Get used to it. You gon' be my main apple scrapple."

"I guess I better get back in the house before my dad gets home and Ma locks the doors up," I said.

Ron watched from the edge of his porch as I walked off, hoping the girls wouldn't notice me in the distance.

"Ron-oh!" one of them yelled.

"Lil' Bits over there wichu?"

I knew they saw me walking away from his porch, but they didn't acknowledge me. They must have figured I had just stopped over there to borrow something or to visit one of his sisters. Then one of them did notice me.

"Ray-Ray?" Nellie shouted. "That you, Ray-Ray? Little Mooslem ass better get your ass in the house and eat a goddam bean pie or something. You know you can't be out here after the sun goes down."

"That ain't her," I heard someone else say.

"Ray-Ray!"

I waved and hurried around the corner of the courtyard to creep in the back door. Headlights were pulling up the alley. I hoped it wasn't Dad. I ran and disappeared down the basement steps. No sooner had I closed the door behind me, than that car screeched to a halt at the gate of our house. I heard the door slam and the gate hastily fling open. Feet scrambled down the back stairs and the banging on the door scared me.

"Joe Tate!" an angry voice boomed.

I was scared silent. I didn't recognize the voice. The man banged so hard I was afraid he'd kick the door in. I said nothing, but he must've heard me scrambling around the drum set, which was part of the band equipment that cluttered the basement. Dad and his band rehearsed there several nights a week, and they often had visitors watching, friends who stopped by to buy weed. I knew men stopped by for other things, too, but I wasn't supposed to know about that. I knocked over a silver-and-white balance scale that shouldn't have been left out on the table. The man banged on the door again, then I heard his feet shuffle up the stairs. Then there was banging on the kitchen door at the back of the house. My heart was racing and I would have been crying; except I was too busy to cry. I flicked on the kitchen light, and as I was searching the kitchen for the large knife I used to dismember fresh chickens, the man continued banging at the back door. I heard Ma coming down the stairs.

"Joe Tate!" the man yelled.

"Sonsyrea, go upstairs," my mother said, bristling past me, going to the back door empty-handed.

I crouched down on the steps, clutching the knife, ready to pounce if Ma opened the door. I would stab the man and keep stabbing until he stopped calling my dad's name.

"Would you stop banging on my door. My children are sleep," my mother said through the closed door.

"Send Joe Tate out here."

"My husband is not home."

"Where is he!"

"My husband is not home. Please get away from my door or I'll have to call the police."

I wished I knew Ron's number. He was right next door. I figured he still had the pistol he'd once given to my brother to protect me.

"I want to see Joe Tate!"

"*Yusef* is not here!"

My mother needed to believe that her husband was the ideal, prayerful, former Nation of Islam man she had married, not the street-savvy musician he was becoming. I was beginning to realize the truth my mother refused to accept—a girl might have to take care of herself in this world. The very man she might expect to protect her, her very own husband, might be the one bringing trouble to her door, and inside her house. I was wishing I could call Ron to my rescue, but some part of me was realizing that as surely as a day found me sitting on a step with a knife to protect my younger siblings, life might call on me in the future to protect myself with no man around.

"Tell Joe that Percy is looking for him!" was the last thing I heard. I sat there frozen with my fingers sweating around the butcher knife. If the noise had disturbed any of my younger sisters and brothers, I wouldn't know because no one came out of their room, and the incident was never discussed. It would be more than fifteen years later when I broke down crying telling my father how I was tired of praying for him, trying to protect him, and trying to protect and provide for HIS kids, my younger siblings. That day, sitting on those steps, changed the way I saw myself in the world. Until then, I had a fancy idea that I was surrounded by my father, my big brother, and my uncles who'd always protect me. In an instant, sitting there on the steps in my teens, I knew better.

"Didn't I tell you to go to bed?" my mother shrieked as she walked back past me, going back to her room. She had no idea that in that instant I became no longer her little girl. More importantly, in that instant, I became no longer daddy's little girl.

Chapter 4
A Hell of a Marriage

In my marriage I felt like I was doing all the giving—except in bed where I felt like I was taking it real good. Sex was better than what I had heard my mother and her sister-friends describe. Now I understood why they kept getting pregnant. Who could stop having sex? It was too bad they believed all that religious nonsense about birth control being a sin. I figured some men made it a sin because they wanted to have as many children as they could for different reasons throughout history. I figured when men needed children to help grow food to sell and eat, they needed as many as they could make. And in the Nation of Islam, the men said they needed to procreate to build up an all-Black nation. I didn't buy any of that nonsense. To me, kids drained what little resources you had—financially and emotionally, and kids were not some things you created for your own purposes.

I knew Ron had a four-year-old daughter before we got married, but I did not know she would become a part of my life. Kia looked just like Ron, a banana-colored child big for her size. She was quiet, though. Her mother was anything but quiet, a real drama queen, tall, dark, thin, and wiry. She dressed like she thought she was a Barbie doll—high fashion, too much makeup, and her tongue was sharper than Ron's mother's.

"I'm a tell the muthafucka, I don't give a shit about him or his wife. He need to spend some time with his daughter!" I heard her say once when she was dropping Kia off for the weekend. Ron wasn't home, and Saundra had let them in after I'd pretended not to hear her knocking on the door. Once Kia came up to the room, I couldn't be mean to her. I loved kids, whoever's they were. I heard her mother's motor mouth still going down in the living room.

"And tell them she needs some shoes! Shit, I buy her shit all year long. He got a wife now, let her buy some shit if his ass still broke. Who the fuck would marry a broke-ass nigga!" I heard her laughing as she left.

At least I wasn't fornicating, paving a path to hell, I thought. At least people would respect me because the man married me rather than try to use up all my sex, then go on to the next woman. But I seemed in more of a hell right now than she did. Maybe she didn't have any man's respect in the form of a marriage license, but she sure was making men pay for being with her. I heard her talk about this one who bought her shoes, that one who took her to a concert, or another who took her on a vacation to the Bahamas. I had a marriage license and nothing else.

I heard the car door slam and her screeching away. How could such a foul woman have such a pleasant child?

"Have you had breakfast, Kia?"

I sure hoped so.

"Yeah, we went to McDonald's."

"Well, I was going to study for a little while, then we'll go over to the park, okay?" I said kindly.

"Do you know where my daddy is?"

How could such a foul, ghetto-ass woman have such a sweet, proper-talking child? I knew Kia's mother, Kim, grew up in the suburbs, that both her parents worked government jobs, and they took good care of their grandchild, but I wondered how they had failed to keep Kim out of trouble. It did not occur to me that Kim and I were similar in some ways.

"No, Kia. I don't know where your daddy is. He didn't come home last night and I haven't heard from him. I guess he'll call later," I said, thinking I could just talk out what was on my mind, that it would not register with her because she was too young to really know what I was saying.

She sat on the edge of the bed, facing the window.

"Can I watch cartoons?"

"Cartoons are all gone off now," I explained. "I have some paper you can draw on. You can make your own cartoon people," I said, reaching into a box of supplies in my closet.

"Can I color, then?" she asked.

"Um, I don't have crayons."

"I brought my crayons and my coloring books," she said, reaching for a suitcase she had brought in with her. I picked up the pink suitcase with a Black princess doll on the front and laid it flat on the bed to open it and see just how much her mother had packed. Was she trying to leave her here for more than a weekend?

"That's my dress, in case we go to church," Kia said. "My mommy said I should bring it in case you and my daddy take me to the Mooslem church. She told me to hang it up when I got here. Can I put it in the closet?"

I shook the blue flowered dress from its folds and found a hanger for it. I couldn't remember the last time I had been to the mosque. Muslims' real worship day is on Friday, but in America, because the rest of society worships on Sundays, we had service on Fridays and Sundays. I didn't go to either because it just did not seem necessary. I did not like having to sit behind the men during the lecture. And when we stood to pray, guess whose butts were in our faces? The men lined up in front of us. But that was just one of the things I didn't like. So much had changed. I was sure things would change again, but I needed something steady in my life.

The building where I first went to worship looked the same on the outside, a two-story tan brick building with an arched roof. But inside, the chairs, which had been set up neatly though divided with one side for men and the other side for women, were removed and replaced with a green carpet on the floor. When Elijah Muhammad died and his son led us into Orthodox Islam, we were told to sit on the floor like the Arabs did. I didn't like that. I had grown up learning to dislike the Arabs almost as much as we disliked Europeans, and for the same reasons. They had no respect for the darker peoples of the earth.

Anyway, not only did the furniture arrangement and the color scheme change—going from Elijah Muhammad's favorite colors, red and white, to Prophet Muhammad's favorite colors, green and white, but too much had changed. We no longer were establishing our own unique culture based on our unique likes and needs as African Americans. We were buying into a foreign culture—the Arabs'. I hated that most of all.

Of course I could not explain all this to a four-year-old child. I put her dress in the closet and explained that we would say our prayers together at home.

"With my daddy?" she asked.

"If he comes back tonight we'll pray with him. If not, it'll just be me and you."

"My daddy doesn't live here anymore?" she asked.

"Yeah. He just didn't come home last night," I said. That wasn't the first night, but now he didn't even bother to call and pretend to be hanging out with my brother or at his grandmother's house. "He'll probably call in a little while," I said.

"What if he calls when we're at the park?" she asked.

"Do you want to wait until he calls before we go?"

"I don't care." She shrugged her shoulders.

"We'll have some fun whether he calls or not," I assured her. "You know how to play tic-tac-toe?" I asked.

"What's that?"

"Here, I'll show you."

I put a sheet of paper across a book for surfacing as we sat on the bed and I showed her how.

"Oh, you're a smart girl," I said as she caught on.

"My grand nanna showed me how to play blocks. Do you want me to show you how?"

Blocks was another game we could play on paper, connecting dots to form blocks, scoring when a line you drew completed a box.

We went to the park later. I let her help make tuna macaroni salad for dinner. She wondered where everybody else was, since her aunts and cousins were nowhere around. And I promised to read one of the books her mother had packed when we got in bed. I bathed her, read her a book titled *Honey I Love* by a Black author and wondered who had the good sense to buy her books about Black kids. Probably not her mother. After Kia was asleep, the madness that had been building in my heart and head for Ron suddenly felt heavy and choked me. I couldn't help but think how stupid I must look taking care of somebody else's child while they're probably both out partying, and what if they were partying together somewhere?

I showered and got dressed for bed and noticed the small clock in the window said 12:20; past midnight. I was mad as hell that he had not called all day and wasn't at my grandmother's or his grandmother's or at my parents' house when I'd called looking for him to tell him his daughter was here for him. I had called his aunt's house, and his mother's house, and nobody had seen him. I cried myself to sleep, then was awakened by the bedroom door opening. He flicked the lights on and I could see he was wide awake.

"My two favorite girls!"

"She's sleep!" I hissed.

"Wake up! Big Daddy's home!"

"She's sleep, Ron! Don't wake her up!"

He snatched the sheets off the bed, ready to play.

"Kia. Big Daddy's home! Hey!"

He started tickling her and she woke up delighted and hugged him around his neck.

"What took you so long?" she asked.

"Big Daddy had to take care of some business!" he said, beaming. "Come on downstairs. I got something to show you."

"Can you give me a piggyback ride downstairs?" she asked.

He did that happily. Hiked her on his back, leaned over smooching his lips on mine, then took off.

"Br-br-br-brooooom!" He took off.

"Ooooowh, Daddy! But I already have a bike!"

"Well, now you got two!" he said.

I went downstairs and saw a pink-and-purple bike with training wheels that looked new. I could just imagine Kia's mother cursing him out for giving her daughter something she'd accuse him of having stolen. Of course, I would never accuse him of anything like that. Even if I thought it was true, I knew better than to say anything. Kia's mother would fight a man. I wouldn't. At least, I didn't think I would.

"Where is everybody?" Ron asked.

"I don't know."

"Oh. So, I can have my wife all over the house tonight?"

The nerve.

"I was almost sleep. I'm 'bout to go back to bed," I said.

"I'm gon' put Kia back to bed, then me and you can hang out down here," he said.

"I'm going to sleep," I said flatly, rolling my eyes. I moped back up the stairs, spread the covers back across the bed, and slid under them.

I pretended to be asleep when he piggybacked Kia back to bed, tucked her in bed on my right side, then climbed over me and lay down on the other side of me. Since I wouldn't hang out with him downstairs, he decided to join me in bed.

"Hey. Apple scrapple. Wake up and make love to Big Daddy," he whispered in my ear. I turned over and pulled the covers up over my head, and heard him get up and quickly undress. The next thing I knew he was under the covers, his dick as solid as a rock.

"Didn't you miss me?" he whispered, kissing the side of my face he could get to.

"Ron, get offa me," I said.

"Come on, girl. You know you missed me. You know you want this," he said. He smelled like weed, and I could tell he was still high.

"I said, get offa me."

The next thing I knew he'd turned me on my back, pinned me down sprawled beneath him, and was squirming all over me.

"Get offa me!"

"Girl, you my wife!" he snarled.

I was crying and struggling but he was heavy, then inside, then exhausted, and rolled off. I turned over and curled up in a knot. I couldn't believe what had just happened, and while his daughter was right there in the bed with us. She didn't move, but I doubted she was really asleep. I couldn't move. My body felt so heavy. My heart ached. My head spun. Tears streamed, but I muffled my cries because a child was next to me. I tried to curl up tighter but there was no room in the bed. I felt myself curling up in a tight knot on the inside.

I was still awake as the sun came up, but I planned to lie in bed until after he got up and got out. I wasn't sure what I would say or do. My chest felt tight, my face, too. I lay there thinking. I know the Quran says a woman's supposed to please her man, and she's not supposed to deny him sex, but what about when he doesn't do what he's supposed to do? It's not like he's really being a husband taking care of me. I'm taking care of us. And even if he was taking care of me, he shouldn't have a right to just take it when I say no. This ain't no kind of marriage. I felt too heavy to move.

This had not been the first time he "took" it. Come to think of it, now that I thought about our relationship, I mean really thought about it the way it was, not the corny little fairy-tale story I liked to tell about how I married the boy next door, I realized our relationship had started out this way.

I remembered losing my virginity to him while standing in front of him while he sat on the bleachers at the football field across the street from my grandparents' house. He'd fingered me that day, then pulled me onto him. I didn't bleed that time, and my cousin later assured me that he must not have gotten all the way in because if he had, I would've bled. I remembered screaming to high heaven in the back of his mother's Firebird one night when he pulled into a parking lot across the street from my grandparents' house just moments before my curfew. I remembered another time when I was visiting at his mother's house, he invited me to his room in the basement, and before I knew it he had me pinned to the gray cinderblock wall, pulling down my pants. I struggled and resisted, not wanting to get caught in his mother's house, right next door to mine, but he proved stronger. It was all I could do to scratch lines of blood on his neck as he pumped my body against the cement floor next to the washer and dryer. Less than an hour later, he was calling me from his mother's kitchen, asking me to give him a haircut. I fucked his head up with parts everywhere and walked out of there as cool as a breeze.

The next day, his mother saw me in the courtyard and said, "Ray-Ray, I don't appreciate what you did to my son."

"You should ask your son what he did to me," I said, barely breaking my stride. I'd left deep red scratches on both sides of his neck, and he'd had to skin his head bald because I'd cut his hair so bad.

That was before the movie *The Color Purple* came out showing a young woman ready to give her abuser a face shaving at his request. She contemplated cutting his throat but didn't. I had not heard my mother or her sister-friends talk about marital rape. In fact, they taught us we were obligated as wives to fulfill a husband's pleasures, but I instinctively believed I had options. These thoughts dawned on me the morning after the latest fight with Ron.

"Salaam Alaikum," he said, getting up. "Let's make Fajr."

"Fajr went out an hour ago," I managed to say out of my still choked-up throat.

Fajr is the Muslim morning prayer that is supposed to be performed at the crack of dawn. My dad used to wake us up for Fajr. But I had since wondered if that practice of praying at dawn was started by people who lived at a time, or in a society, where people got up early to go out and work in the desert or on farms before the sun got too hot. We lived in a different time, a different world. School didn't start until nine, which meant we didn't need to get up until seven, so why get up at six just because people in some foreign faraway country did that?

And, hell no, I did not feel like praying with this man who had just forced himself on me.

"We can still make it," he said. "We need to make salat."

I was thinking, *You go to hell*, but didn't say it.

The nerve. He didn't *need* to come home the night before. He didn't *need* to look for a job. He didn't *need* to do the cooking and cleaning around the house since I was the one working. And he didn't *need* to get off me when I asked him to. He didn't *need* to show me at least that much respect. We hadn't even talked about that because I hadn't wanted to bring that up in front of the child.

"I'm not making salat," I said.

He shook his head and left the room. I lay there wrestling with my thoughts. I had gotten myself into a mess, trying to do the right thing but for the wrong reason. I had not known getting married for sex was wrong. Even my Christian grandparents had said over the years, "The Bible said it is better to marry than perish." In Islam, kids were encouraged to marry young to avoid sex out of wedlock. Now I was thinking that was some dumb shit. This marriage felt so lopsided, like I was doing all the giving. I had the only income so he expected me to share. I was the woman, trained in the domestic arts even, so he expected me to cook and clean, too. I was his wife, so he expected nookie on the regular. For his part, he was just The Man, which meant he was entitled to whatever he thought was his due. These established rules, I was beginning to understand, were about as weak and hollow as the noodles I bought just because they were cheap. Our relationship was as unhealthy as the noodles I bought. Our sex was like a seasoning. It gave our otherwise empty relationship flavor. I began realizing that we had nothing else in common. No common goals, and our values—what we considered important in life—were mismatched, as well. Sure, we both were in survival mode, but I was beginning to realize we had different ideas about how best to survive.

I was glad I had been at least smart enough to stay on the pill. School, and mainly the experience of getting pregnant and terminating the process—had at least taught me that life offered choices. I could choose now to avoid pregnancy until much later in my life. Neither school nor my life experiences, so far, had taught me everything I needed to know, however. Some wisdom I had yet to grow into, and some conventional wisdom that no longer served good purposes, I had yet to grow out of. I had not yet learned, for instance, that honesty didn't necessarily mean telling everybody everything just because it was the truth. I'd have to learn that sometimes the urge to purge came from a need to assuage my guilt. But sometimes guilt should just be spat on the ground and stomped on rather than spat in somebody's face.

One night, lying in bed after good loving, I told Ron about the abortion. I told him I didn't regret it because I thought we weren't ready then for a child, and obviously I was right, because look at us now. We were barely able to take care of ourselves. I was glad he remained calm and I had expected him to. He pulled me closer into his chest and held me tight. He didn't say anything about it, and in moments, he was asleep.

But a few weeks later, in our first big argument, he threw it all back at me. I don't remember what the argument was about at first, or how it started. But I would remember how it ended for years because the end of that argument was the beginning of our pulling apart. The argument started in the kitchen so it probably began with me complaining about his sisters eating my food again. It ended with him pulling me by my arm into the bathroom, flushing the toilet, and screaming at me, "You killed my baby! That's what you did to my baby!"

I was stunned. Standing there, I must have looked like a wide-eyed doe.

"What! You think I can't take care of a baby! You thought you was gon' hafta take care of me and a baby! You think I'm not a man!"

He slammed his hand on the wall, then pushed past me, and out the door. I stood there trembling with tears running down my face. His sister Kim heard the commotion and came running down the stairs. "Ron, what you doing to that girl? Ray-Ray, don't let that nigga talk to you like that."

"Fuck that girl!" he said. Then he left the house.

He started staying out overnight more and more. I didn't feel guilty about what I had done, though. I was mad as hell at his reaction, but I still believed I had done the right thing. The more I thought about it, the more sure I was. And the more I thought about our marriage, the angrier I got.

One night when he didn't come home, I stood at the window with hot water waiting to dump it on his head when I heard him at the door. I reheated the water over and over again for a couple of hours, then got tired and went to bed. Other nights, I put a pair of scissors under my pillow thinking that if he came in high or drunk assuming he was going to "take" it, I'd cut his ass. Even if he didn't I just might cut his ass in his sleep for making me miserable. One night he came in and nudged me out of my sleep for sex, but I didn't wake up angry. We made love, but at some point the pillows got jostled and he saw the scissors and it scared the shit out of him. He jumped up out the bed.

"Crazy bitch! What the hell you got scissors in my bed for!"

I looked up at him with what must have looked like a crazy smirk because he hauled ass out the room. The next morning I got up and dressed for work like nothing had happened. He was sleeping on the couch downstairs and called to me as I was going out the front door.

"Where you going?"

"Somebody has to work," I said.

"Oh, no. We need to talk. You not going nowhere."

I slammed the door behind me. I wouldn't see or hear from him for a few days after that. Then one evening, Kim told me he had gotten arrested on a parole violation. I wasn't mad, I felt numb. What do I do now? I called Ma and asked if I could come home. He would call me there, but I told him I could not run up my mother's phone bill with his collect calls, so he began writing letters. Over the next three months, he wrote letters telling me how much he loved and needed me now more than ever and he would do better when he got out. He would find a job and try to be the man I deserved because I deserved the best and he understood that I didn't want to settle for less and I shouldn't and please, baby, please.

I had a lot of time to think back at home. I didn't talk much about the mess I was in, having moved out of the comfort of my grandparents' nice, large, middle-class house into a hell hole with a no-good husband. I hadn't felt comfortable in my grandparents' house. Everything was sterilized, right down to people's real thoughts, emotions, and complexities. It was like living on eggshells, afraid to say or do the wrong thing. In Ron's house, which was nasty as hell, so nasty that my girlfriends would not sit on the filthy couch that had old chewing gum patches here and there, we all felt free to be ourselves—our worst selves, but ourselves.

Back home, I moved back into my old bedroom on the top floor of the four-level house, a room that had no window. It really was a storage room that Ma turned into our library with two bookshelves and large pillows for sitting. I slept on a mattress on the floor and stored my clothes in the basement on racks that wouldn't fit in the small room filled with books. I'd lie in bed thinking for hours when I couldn't sleep and didn't want to be bothered with my siblings downstairs.

I thought about how much I had opened up to Ron and how much he had opened up to me. We had laughed over games of Monopoly just between the two of us. My grandparents played Dominos together every evening after dinner so playing games across a table seemed like a good thing for couples to do. We would lie still some nights after a good round of sweaty sex just talking. He would recall some of his most painful memories, and I would listen, still too choked up on mine to discuss them.

Beneath all his bravado, beneath his mustache and grimace, behind his hard stare, I had learned that Ron was a sensitive man, still reeling from the pain of some things his father had done. He couldn't understand why his father, who had been in and out of jail since Ron could remember, sold everything he got his hands on. Ron told me about his father selling his basketball. He had loved that basketball, the one thing that was his. I heard his voice tighten as he talked about learning that his father had sold it for dope. His mother tried to explain an addict's need, but expecting a twelve-year-old to be compassionate about somebody the whole world scorns is a bit much. In school, on TV, from all the law-abiding adults in our world, we learned that drug addicts are the scum of the earth—trifling, selfish, stupid, ending up on drugs due to their own weak character.

I couldn't tell Ron about loving his father more than some basketball because I still was angry as hell at my own father for some of the same reasons. His addiction embarrassed the hell out of me. I never will forget my first semester in college. I was taking a photography class and had bought a special camera with money saved from my summer job, and somebody stole it out of our house. I never found out if Dad had stolen it and sold it or if one of the addicts he invited into our home for evening prayers stole it and pawned it. Whoever took it took the whole camera bag—lenses, film, and everything.

My heart and Ron's heart were broken in some of the same places, and I don't care what folks look like on the outside—good girl, bad boy—hearts know what they are and they find their twin. People wondered, "How could she marry him?" But my heart knew Ron long before my mind realized what was happening. My heart knew immediately what it might take my mind twenty years to accept. My heart knew that he was courageous and indomitable. His heart knew that I was smart and promising.

Ron had dreams that looked foolish to everybody but me and his mama. How you gon' be a businessman when you got no business?

I remembered how he strutted around swinging his briefcase, changing from one lanky arm to the other as he walked briskly to the bus stop. He had likely put a gun to some white man's head and snatched the briefcase. I knew he hadn't gone into a store and bought it. I realized Ron stole, like a few of the folks in our neighborhood, but it wasn't something I judged or condemned. I hadn't stopped to consider that the gun he loaned my brother once had been obtained for more than just protection. His protection would be mine as well, and more than anything these days I needed protection.

I managed to work twenty hours a week at a good government job I got through school. I applied for a job through the "Stay-in-School" program, designed to help poor kids working their way through college, and got assigned to a clerk position at the U.S. Department of Energy. I worked in DOE's Congressional Affairs office, and was delighted to be working with Black women who had the kinds of jobs I'd wished my mother had. Some of the women in my neighborhood worked good government jobs, and it seemed like their kids, my friends, had the best of everything—more clothes, more spending money, and more free time. It would be years before I would appreciate the wealth of my mother's attention and intentions. My mother's own mother had worked so much, my mother decided to stay at home and make raising her kids her full-time job.

I also took a full-time course load at school so I could remain qualified to receive a grant from the state large enough to cover tuition and leave me with about a thousand dollars of spending money for the semester. On top of that, once a week in the evenings, I went to work at the Capital Children's Museum, where they allowed a group of teenagers to produce our own radio shows that broadcast on commercial and public radio stations. On Saturday mornings, though, I got up earlier than any other day to hurry downtown to get the one bus heading out to the jail in Lorton, Virginia—about forty minutes away. That's where Ron was.

He was out of jail in what seemed like no time, and moved into the tiny bedroom in my parents' house with me until I found us an apartment nearby.

I searched *The Washington Post* classified section for apartments I could afford on the salary from my stay-in-school job. Ron and I looked at a few apartments together before I realized I would be better off looking on my own since landlords seemed skeptical about a man moving in with me who had no job. We explained that we were married, but except for the big passion marks I liked to sport around my neck now, we didn't think to show proof that we were a legitimate married couple. We couldn't afford wedding rings. I finally found an old woman to rent me an apartment for $360 a month. It was a spacious one-bedroom apartment with hardwood floors; except in the bathroom and kitchen. It had a screened-in back porch that could be used for storage, a separate living room, dining room, bathroom, and galley kitchen. It was in an old four-unit building that had not been renovated in at least twenty years. The yellowish-beige linoleum on the kitchen floor looked pretty raggedy, the refrigerator and stove were old models, and the large dingy water heater needed something to hide it from view. I liked the place because it was on a quiet street lined with uniform four-unit buildings, front yards, and trees. Also, it was located about eight blocks from my family's home, a neighborhood where I was comfortable.

Chapter Five
Brother, Please

Ron was excited that his main apple scrapple found us a home. He had his friend Derrick, whom I'd not met before, help him bring in furniture his aunts and mother gave us. His mother gave us an old bed frame and two mattresses, one of his aunts gave us a blue-and-brown plaid recliner, and Derrick's mother gave us a blue sleeper couch. Derrick reminded me of Al Pacino, short, scrawny, quick, and super-cool. He looked part Italian and part African American with slick black hair and milky skin. I had met only two of Ron's male friends, a dude he called "Ahk," and now Derrick. Ron's cousin Walter had tried dating me before Ron staked his claim. Walter was dark and cute but really not my type. He had a reputation for robbing people and soon after I met him I heard he was in jail charged with a rack of murders.

All Ron's friends clearly were hustlers, and proud of it. It was in their swagger, their steely eyes, their general mannerisms. I knew the signs because two of my uncles were bona-fide hustlers, having served time for bank robbery and petty crimes. Derrick's main hustle was selling clothes, shoes, leather coats, and electronics stolen from department stores. That lifestyle didn't bother me either because I had a cousin who used his job at a department store to give his friends access for large thefts, and I had an uncle who often bought stolen goods to keep his wife and girlfriends on the side happy. Besides, it wasn't really stealing to take back a little something from the large corporations that exploit poor folks' labor, paying minimum wage with little or no health benefits and crap. And Ron's friends respected me.

"That mutha fucka…oh, sorry 'bout that."

Usually I'd stay in my room when they were hanging out with Ron, smoking weed and talking shit in the living room. They'd leave late at night, Ron would come to bed to get a piece, then I'd get up and go to work and then school the next day.

The first weekend we were in the apartment, I went shopping at a Zayre bargain department store when I knew my girlfriend was working the cashier. I got in her line with a cart overflowing with household stuff—an iron, ironing board, sheets, glasses, flatware, pots, pans, casserole dishes, bath towels, washcloths and matching throw rugs to fit around the toilet and next to the bathtub, curtains for the living room, sheer valance curtains for the bedroom and curtain rods, paper to line the kitchen cabinets, wallpaper for decorating the cabinet doors, Ajax and sponges for cleaning the bathroom, gloves, wood oil for dusting, a large box of Trend soap powder, a large bottle of bleach for laundry, dishwashing liquid, an electric can opener, a toaster, a broom, a mop, deodorant, lotion, and a stock of soap and toilet paper. I had gotten everything on my list, scratching off each item as I put it into the cart, and arrived at her cash-out line holding on to items to keep them from falling off the pile loaded into the cart. We pretended not to know each other, and she pretended to ring up each item I set on the rolling belt for her to charge. She and I had been busted once before for stealing from a department store when we were thirteen, but this didn't seem like stealing.

When we were thirteen, and finally allowed to take a public bus downtown to shop on our own, we spent all our money on Tinkerbell lotions, lip glosses, and nail polish at a semi-exclusive department store we called Woodies (short for Woodworth & Lothrop). Then we went to the five-and-dime where our mothers had sent us to get back-to-school supplies and ended up stealing the panties, socks, training bras, and stockings our mothers had put on our list of things to buy. It didn't matter to me that my friend had her younger sister and I had one of my younger brothers with us when I came up with the bright idea that we could get what we needed without paying for it.

"Don't pay for that," I said. She looked confused.

"Just drop it in your bag like it's just too much for you to carry. I told you how to do it," I said. We both had paid twenty-five cents for large shopping bags with the Woodies logo on it so we would ride back through town looking like we had been shopping at the fabulous Woodies. I also had heard big girls in our neighborhood talk about "boosting" or stealing stuff to sell.

My friend was too afraid to do as I'd instructed, so I came up with another idea. I told her and her sister to follow me into the ladies room, and I left my little brother standing guard outside the bathroom door. He knew what we were planning because on our way from the big department store, I'd told my friend that I had heard it was easy to steal from the cheap store.

In the bathroom, I promptly opened my shopping bag for my friend and her little sister to drop their things in. We were barely out of the restroom when a pair of security guards, one black, one white, grabbed me and my friend by the arm and led us all down a narrow aisle and around a corner into their office, where the white guard left and the black guard took over. "What? I ain't do nothing. We, we, we..." My girlfriend was beginning to stutter, which she did when she got too excited or mad or stressed. "I, I, I, wh, wh..."

The officer motioned for the little ones to sit in a waiting area while he took my girlfriend and me into his office. We sat in the two chairs in front of his desk, and he walked around and sat behind his desk.

"Young ladies, I believe you have some things in your bag that don't belong to you," he began patiently.

"We have our receipts, sir," I said. He motioned for us to hand them over and we did.

"Empty your bags on my desk," he said, still kind. We did, and he began placing to one side of his desk all the stuff we had that wasn't listed on our receipts.

"Young ladies, this is shoplifting. Do you know the consequences for shoplifting?"

"Uh, sir. We weren't shoplifting, we put that stuff in the bag because it was too much to carry. We was going to pay for it. We have money."

"Young lady, we have it all on camera."

I was stuck.

"We were going to pay for it, sir. We just put it in the bags because it was too much to carry in our hands. We didn't get a cart because we didn't plan on getting so much stuff, then it was just too much to carry, so we put it in the bag until we got to the line. We were going to pay for it, but you snatched us and pulled us in here before we even got to the checkout line."

When he confirmed that all the money we had left between us barely amounted to bus fare for four, he said our parents would have to come pick us up. He took out some papers from his drawer and began asking personal questions. My friend gave him a fake name and a fake phone number and I couldn't help giggling hearing it. I gave him my real name, and lied, saying our phone had been cut off months ago. After he called the number my friend gave him and realized it was a wrong number, he got mad.

"That's why your friend is sitting over there laughing. She don't know I'll lock both of ya'll Black asses up!"

He was as Black as us, and I thought he had a nerve calling us Black like it was something bad. He went and got the little ones and got my friend's number from her little sister. I gave my brother a look that said he'd better not say a word. He looked terrified. I didn't think he could possibly know what was going on, being only eight years old, but something told him that something was very wrong. Maybe the man's deep voice and blue uniform scared my brother, I thought. I'd often seen our dad on his job as a security guard at a hospital, so uniforms didn't scare me. Years later he told me that he was afraid of what our parents would do when they got a call about us shoplifting, embarrassing them and shaming our family name. He knew what being a Tate meant. Our uncles Hussein and Wallace were role models in our neighborhood because they kept jobs and went to college and respected adults. We were expected to do the same, but I got caught up in a moment of fun, and the idea of getting something free.

The guard finally reached my friend's mother on the phone and told her that we would only be released to a parent. She said she would pick us up, and the store closed before she arrived. The guard told us to wait out front and although we knew he was leaving, we knew better than to leave ourselves since my friend's mother was on the way. I wasn't scared. I would stick to my story and tell my friend's mother that we'd put a few items in the bag before paying for them because it was all too much to hold.

My friend's mother, Ms. Dorsey, a prison guard, arrived visibly angry. She got even madder when she found that the door to the store was locked.

"I know Ms. Tate's daughter don't steal!" she said, fuming. She thought her daughter might steal, but couldn't believe some over-zealous security guard had accused Mrs. Tate's goody-two-shoes daughter of shoplifting. I swore I was innocent. She took us home and came to my door to explain it all to my mother. She assured my mother that she would have given that security guard a piece of her mind if he had not left early.

That was when I was thirteen. Six years later, married and in college, I still got a thrill out of trying to get something free, so there I was in line for this same girlfriend to give me all this stuff for less than half the cost.

I had taken a hundred dollars—five crisp twenties budgeted for household stuff, but that hardly would have covered everything we needed. It didn't occur to me that I could have bought just a few things at a time, the things on sale that week, like my grandparents did. It didn't occur to me to borrow money from my grandparents, because they would have assured me that I did not need everything—and so much of everything—all at once. It didn't occur to me, either, that I could save a few dollars here and there for a couple months, then go on a big shopping spree like I'd also seen my grandparents do. All I knew was that I needed all this stuff and could have it with a little help from my friend who worked at the store.

She slid each item across the belt, pretended to punch the numbers into the cash register, then told me my bill was thirty dollars. We had heard that those cash registers had cameras in them to catch employees doing stuff like that, but it didn't occur to us that we could get caught.

I rolled out of the store with all my stuff in bags, hailed a cab, and felt good about getting away scot-free.

I didn't consider shoplifting breaking the law in the way Ron broke laws. To me, shoplifting was just a little something to do to get some basic things I needed and wanted. I cringed when I thought about Ron breaking into people's homes, selling drugs or robbing people. That was bad. The shoplifting I did was just stupid. But, I guess the shoplifting was an indication that I felt as desperate, as entitled, as unbound by laws as Ron felt. But I didn't realize this at the time.

My grandparents gave us a cordless phone and dishes as a belated wedding present, although they were mad as hell that we had eloped. My uncle, who knew where to get stolen goods, helped me furnish our dining room with an exquisite cherrywood dining table and chairs, and an entertainment center for the living room. I got a phone line installed under my name, and called the electric and gas company to put those services under my name, too, just as I had promised the landlord.

I knew my granddad used to take meats and breads from the kitchen where he worked. He didn't have his company's permission to take it, so that was stealing, too, when I thought about it. It seemed to me that everybody broke some little laws in small ways, and the shoplifting I did to make ends meet was no different.

Chapter Six
Not Half My Faith

The first few weeks in our new apartment were exciting. I still did all the grocery shopping and all the cooking and washed our clothes by hand in the bathtub rather than get a cart to take them to the Laundromat around the corner.

I cooked meals on Sundays and stored a couple in the fridge—fried chicken, rice, and greens for one meal; spaghetti and meat sauce for another—as my grandmother had done when she was young, married, and working. Never mind that her circumstances almost fifty years ago were completely different from mine. Her husband worked, for one thing. She wasn't paying all the bills and doing all the housework. I didn't have time to think about what needed to be done and who should do it; I just did what needed to be done. I didn't have time to fuss and fight over it either. It was easier just to do it.

Within a couple months of moving into our apartment, Ron came home in time to eat dinner with me less and less. He'd come home in the middle of the night, grab leftovers from the fridge to munch on, crawl into bed, try to get some, then be knocked out when I got up to go to work or school in the mornings. When he was home in the evenings, the place was noisy with his friends, or he was pacing the floor on the telephone making plans with one of his buddies or fussing with his ex-girlfriend about child support, which he hardly ever sent.

"Kim, why you startin' up with this bullshit again! You think I don't *want* to support my kid? You think some fuckin' courts could make…

What's that bullshit gon' do? I told you I'ma get the fuckin' money…"

They went through that at least once a week, it seemed. I'd go into the bedroom, shut the door, and read one of my assignments for school. Sometimes he'd call one of his buddies next, and before I knew it he had a ride out front. I didn't even bother to answer the phone because I didn't want to deal with his ex-girlfriend. One night she called about 10:30 claiming some guy was stalking her and Ron needed to come protect his daughter.

"She lives at home with her parents. Her father's there. Why's she calling you?" I said to Ron.

"My daughter's my responsibility!"

I knew it was bullshit, but couldn't do anything about it. I had class-work to tend to. More than keeping a sorry-ass marriage together, I was determined to become a reporter and then maybe write plays. I also was determined to become a writer like Maya Angelou or Nikki Giovanni. I planned to work at a newspaper to pay my bills. I had it all figured out. A husband didn't really matter as much. Marriage was just to make sex legal. As a teenager I had imagined that I could get married and have my own house separate from my husband's. We would have separate lives but get together for sex.

I was taught in Islam that marriage is "half your faith" and that's why it's so hard. Bonding with another human being is challenging and difficult, but it's practice for bonding with God. I had no intention of working hard at a job all day, then coming home to work at a marriage.

In Islam, Muslims jumped in and out of marriages like regular folks jump in and out of romances. It was common for men and women to marry three and four times because they married for the wrong reasons. I married once for sex and quickly knew I would not do it again. When I got through with Ron, it would be a long time before I put some paperwork around a mess and call it a marriage. If I was playing and just wanted to have sex, I'd call the relationship what it was. If there really was a God, all I needed Him to do at this point was get me out of this mess with Ron.

Ron's ranting and raving and scheming on the phone, creating all kinds of chaos in my home, the place where I was paying all the bills, was starting to get on my nerves. Most of the time I said nothing. I could simply bury myself in schoolwork, but sometimes PMS kicked in hard, and without my knowing that was what was stirring up an uncontrollable rage, I'd snap. Well, PMS and his trifling ass. That was enough to make me snap.

We fought about something once, and all I remember was his hands around my neck, pinning me against the wall with my feet above the floor. I felt as limp and helpless as a rag doll. Another time I slapped him real good but he simply turned and walked out the door.

Some nights he came home close to dawn, or after the sun came up, clearly high as hell. It was all I could do to stay in the bathroom pretending to be getting dressed until I was sure he'd crashed in bed. Between his two hustler friends in and out of our home at all hours of the night, him staying out all night, and watching his engagements with his ex-girlfriend, I started praying to God to get me out of the mess.

The good times were few and barely good after all. Ron called me late one Friday night, for instance, telling me to get dressed quickly to go out and party with him and one of his cousins who was home from the army for a short vacation. His cousin Kenny and his wife were in their mid-twenties, but seemed older than us in some way. Ron was all excited about showing his cousin some club called The Chapter III in Southwest D.C. I put on the same outfit I had worn to work that day—blue slacks; a light-blue, button-down shirt; and blue pumps with a low heel.

"Baby, wear that dress I bought from your uncle," Ron asked, full of laughter and fun.

I did not feel like wearing the turquoise-and-green-striped silk dress Ron had bought. For one thing, the damn thing really wasn't my size. Besides that, I wasn't in a party mood. Ron was already high, his eyes bloodshot like he was high on weed, but he smelled like beer. We piled into the back of Kenny's small red Toyota and took off. Standing in line outside the club, Ron wanted to be all lovey-dovey like Kenny was with his wife, but I wasn't feeling it. I really wanted to be home in bed with one of my books. Ron was a live wire—high as hell, happy as hell, having enough fun for the both of us. He tried kissing me on my neck and I inched away. We finally got past the two guys at the door who collected bills and stamped the backs of our hands in case we needed to leave the club and return. I could see that the place was grungy, even in the dark. I had never been to a nightclub before, and sure as hell wasn't impressed with this place. Ron pulled me to a table near what looked like a dance floor, and Kenny and his wife followed. People all around were looking for somebody or someplace to sit or forcing their way up to the bar, which was crowded. All the stools were filled and people were standing waving money over the heads of the people sitting. It looked like madness.

"Hey, baby. How you doing tonight? Oh, this is my wife, Sonsyrea. Sonsyrea, this is Dottie. Dottie, this here is my main man Kenny and his wife. Kenny's home from the military. I know you gon' set him straight. Sure ya right. Oh, and this is his wife, Neicey," Ron said. I'm wondering who the hell is Dottie, and how does he know her so well. "Hey, hook my man up with a rum and Coke. You know how to do it. And get my wife here a daiquiri," he continued. I had tasted a strawberry daiquiri once when Uncle Wallace took me to lunch to celebrate my high school graduation. He had taken me to a restaurant in Georgetown, an upscale shopping district, and ordered me a virgin daiquiri so I could feel grown up. He and Uncle

Avon would tell me, "Remember, Ray-Ray, you're not a McDonald's kind of girl, you're an O'Donnell's kind of girl." O'Donnell's was an expensive seafood restaurant way uptown. Uncle Wallace was the one who actually took the time to take me to a couple of them.

The music was loud—no, down-right noisy—and the ladies looked like hoes if you asked me, but Ron was having a ball. Kenny looked like he was scared to turn his head, like his wife might hit him or something if he started having fun. Ron noticed, too, and teased him about it.

"I told you not to marry that girl," Ron said, laughing.

"Aw fuck you, triflin' son-of-a-bitch…'scuse me, Sonsy, Sonsy, what? I don't mean no disrespect, but how the fuck you end up with a trifling nigga like that."

I didn't even try to answer that, since I'd been asking myself the same question the past few weeks.

"Man, you goin' let your lady step out there like that? You better git her. Sure you right." Ron laughed.

A DJ was talking over a loud speaker, the music was blasting and the crowd was moving every which way. The next thing I knew a half-naked man was on the dance floor stripping and women were cheering him on. My strawberry daiquiri was more bitter than the drink I remembered from my graduation celebration. Within moments, it even made my head hurt. Between the noise, the drink, and the rowdy people, I was wanting to leave, but I could see Ron was having a good time.

"Baby, go up there and put this in his G-string," he said, handing me a dollar bill. What the hell was a G-string?

"Go 'head up there, baby. Sure you're right."

"Man, you better take that little girl home," Kenny said. I didn't care what he thought of me, too young, whatever, I really did want to leave.

71

"Go 'head up there, baby," Ron insisted. I went to the bathroom, which was smoky as hell and filled with the ho-looking ladies primping in the mirror. They wore their hair teased out, big bangle earrings that looked like door knockers, leggings that looked like tights with the feet cut off, and short skirts way up past their knees. You could see the bottom of their behinds if it wasn't for the leggings. I was no more comfortable hiding out in the ladies room than I was back at the table with my high-ass husband, so I returned to the table and managed to tune out until it was time to leave. At home that night Ron and I fought again because he was horny as hell and I didn't want to be touched. When he fell asleep I got up and went and slept on the couch. I woke up praying to God to get me away from this man.

Chapter Seven
Norma Knew

At work one of the secretaries, Ms. Norma Jean, who had been in the government probably since I was born, saw me flipping through a book called *The Billings Method.* She told me, point blank, "Honey, you better get yourself some birth-control pills, 'cause the last thing you need at your age is a baby, and you don't want to be messing around with none of those so-called natural methods. Get yourself to the doctor and get you some pills. That's what I told my daughters. Ya'll got too much going for you to be getting saddled down with a no-good nigga and some kids. These men out here ain't worth a damn."

I felt a little embarrassed that she caught me reading a book about birth control. I managed to tell her in what must've been a whisper that I actually was married. She shot that to hell.

"Honey, please. You ain't wearing no ring. If a nigga can't afford to at least put a ring on your finger, you know he ain't worth a damn. I told my daughters, don't be foolin' 'round with these broke-ass niggas. They'll promise you the damn moon. You got too much goin' for you, sweetie. You a smart girl. I can see that. Now, whoever this little nigga is be calling up here for you, I can tell you he ain't no damn good. I can tell it in his voice. I don't even need to meet the nigga. I can tell he ain't no damn good. Don't you get yourself knocked up by that nigga."

The Billings method was a birth-control method that required you to keep track of your menses cycle and chart the days when your body ovulates and refrain from sex on those days. I knew that wasn't a reliable method in my situation since Ron might take it whenever he got high and horny enough.

At night when he didn't come home, I thanked God. When he didn't come home for two nights in a row, I got mad, cried, then thanked God for keeping him away two whole days and asked if maybe God could keep him away longer.

Once, while he was gone for two days, I rearranged the furniture in the living room, anything to keep myself busy to settle my thoughts. I cleaned the apartment from one end to the other this particular night and no sooner than I had fallen out, exhausted, in the recliner, the phone rang.

"This is the operator calling collect. Will you accept a call from Ronald Bates?"

"Uh, okay," I said with hesitation.

"Sonsyrea, they got me. You gotta come get me. They nabbed me on some ole bullshit last night. Look, here's what I need you to do. Call Kim so she can call Akh to bring ya'll out here. My hearing's not till the morning but the bond on this ole bullshit is going be about a thousand. All you gotta bring is a thousand dollars, and that'll get me out. I can work on getting up the money for a lawyer when I get out, and…"

"Ron, I don't have a thousand dollars," I said calmly.

"You can use your credit card…"

"Ron, I'm not charging up my credit card. I gotta pay that back."

"Did you hear what I fuckin' said! They got me trapped up in here! When I get out, you'll get your money. This ain't about no damn money. I'm talking 'bout my freedom they trying to take!"

Listening, all I could think was, you shoulda thought about that when you was out there hustlin'. It was ironic that he talked about his freedom. Sometimes I thought my granddaddy Tate, who died when I was four years old, must turn over in his grave to see what young Black men do nowadays. Black folks used to leave whatever they had—a shack of a house they called home—to escape to freedom. Now, Black folks risked their freedom to acquire material stuff. This was the 1980s and it seemed ironic to me that young men risked going to jail to afford bulky gold chains to wear and to give to their girlfriends. They sold crack, robbed stores, and stole cars for parts to sell in order to buy clothes and jewelry. In twenty years a few young men would emerge with profitable record companies and businesses that traded diamonds in Africa, but tens of thousands of young Black men were killed on the streets in the meantime. Ron was one of those young men caught up in the streets.

I hung up on him. The phone rang and rang again, and again. I didn't answer. I turned the TV on and watched the nightly news. More depressing. More homicides, and another big bust of crack dealers. I had missed *The Cosby Show* earlier because I was so busy cleaning and fuming, I'd forgotten to turn it on. *The Cosby Show* was one of the few shows I liked. I also enjoyed the sitcom that came on after it, *A Different World*, and another show, *Family Ties*. My world used to seem like those worlds in a way. My family was loving, and my parents worked well together. Dad went out and worked every day, and our mother worked at home, babysitting so many other people's kids that our house became an unofficial day-care center. I didn't see us as any different than the white family in *Family Ties* either. In fact, the smart-aleck son reminded me of myself. He was the one taking college and success more seriously than anyone else in his family. That was me. My sisters and brothers and I had picked our soul-mates on *The Cosby Show*. They thought I looked like Vanessa, the weird one. I thought I could grow up to be like Clair, the accomplished attorney, who didn't let her family ties hold her back.

I turned off the news and went to bed, turning on the clock radio on the floor next to my bed. I enjoyed listening to "The Quiet Storm." A song came on and reminded me of the good times with Ron:

Please remember, what I told you to forget

There's a man on the phone and he wants to come home

I hated Ron for leaving me alone, for embarrassing me, for screaming at me, but the song reminded me that we had been happy sometimes.

I heard knocking at the front door, then yelling at the front door.

"Ray-Ray, I know you in there. Ron wants me to talk to you."

After a long hesitation I opened the door and let Ron's sister Kim come in with her own brand of madness.

"You s'posed to stand by your man. What kinda shit is that? Soon as your man's down, you tryin' to turn your back on him. You know he loves you. Ron loves you more than he ever loved any girl, and he needs you now. You gotta be there for him. My mother said I can use her car to take you to bail him out in the morning."

"I'm going to work in the morning. Ain't nobody else goin' pay my bills," I said, without losing my calm, cool demeanor.

"Ron gon' *take* good care of you when he get out. That's why he's trying to get out. He's out there making money so he can get *you* nice things," she said.

She didn't know? She might've been getting shoes and jewelry and purses from her boyfriend, but Ron hadn't given me shit, except a couple dresses he bought hot from my uncle. He might've been buying stuff for his ex-girlfriend and that woman who was letting him drive her car, but he wasn't giving me stuff.

"I'm sorry. I don't have that kind of money, and I can't afford to run up my credit card," I said.

Then she snapped.

"Yeah. That is some sorry-ass shit. Soon as your man down, you turn your back on him. All he do for you. I don't know why he fuck wit a woman like you anyway. Punk-ass woman, won't even help her man when he down."

"Kim, I gotta go to bed. I gotta go to work in the morning."

"That's some sorry-ass shit, Ray-Ray."

I opened the door and she got the message. I went to bed, thanking God for answering my prayers. I felt delivered from the mess. Yes, God was keeping Ron away from me, I figured.

Another song that was playing when I got back to my room had me feeling confused about my feelings for Ron. I was mad as hell at him but didn't he rock my world with the good sex, and didn't he help me survive the fall-out in my household when Uncle Hussein was dying and Dad was about to go to jail? Hadn't he taught me that men have feelings, too? I had known men to be good providers and protectors, but Ron, when he broke down crying about the abortion—I mean cursing me out, but also crying, his emotions seemed genuine.

A Peabo Bryson song came on and also made me think of special moments with Ron. Peabo Bryson might as well have been singing that song for Ron. Ron used to tell me I was the best thing that ever happened to him. I used to think men sang those songs just because they knew women would buy them, but when I thought of Ron, those words had real meaning for me. For now, though, my own feelings were all I could focus on. I turned the radio off, hoping to get some sleep. I tossed and turned throughout the night and woke up exhausted in the morning, but I managed to get to work on time and complete a few things I needed to do.

In the evening, Ron called, and I declined his call when the operator asked if I would accept. I declined the next day, and the next, too. About a week later his mother called and told me in her high-pitched voice that she didn't understand how I could turn my back on her son.

"Ray-Ray, I wasn't gon' say nothing to you, 'cause Ron told me not to, but it's just not right how selfish you been. You been that way through the whole marriage. You act like Ron don't have a job because he don't want a job. Ron loves you. He just can't get a job. When my husband wasn't working, we split my check. He didn't have to beg me for help like Ron hafta beg you. A husband and wife's supposed to be a team, Ray-Ray."

"Ms. Bates, I don't mean no disrespect, but my mother told me I don't have no business trying to take care of a grown man…"

"You think you taking care of Ron just 'cause he need a little help now and then. What's yours is s'posed to be his…"

"Ms. Bates, I can't do nothing for Ron. He got himself in jail. I don't think it's my responsibility to…" She hung up the phone on me.

By my second weekend alone, without worrying where my husband was or what mood he might be in when and if he came home, I was beginning to enjoy myself. I watched TV more, and listened to the radio more. I called my girlfriends whom I hadn't had time for while dealing with my triflin'-ass husband.

His mother had the nerve to call again one day out of the blue, telling me his trial was the next day and I needed to be in the courtroom with them to show some family support. If the judge looked around and didn't see any concerned family, Ron wouldn't stand a chance of getting out.

Against my better judgment, I took a bus to the courthouse and found which hearing room Ron would be in. I was glad I went. I mean, at first I felt hurt when I looked up and recognized the woman whom I'd seen bring him home just after the sun came up one morning. She was the woman who loaned him her car sometimes: Karren. She sat on the same side of the courtroom as me, but she was up front, tacky in a dirty scarf around her hair and an oversized shirt over baggy pants, trying to look like a Muslim woman or something. I sat in the back, thinking I must be stupid as hell to stay and show some support for this man while he already got another woman there doing the same thing.

When he was led into the room by a security guard, wearing a baggy blue jumper, his hands cuffed in front of him, he smiled at me—and at her. He then sat at a table in front of us, his back turned to us until he took the witness stand and tried to tell what happened. He swore to the judge that the police report was all wrong. The report said that someone called police to report a burglary in progress and when the police got there, they saw Ron, wearing sweatsocks on his hands, prying open an apartment window while his friend, a short, very light-skinned man, stood guard near a getaway car. The report said police witnesses saw Ron raise his "gloved" hands in the air to signal his friend when he got the window open and that's when police rushed in and arrested them both. Ron swore to the judge that what police saw was him raising his hands in the air, calling his friend to come pray. They were in the neighborhood and realized they had missed salat, and his friend had already gone to the car. But Ron found a secluded space next to the building where they could make salat, so he was motioning his friend to join him.

That's when I got up and left. I figured if this man could get on a witness stand in a court and lie on God, he's a dangerous dude. I didn't want to be near him when God struck his ass with lightning, and I didn't want to be living in the same home with him when the what-goes-around-comes-around karma theory kicked in. I wouldn't want somebody burglarizing *my* home.

I walked out of that courtroom feeling convicted, as my grandmother would say. At that point I knew what was the right thing to do, and staying married wasn't the right thing.

My conviction didn't last very long once Ron started calling again and I accepted his call. He convinced me to at least stay with him until he got out of jail and got back on his feet. He explained that Karren came to court to show some support since he wasn't sure I would show up. He begged me to call the parole office, find out who was assigned to his case, and plead for leniency. He had to serve a few months in jail, then would get out, but would have to be monitored by a parole officer. It took more than a week, but I found out who his parole officer was. It was a woman, and she suggested I come to her office to discuss my concerns.

When I visited the parole officer, a tall, serious-looking woman, she closed her door, took her seat behind her desk, and talked to me like she knew me, like a school guidance counselor. Before I knew it, I was trying to explain why a smart young woman like me was hooked up with a young man who got his thrills breaking the law. She tried to explain his behavior and help me understand mine.

"But I don't know why he treated me like that when I was trying to do so much for him," I said.

"You were more of a man than he could be and he resented you for that," she said matter-of-factly. The words went straight to my heart, where they would be remembered forever. "You were able to do more for him than he could do for himself. No man wants that."

The parole officer reached into a manila folder on her desk, pulled out Ron's record, and told me I shouldn't be wasting my time with a young hardhead like Ron. His record was pages long, and included petty thefts, auto thefts, burglaries, attempted robbery, attempted murder, probation violations, and a murder. I was shocked.

I left her office feeling dizzy, but wiser—a little. I still couldn't completely give up on him since I wasn't as mad as I was when he first got arrested. Now, I didn't see any harm in making a few calls on his behalf, and accepting his calls a few days a week. The parole officer's advice to leave Ron alone didn't seem as important to me as her explanation of his behavior. She explained that his hurting me had more to do with him feeling hurt himself. That took the sting out of the harm he'd inflicted on me. I felt compelled to help him.

He asked me to call the newspapers and tell a reporter to do a story on how the system was discriminating against him. I didn't see any harm in doing that either. When I could get a quiet moment in somebody's office while they were out to lunch, I called *The Washington Post*. First I asked the person answering the phone in the newsroom which reporter might be interested in this story. I was told that either of the Black columnists on the Metro desk—Courtland Malloy or Dorothy Gilliam—might be interested. I wrote down their names and called every day trying to reach them.

One day I noticed that the person on the other end of the line sounded young like me, and I asked her how she got to work at *The Washington Post*, being so young. She told me she wasn't a reporter, that she worked there as a copy aide. I had not heard of such a job, but she told me about it and how I could apply. We became friends on the phone and she told me her boss' name and extension. My job for the next month wouldn't be typing letters from the in-box at my government job. All my effort during those four hours each day would instead be trying to reach the copy aide supervisor to get him to at least give me an interview.

Eventually, he took my call and told me to mail him my resume. I did, and began calling again a couple days later when I was sure he'd received it. I called him every half-hour, and sometimes heard him in the background saying, "Tell her I'm not here." But finally, he took my call and gave me a date and time for an interview. At my government job, my boss overheard me telling Ms. Norma Jean how excited I was to get an interview at *The Washington Post*, and he called me into his office to tell me, in a fatherly kind of way, not to get my hopes up too high because a career in journalism was very competitive, especially trying to get in someplace like *The Washington Post*.

He said I should have a backup plan, like becoming a teacher, or even developing my typing speed so they might hire me permanently in the government. I was sure I could get a job in journalism. God had told me directly. I remembered the prayer I made one time when it came to mind as crystal clear as if I had been on a telephone talking to God. I was going to have a job in the media. Didn't know how, when or where, but I knew that was God's plan for my life. Ma had tried convincing me that God's only plan for women was for us to get married, have children, and support our husband's dreams, but I knew better. I knew there would be something better for me.

Chapter Eight
I Dream a Life

I was surprised to meet the copy aide supervisor. He was absolutely gorgeous, and immediately, I fell in love with him. Turns out he was Black like me, and cool yet smart and successful like some of my uncles. He eased my nervousness by telling me he graduated from Anacostia High School in Southeast, which rivaled my Northeast school in football to make it to the citywide championship. He asked where did I see myself five years into the future, and I confidently told him I would be graduated from college and working as a television producer after working a few years at a newspaper to sharpen my writing skills. The internships I had done at a radio and television station seemed to impress him. He also seemed impressed that I had co-produced a youth radio show broadcast on a popular radio station. It occurred to me on my way back to campus after my interview that my passion for my career had been my saving grace through my messy marriage.

I hadn't stressed too much over Ron in recent nights because I mostly lived for going to class and work the next day. I enjoyed feeling like part of the big, wide world. Working in the government, I felt like I was part of that Big Brother/Uncle Sam monstrosity my family feared was designed and maintained to destroy Black people. Inside the monster, I could see it wasn't so bad. There wasn't a bogey man in a closet. It was a complex organization of individuals—just people. Ambitious people, lazy people, intelligent people, dim-witted people. White men arrogant as hell, white women doing their best to get by, some mousy as hell. There was one white woman, Bonnie, who was a secretary with her own office. I felt sorry for her. I was sure her husband was abusing her. She walked around hunched over, looking afraid to speak or deep in thought most of the time, and sometimes she had big bruises on her leg, which you could see through her stockings. The Black women who were contractors seemed particularly anxious, running around hustling up business as if their lives depended on their work. Some of the women seemed to be growing bitter, settling into their meager jobs like it was the best they could do just to hold on until they're eligible to retire.

Sitting on the bus heading back to campus after the job interview, I felt excited, like my career finally was going somewhere. I was going to college, which no woman in my family had done before, and I might be going to work in a professional job, something else no woman in my family had done before. My Aunt Carolyn and Aunt Nell had worked good government jobs since I could remember, and Grandma Thomas had been semi-professional, working as a nurse after stints in government and a few years cleaning homes. But all the other women ordered their whole life around having children and staying married. I was about to work at something I'd chosen.

On the bus, I daydreamed about what kind of life I could have. As we rode through the downtown business district, then past increasingly elaborate houses and apartment buildings, it occurred to me that I couldn't move into one of those houses, or even one of those upscale apartment buildings if I was still fooling around with a guy like Ron. He wouldn't want to move uptown because he resented so-called "uppity" people; and he'd never get a good job with his police record.

I realized with growing certainty that I couldn't stay married to Ron, but I couldn't make a quick clean break with him locked away in jail. He could play my heart strings over the phone, and did. I got the job at *The Washington Post*, and somehow, Ron got the phone number to call me there during the day if he couldn't reach me on the phone the night before. I hadn't given him my work phone number, but he called me there. He managed to convince one of the security guards to let him use the phone so that he didn't have to call collect. He'd reach me at my desk and always knew just what to say to send me rushing into the bathroom to break down in tears.

Often, he complained about me not sending him enough money for cigarettes and soap. He fussed about me turning my back on him just because he got in a little trouble, and how was a Black man going to survive this racist white beast if his own woman could be turned against him. He added that this never would have happened if I had been more supportive in the first place, and this never would have happened if I had bailed him out when he told me to. Since I didn't come through when he needed me, he ended up going back to court for a bond reconsideration, and while he was in the court-room for that, a man who had prosecuted him on a murder charge recognized him and wondered how Ron had gotten out of jail to commit another crime when he was supposed to be serving a twenty-five-year sentence in Maryland. There had been a mix-up between D.C. and Maryland, and Ron had mistakenly been released, but the twenty-five years he was supposed to serve was still on the books. Ron said it was my fault he was looking at having to do all that time. If I had believed in him, I would have moved to the Caribbean with him when we first got married. He'd said we could move to one of the islands, find jobs, and live happily ever after. I was at least smart enough not to go that far away from my family with a man who had no job. The sex was good when it was good, but not good enough to go that far.

"You ain't no kinda wife! You never believed in me," he would say through clenched teeth as I sat at my desk holding the phone to my ear, holding back the tears. "You ain't half the woman my sisters are. You got all that college knowledge, but don't know how to survive on the streets. You turn your back on a nigga."

I'd run into the bathroom and cry.

"Mizzzz Tate, you okay," Len would ask, noticing my red watery eyes when I returned. Nobody on my new job at the *Post* knew I was married. I had not reached either of the columnists on the phone all those times I'd called, and by the time I got hired, I'd found out about Ron's rap sheet and decided against pleading his case.

Somehow, Ron still convinced me to come see him and bring him more money when I got off work in the evenings. I had to go in the evening because the bus didn't run out to Upper Marlboro, Maryland on weekends. It ran only through the week for suburban workers.

I was nervous walking the cold, dark, mile-and-a-half stretch from the subway station to the detention center in Upper Marlboro. No bus traveled this route for obvious reasons, and, yes, I felt quite pitiful, foolish even. I had not gone to a prison to visit my own father, not to see my own brother. Now, here I was trekking out to some far-off jail in the dark to see some no-good man who didn't treat me right when he was on the outside. I could feel my shoulders slumping under the weight of my thoughts, the weight of my thick tan parka, and the weight of my leather-like attaché hanging from my right shoulder. The lampposts along this stretch did little to cut the eeriness held by thick woods on both sides of the road. There was no walkway, because it wasn't meant for folks to walk this road. Cars whizzed by in a rush to the same destination as me. Once I got lucky and a young woman in a white Mercedes-Benz slowed down because she thought she recognized my coat from behind.

"'Scuse me?" she called out. "You goin' to Upper Marlboro?"

Upper Marlboro was the nickname for the city's detention center where the accused were held pending trial.

I looked and noticed her perfectly coifed hairdo, a precision bob squared about two inches up her long, slender neck. "You want a ride?" she asked.

"Sure," I said flatly. I recognized her face from the visiting room the week before.

In the ten-minute ride down the rest of the stretch, she managed to tell me more than I needed to know about her boyfriend and about herself. Her boyfriend, Reggie, was accused of raping a white woman in a park in suburban Virginia, but, of course, the police got the wrong man because what would he need with some skinny ole white woman when he had her fulfilling all his needs. Reggie wasn't no ugly man, and even if she wasn't giving it to him anytime he wanted, he wouldn't need to take it, she insisted. They had been going together two years, and he had two kids by some other woman who couldn't fulfill his needs, but he had been good to Carla and Carla had been good to him. Carla could afford to be good to him because she lived in her grandmother's basement and didn't have to pay for nothing but her car note and insurance. More than I needed to know. I didn't feel like talking about Ron, and Carla must've sensed this, because she kept right on talking.

I nodded on cue as if I was listening, but really I was wiggling my toes to thaw them and feeling tired and thinking about a school assignment due in two days, and the article I needed to finish for work. Fearing Ron's wrath, I also was thinking about how he'd gotten progressively worse in the last few weeks. Just last week he'd called and cursed me out for sending him a picture of me and my girl-friends at the club. He'd asked for a photo and I sent him one that my girls and I had taken last spring. But that infuriated him. He'd called me, fuming, saying I didn't look like no Muslim wife and even his friends said so and what the heck was I doing out at some club shaking my behind with some other niggaz. I dreaded going to face him again.

Carla parked, and popped out of the car with a quickness, grabbing her Gucci purse, pulling her stylish black leather jacket close to her tall frame. I grabbed my leather-like bags and tried to keep up, rushing up the walkway to the green metal doors of the two-story, red-brick building surrounded by grass and shrubbery. Carla snatched open the door, and I followed closely behind her.

"Damn!" she said, surveying the long line of mostly women, many with babies or toddlers, waiting to be searched. "I called myself leaving work early to beat the crowd." She sighed.

"It's usually died down some by the time I get here," I said in my still flat, monotone voice. My throat was tight, choked up by thoughts of what might be waiting for me, choked up by being in this place.

Carla and I signed the guest book and got in line.

"Oh, you want to take my number so I can pick you up next week?" she offered, friendly as if we'd known each other from school or something. "No sense in you having to take the subway and walk. I can meet you somewhere or pick you up."

"I live in Northeast, over there by Gallaudet," I said.

"I live uptown," she said proudly. "But I don't mind picking you up."

I handed her one business card to write her number on the back and one to keep.

"You work at *The Washington Post?!*" she screeched.

"Um-hmm," I said in a low voice, hoping to quiet her some.

"You think you can get somebody to do a story on what the system is doing to my man?"

I lied and said I would try. It was soon my turn to step up and open my purse and attaché for the woman in the uniform to search me.

"I hate them ole freaky thangs patting me down," Carla said. "Reggie's gon' owe me big time when he gets out!"

We found chairs side by side in the waiting room and waited for our names to be called. Carla was called in a jiffy, but I waited and waited, growing anxious as the second hand on the wall clock in front of me ticked slowly. I was hungry, but had no change for the soda or snack machines near the entrance. Finally, my name was called and I moved—heavily, as if burdened—into the visiting hall, a narrow aisle with stools at a counter in front of a large Plexiglas partition. The "residents" sat on stools on the other side of the partition. I could tell Ron was angry by the snarl on his face as he approached his stool, his bright orange, prison-issue uniform hanging on him loosely, his white crocheted kufi pulled down over his hair looking like it hadn't been cut in weeks, and his mustache looking scraggly. I sucked in enough air to breathe a few more minutes, and grabbed the black telephone to talk through the glass.

He was gritting his back teeth, jaws flinching, as he sat down.

"Why didn't you answer the fucking phone last night!" he began through clenched teeth.

"I was sleep," I muttered weakly.

His face tightened even more. He stood and leaned into the glass. "You wasn't sleep!" he fumed. "Who was you sleepin' with!"

"Nobody," I muttered, my eyes cast down, thinking I could avoid part of this wrath just by not looking at him directly.

"You lying!" He hit the glass.

I was shaken.

"Look at me when I'm talking to you, goddamit!"

I couldn't look at him, couldn't speak. I wanted to tell him about how depressed I had been feeling the last two weeks. Wanted to tell him I stayed in the bed all day on weekends and if I wasn't at my job, all I could do was stay home under the covers trying to sleep to escape the agony inside. And that last night I'd taken half a bottle of painkillers hoping to kill all the pain and myself.

"You hear me talking to you! Answer me, goddamit!"

"I couldn't get up last night because I took some pills, but I guess

I didn't take enough," I shot back, half hoping he would feel sorry for me and let up.

"What?! You took some pills?! What, you tried to kill yourself?! What!?! You better not be coming in here telling me no punk-ass shit like that! They got me locked up like a fuckin' animal, and you tryna do what!?!"

He slammed the glass with the palm of his hand and I jumped.

Maybe it was sad that he couldn't get up and walk out of there like I could, but what about me? Bastard. He embarrassed the hell out of me. My husband was in jail. All my girlfriends knew, the neighbors back in my old neighborhood knew, my family knew. My husband was back in jail. How could I have been stupid enough to marry a criminal? Was it true that all my book learning had made me dumb when it came to real-life stuff?

"I said listen to me, goddammit!" He slapped the glass again. His verbal assault woke me the fuck up, and I stood up to leave. I stood right there and stared at him, strength coming from God knows where. My face might've still looked soft, but I could feel my eyes and my heart growing harder. If he could read my mind now, he would hear no plea for his sympathy. He would hear, "How dare you, stupid muthafucka. Your ass was out there breaking into other people's houses while I was home lonely as hell. So-called married, but lonely as hell for real because my stupid-ass husband is out there breaking into other people's houses!"

If he could read the writing in my eyes, or touch the words being inscribed on my heart, he would be mad to find that I was happy as hell he was locked up at last. He would know that those times he came into the room high on cocaine, explosive, crazed, he'd scared the hell out of me, and I'd prayed in my heart of hearts, "Allah, can you hear a sistah? Can you help a sistah out of this mess?"

He slapped the glass between us again, pointing to the phone, telling me to pick it up again. I stood there thinking, *Fuck you!* I could hear him through the Plexiglas even after I hung up the phone.

Carla's boyfriend ran down from the other end of the hall and tried to take the receiver out of Ron's hand.

"Man, you can't be talking to that woman like that," he told him. "You can't be disrespecting your own woman..."

"Nigga, I got this!" Ron shot at him "This *my* woman doing some punk-ass shit!" He turned back to me. "Sonsyrea!"

I was embarrassed as hell, and mad as hell, and a tear streamed from my eye.

"Sonsyrea!" he yelled again into the phone, knocking on the window. "Put the phone back to your ear, goddamit! Look at me!" His snarling and arms carrying on made his message clear.

"Man, calm down for they come pull you up outta here. You don't be talking to your woman like that."

"Man, fuck that girl! She need to cry. Act like she don't got no goddamn feelings. Her ass need to cry."

I had not been the crying type before now. I had been the think-it-through type, the burn-you-with-a-pot-of-hot-grits type, the cut-patches-of-your-hair-in-your-sleep type, but not the tear-dripping type. I had not seen either of my grandmothers cry, had never seen my mother cry. Not ever. At least, I had not seen them cry tears. Maybe Ma was crying when she yelled and screamed at us kids daily through the years when her life seemed to be spiraling out of control. Maybe she was crying when she slapped my teenage face for demanding of her answers she did not have, answers she needed but could not get. My grandmothers must've cried at some time in their lives, at some time in my life, even. But I'd never seen them cry tears, so it irritated me to my soul that this man had moved me to tears. I had not cried tears since I was eight or nine, and a very tender-headed girl. I cried when Ma combed my nappy hair, nappier after washing it. But I learned to do my hair myself so I wouldn't have to sit there and cry.

His words resonated in my ears and tears streamed down my face. "She need to cry," he said.

I wiped the slow trickle from my face and turned to leave. Ron banged on the glass and a uniformed guard came and took him back to his cell. I grabbed my bags and rushed out of the visiting hall, across the waiting area in the lobby, straight to the bathroom, where I let loose and cried like a baby. Leaning against the wall, trying not to see myself in the mirror in front of me, I cried and cried, aching in my chest and throat. I cried and cried, thinking that nobody could be as stupid as I was. I cried and cried. All I tried to do for this man and this was how he was treating me? I cried. I'm the one in college and working, his sisters are lying at home having babies, on welfare, and he's saying I'm not half the woman they are? I cried. How could he hate me so much? He used to say he loved me, now it was clearly hate.

I remembered a nasty card he had mailed me, a hand-made card he or one of his cellmates had made. It had a coloring of a beautiful apple on the cover, but when I opened the card the apple had a nasty worm oozing out with the words: "Deep inside, you're no good." How could he say I was "no good"? He was the one out robbing people and breaking into people's houses.

Another time he sent a letter that emitted a very foul smell when opened. He wrote that he had ejaculated onto the paper and said I had become a "come bucket" for whatever man I was probably sleeping with. How could he be so mean? God, what was going on? Why did I even care what he thought about me? How could I be so stupid? How could I be so weak? My mother and grandmothers never would have been so dumb. I cried and cried, with my back against the bathroom wall there in the waiting room at the jail. It was all I could do to stay on my feet. I was sliding down the wall, my knees buckling. A white woman with her hair obviously dyed blonde and big-ass ghetto-girl earrings came in and walked past me with hardly a notice.

A young Black woman about my age came in balancing a baby girl on her hip. She seemed too busy to say hello. As she set the toddler on the floor, then turned to put on makeup, I looked at myself in the mirror and decided I didn't have to stay stupid. I was suddenly happy that at least I wasn't lugging around Ron's baby. I thanked God I didn't have a baby.

"In the name of Allah, Most Gracious, Most Merciful. You gotta get me out of this mess," I prayed. I started with the formal prayer I had learned growing up, then let the words come straight from my heart. I washed my face and dried it with one of the hard brown hand towels provided. I wasn't wearing makeup. I looked plain-Jane, as usual. I snatched open the door and suddenly knew I wouldn't be coming back to this place to subject myself to that kind of abuse.

As I walked through the lobby, I noticed a familiar face standing in line to get inside the visiting room. It was Karren, the same woman who'd driven Ron home in the wee morning hours sometimes, the woman who'd loaned him her car, and who showed up at his hearing to show her support. She was good and pregnant, too. Had another raggedy scarf tied on her head and baggy clothes, looking like a Muslim woman. I marched right over to her.

"'Scuse me. Are you going to see Ronald Bates?" I asked calmly. She was calm, too. Not exactly ghetto like his sisters. She nodded. "Oh, is that his baby? You look like you're due."

"Excuse me?"

"Oh. I'm Ray-Ray, his wife. My brother told me he had a baby on the way by you, but Ron denied it."

"He asked me not to tell you until ya'll got your marriage back on track."

"Oh. Our marriage is over. Have a nice life."

I walked out of there feeling much different than when I'd walked in. A song that once played when we were screwing in the backseat of his mother's car came to mind.

Through the fire, to the limit, to the wall
For a chance to be with you, I'll gladly risk it all.

Not anymore. I was done with Ron and his brand of hell. One of my schoolteachers used to say what doesn't kill you makes you grow stronger, and I knew I was stronger now.

I thought Ron was right where he belonged, and maybe somebody would rape him so he'd know the feeling. Years later, I realized in some way he'd already felt helpless and that's why he put that on me. I prayed that he'd become empowered instead. I read somewhere that hurt people hurt other people, so I prayed for his healing. I also later understood that one man couldn't possibly get all he needed from one woman—nor could I get all I needed from one man. Our humanity and divinity were too complex to allow for that. I had needed something different from six different uncles growing up. My father had ten kids and a wife, and a job, and a passion for making music and making money, so he had only minutes here and there to give me his undivided attention, but my uncles Hussein, Wallace, Avon, Sharrief, and Butch all had added richly to my life. I had needed more than one mother, too, and got mothering from aunts and my own girlfriends. Our humanity was too complex to map out in neat little relationships, strictly defined by certain parameters. I was beginning to think about all this stuff.

Chapter Nine
God Damned

By the time I married Ron, I had worshipped three different gods—pretty much—if you consider religion to be a god, which I did since it dominated my every thought and movement. I had been raised in the Nation of Islam from ages three through ten, then practiced the Sunna Islam (as practiced by Prophet Muhammad and his Arab followers) until I was about eighteen. Then a new interpretation of the Quran was published and I was told the old Sunna Islam was questionable, that the Quran didn't really require women to wear veils or marry at the onset of puberty. The new interpretation of the Holy Quran claimed the number nineteen was God's most important number, not the number three, as we initially believed. So much nonsense. I wasn't sure I wanted to be bothered with any religion at all.

I had time to think about all this stuff now. Sometimes I thought about it while standing at my kitchen stove stirring dinner. I thought as I washed dishes, as I cleaned my home. There was so much to think about, now that I had time for just thinking, and wasn't so caught up in surviving day to day, worrying about my husband's next move. Thinking time was good for me.

I thought about how some Muslims swore by Allah and swore by Islam. Swore that Islam—its doctrines and philosophies, its rules and regulations—is the most life-giving force anyone could hope to have. Muslims said Islam was the most peaceful religion, the most enriching, empowering, and soul-stabilizing thing in the world, but to me it felt more like a sword. It was the cause of internal conflict, external embarrassment, and a tense struggle to reconcile the Arab Islamic culture being forced on me with the African-American culture I had grown to love.

The Hadith, one of the sacred texts Muslims use to study the life, times, and practices of Prophet Muhammad, said Muslim women should be modest and wear veils, for instance. When I was about fourteen, I'd begun arguing with my mother that what was modest in the Middle East was hardly modest here, so we were violating the spirit of that law.

"Ma, the dictionary says 'modest' means behaving so you don't draw attention to yourself. These Muslim clothes here in America draw everybody's attention to me. Like I'm trying to make a statement, like everybody's got to know I'm a Muslim because that's supposed to be special. That's not being modest," I argued. "Anyway, Uncle Hussein says, 'when in Rome, do like the Romans.' Wearing these clothes is somebody else's culture. A lot of this stuff we do—taking off our shoes to come in the house, sitting on the floor to eat instead of at a table, eating with our fingers instead of a fork, that don't got nothing to do with my relationship to my God. That's somebody else's culture." The prophet Muhammad and his friends ate with their fingers, I argued, "because they didn't have silver spoons and forks back then! That was four hundred years ago! They ate on cloths on the floor because they couldn't afford a table! Why are we trying to live like people lived four hundred years ago?" I couldn't articulate it clearly enough at the time, but I was thinking that our modern conveniences were divinely inspired and should be appreciated as such. Why should we live stuck in the past?

Of course I was mad as hell when just a few years later she read these same insights in a book and accepted them. I'd been trying to tell her, but had no credibility with her because of my youth and because I was her child.

Besides the Arab-style clothes clashing with American styles, Arab expectations of women also were different from what would be required of me as a young African-American woman. My mother had formed my girlfriends and me into a quasi Girl Scout troop that she called Modest Maidens. She organized tea parties so we could practice baking, and planned trips to the movies for us, though we would have to analyze and condemn the behavior of the American teen sex goddesses we saw on the screens. Never mind that where I was coming from—a rugged inner-city neighborhood—and where I was going—into government politics or corporate America, there was no place for damned modest maidens. I would quickly learn away from home that women in these places gotta curse guys out. Give a blow or take one. Better to become thick-skinned, with an edge of anger and righteous indignation than meek and modest. But my mother didn't know that. She had retreated from office politics at the hospital where she worked when I was a baby and would not return to the work force for more than twenty years. She made raising her children her full-time job at home. Teaching me and my girl-friends proper lady-like etiquette was more fun for her than for us.

But her little activities could be fun sometimes. Ma even came up with a song for us to sing when she piled us into her station wagon for trips to the museums downtown. The song went, "M-U-S-L-I-M, I am a Muslim, yes, I am." Over and over we sang it, getting louder each time until it was a scream. "M-U-S-L-I-M! I AM A MUSLIM! YES, I AM!"

I no longer called myself a Muslim once I got to college. I might mention my Muslim upbringing when the occasion called for it. But, I didn't really feel like a Muslim anymore. I felt even less affinity for Islam after my fiasco of a marriage to Ron. We both had misused or innocently misunderstood the religion to destructive ends. My belief that I should get married to sanction sex was a misunder-standing. I had to learn that abstinence could be an option, but most importantly, learn that my sexuality is a gift from God, and my love, too. Religious folks want to regulate everything with rules and restrictions. But love is like air. It just is what it is and simply does what it does. Aunt Brenda liked to say, "We can't control who we love," and I believed her. I analyzed sex restrictions and marriage to the hilt and determined that the leaders of society felt the need to regulate who's responsible for what children and who belongs to what family in order to maintain a civil society, but goddamn, they went too far. But times changed. Birth control devices were created and made available to anyone. I wondered why we still needed restrictions on sex. Some religious folks talked about sex having a spiritual thing to it, something that created a natural bond between the sex partners. But I realized in my twenties that it doesn't take sex to create a bond between folks. Sometimes the bond is there, you recognize it, you feel it, and celebrate it through sex.

My separation from Ron gave me time to reconsider what a marriage was. Marriage certainly could not be declared simply by signing an official document. Marriage was about becoming one with someone else in some way and we never quite did that. We never even fully acknowledged or appreciated what it was that we had in common. If Ron knew, he certainly did not articulate it. My heart knew, but that knowledge had not reached my consciousness.

Being single also gave me more solitude to contemplate my beliefs in God and religion. I desperately wanted to understand what I had done wrong with Ron so I wouldn't repeat that mistake again. I wanted to know and wanted to know immediately, but that understanding would take many years. Meanwhile, my disdain for, my disillusionment with, and my disappointment in organized religion took root.

I was standing at a bus stop one day when a sidewalk ad for a palm reader caught my attention. For only five dollars and a ten-minute commitment, she could ascertain my whole future right from the palm of my hand. Without giving charity to a mosque building fund, or giving a weekly percentage of my paycheck to a religion in exchange for God's inspiration to an appointed minister, I could find out what God had in store for me, personally. It's right there in the palm of my hand already. I had seen the sign many times, but this day I chose to check it out, so I hiked up a very narrow, very steep staircase, knocked on a dirty door painted a dull shade of orange, and was greeted by a woman of obvious Hispanic heritage. I sat at her small kitchen table and offered my palms when she reached for them around a pillar candle. She saw good fortune in my palms and a broken family. She read one line to indicate divorce. I left there excited about the few things from my past that she discerned with accuracy.

"Girl! She predicted I was goin' get divorced! I hadn't even told her about Ron, and she said my marriage line showed divorce!" I told Chee-Chee, whom I called as soon as I got back to my apartment that evening.

"Girl, I told you not to go messing with that foolishness. That's some satanic shit!" she said. "You let that devil in your system and might never get it out. Don't nobody know your future but God. Shit, how much you give that woman? I coulda looked in your damn palm and told you to get the hell away from that damn Ron. Hell, I told you that already. You ain't give me no damn five dollars..."

"She said other stuff that she couldn't have known," I said.

"Girl, your ass is see-through as a damn piece of glass. I tell you all the time you wear your heart on your damn sleeve. Bitch probably read your ass like a book. She probably saw your ass coming. What else she got to do every day but sit up in her window watching all the people at the bus stop, just waiting for some fool to walk up them steps and hand over her five dollars? How long you been catching the bus from that stop? She probably been watching your ass a while. Just waiting. Probably got more than five dollars outta you, too. I know how they do. Get you in there and tell you just enough shit for five dollars to get you spending more money on all they other shit. Tell the truth, Ray-Ray, you probly got the forty-minute special for thirty-five, didn't you?" She laughed.

"Chile, please. I didn't even have thirty-five dollars. I just think it's fascinating that somebody you don't know can know so much about you and your past," I said.

"Girl, you better leave that shit alone."

Two years later, I would find myself drawn to other psychics, and, yes, spending more money for the hour-long special. One day I went to one, a lady who called herself Joy, and she told me so much shit I didn't like, I ran to another psychic, recommended by some folks on my job, so he could release me from the hex I was sure the evil woman had put on me. When I thought about it later, Joy and the psychic I ran to next, George, had both read the same characteristics in my personality, but they had presented their readings differently. For instance, Joy said I was "self-destructive," George said I was "too hard on myself and should lighten up." This Joy woman said I was foolish and repeated the same mistakes over and over. George said I was unconventional and determined in my beliefs until proven beyond a shadow of a doubt that I should change them. I tore up the taped conversation with Joy immediately, and eventually lost the cassette with the conversation between me and George. But the most important lesson I learned from them was that perspective and presentation of any set of facts depends on the agenda and understanding of the interpreter.

Chee-Chee and I would play with tarot cards, interpreting the symbols for each other and for ourselves. I was beginning to learn that my fate is in my hands, that I shape and mold my future based on my own devices. I did not need to rely on text hundreds of years old, or inspirations, understandings, and interpretations from other individuals—in organized religions or corner con-shops.

I was feeling more free to live and enjoy life on my own terms.

Chapter Ten
Heaven in My Heart

A s far as religion went, I figured I could do without it. Increasingly, I became more interested in the spirit of the rules and regulations I had been trained in through the Nation of Islam than through the practice of Sunni (Orthodox) Islam. For instance, I began to appreciate that the idea behind stopping work or whatever we were doing to pray five times a day had more to do with knowing that at least five times a day we could get off the treadmill of life and acknowledge our connection to a source bigger and more powerful than our individual selves. The actual ritual didn't matter to me so much—leaving an office or classroom in the middle of a work day to perform a ritual wash (scrub your hands up to your elbows three times, wash your face three times, up your nostrils and inside your ears three times, rinse your mouth three times, wash your feet three times), then finding a quiet place, facing the Middle East, and reciting a series of Arabic prayers. It would not occur to me until many years later that stopping to pray at certain times, acknowledged by Muslims around the world, created five times a day a fellowship that most religions have established only once a week—Saturdays or Sundays. Later, I could appreciate billions of Muslims around the world praying in one language—Arabic—a plea for guidance and forgiveness five times a day each day. I also would realize, however, that training our thoughts on living in harmony with others by praying five times a day could be as ineffective as once-a-week worship if the believers believed in the rituals more than the spirit of those rituals.

Some of the meanest, most spiteful and vindictive people I knew went to church every week. The main gossipers on campus were often the same people who went to church every week and looked down on you if you didn't belong to one. It was easy enough for me to disregard religious folks like this, and easy enough to disregard the strictness of the religion I was raised with. But leaving a religion behind turned out to be a lot more difficult than simply taking off a head wrap. The religious tenets I had learned had become a part of me. I would find myself zikring (chanting Arabic phrases: *Supanallah al-humdulillah*, which means God is good and God is great) to calm a variety of thoughts racing through my mind. I would decline pork because I figured my body might reject it since I wasn't used to it. I would still wear my clothes loosely and modestly simply because that's what I was most comfortable with.

When I heard my Muslim grandmother talk about preparing to fast during the month of Ramadan, I thought about the spirit of Ramadan. Fasting—refraining from food, drink, and sex during the daylight hours—was good practice in self-restraint, discipline, and mind over matter. But I realized fasting was not the only way to practice self-discipline and enjoy a sense of personal fulfillment. I had to exercise considerable self-discipline in order to manage my schoolwork and job, and I did it.

I realized, too, that some of my favorite pop and R&B songs on the radio were as inspiring and instructive as gospel songs sang in churches and played on gospel radio stations. I bought Whitney Houston's album and played the tracks off the songs that spoke to my predicament at the time.

Yeah, I wanna dance with somebody
With somebody who loves me

Ma had told me on a regular to watch the words I sang because words program the mind toward certain actions and if I sang about sex, I was programming my mind to seek sex. But I realized some of these songs only reflected what my mind and body already were naturally programmed to. As a young woman, my body naturally was inclining toward sex because that's how animals, which humans are, reproduce. I didn't crave sex because of these songs. These songs affirmed what I instinctively knew. Yeah, I wanted to dance with somebody. A dance is about getting in sync with another person, getting a rhythm going.

I wanna feel the heat with somebody
With somebody who loves me

I played Whitney's album over and over and over as I danced around my apartment, cleaning up here and there, cooking, straightening books, hanging up clothes off my bed where I piled them up for days.

Where do broken hearts go
Can they find their way home
Back to the open arms
Of a love that's waiting there

She was singing my songs.

I also bought Kool Moe Dee's album, and his song "How Ya Like Me Now" became another one of my freedom songs.

Get off this stage
I'm in rage
Just like a lion
Trapped inside a cage

I loved having my little apartment all to myself, and loved my new life out on my own. I shopped for more household stuff and clothes. I loved shopping, loved carrying home bags full of little things—stockings, nail polish, new shoes, more form-fitting dresses. I got good at finding bargains at Woodies. They had a clearance floor where I could lose myself for hours picking over out-of-season and irregular pieces with a slight tear or missing button. I was buying clothes more colorful and fancy than anything I'd worn since before my mother joined the Nation of Islam when I was three years old. My favorite was a soft nylon red-and-white pin-striped dress I found on a clearance rack, and I must've worn it to work at least once a week.

I felt more free and more bold with Ron gone. I enjoyed listening to the radio at night. Howard University's WHUR-FM had a "Quiet Storm" of love songs every evening from seven to midnight and I could get lost in the music. Sometimes there was a message in a love song, a message as powerful as any old spiritual or gospel tune. One evening I was reading a textbook for school, listening to the radio, and a tune I loved years before came on with a strong reminder.

You've got to follow your road
Follow your road
Follow your road
And maybe someday your road will lead you far away.

My innocence was lost. In the three short years since I'd left the comfort of my chaotic Muslim home, my innocence was lost—given away, you might say, but gone for sure.

I remembered being innocent. I remembered being sixteen, so ready to leave home, so ready to be different from any of the women I knew, so ready. I remembered.

Chapter Eleven
Can't Leave Home Without It

You can leave home all you want, but home will never leave you. This much I know. Leaving home is what I'd dreamed of since I was thirteen, at least. I didn't know exactly what I wanted, but I knew I wanted a life far different from the one I had. I was a Muslim girl, and my mother thought she was training me to be a good Muslim woman, a domesticated wife and mother. No way. If my mother thought I was going to live the rest of my life changing diapers, cooking for a big family, dressing in long, shapeless clothes that made me uncomfortable among my peers in their fashionable painted-on jeans, and trying to fit five prayers into my every day, she had another thing coming.

I got myself into the local university when I was sixteen, forging my parents' names on the forms requiring their permission. Ma tried to keep me from going away to college, using our religion as an excuse, saying Allah's purpose for my life was for me to become a Muslim wife and have as many babies as He would bless me with, but that was her nonsense, not mine. She and a lot of other women who learned about Islam when it first became popular in the African-American community back in the seventies, believed that nonsense or found it a convenience that allowed them to lie at home having babies, making us eldest daughters do all the work. Ma also thought I was too young to leave home because I was two years younger than most kids going to college, but I knew Dr. Martin Luther King Jr. had gone to college early, and so had my Uncle Hussein.

Ma succeeded in keeping me from going away to school at sixteen, but she couldn't keep me from "leaving" home emotionally, mentally and spiritually. I decided I was going to be *soooo* different from Ma and the other Muslim women, who believed, as they used to say, that "a woman could only make it to paradise if her husband was pleased with her." Hadn't they read the parts in our holy books, The Holy Quran and the Hadith, that said paradise lies at the feet of the mother? Even my Christian grandmother and aunts believed a woman wasn't worth a damn unless and until a man picked her to be his wife, his helpmate, his support, the most honor a woman could hope to achieve in her lifetime.

I knew there was more to life than what I'd experienced so far. My favorite books of philosophy and poetry by Khalil Gibran, an unconventional eastern thinker; and Nikki Giovanni, an African-American feminist poet, had told me so. My favorite fiction, Richard Bach's *Jonathan Livingston Seagull*, about a bird who dared to be different, and Hermann Hesse's *Siddhartha*, about a young man's courage to seek his own spiritual enlightenment, had given me ideas. And the gospel and R&B music I enjoyed suggested there was so much more to life than the Arabic prayers I'd been trained to recite while performing what now felt like rote ritual prayers. My favorite TV shows, including the breakthrough sitcoms, *The Cosby Show*, featuring a highly educated, professional African-American couple raising their kids together, and *A Different World*, about young men and women away from home for the first time, gave me vivid images of other experiences to seek.

Reaching the age of reckoning that every young person must, the age where there are more questions than answers about the hows and whys of life, the age where everything one has been taught about God, religion and life must be challenged for authenticity, the age when one begins to seek one's own self, I had more questions about the Islam my mother had given me than my mother had about the Christianity her parents had given her.

What did dressing like Arabs, eating like Arabs, praying in Arabic have to do with my connection to God, the Supreme Being? Couldn't God, Allah, hear and understand me in my own language? Hadn't God created my African-American self, too? What did removing our shoes at the door when entering a Muslim mosque or household, burning incense throughout the house, decorating our homes Mideastern style with pillows instead of couches and tablecloths on the floor rather than tables have to do with my connection to God, the Most Magnificent, Most Merciful? There was a difference between preserving a particular culture and following a certain doctrine, right? Sure there was. Author Gibran, who was from Lebanon, had informed me so through his books. There also was a difference between strict adherence to religious texts and rituals and individual, authentic spiritual pursuit, I was sure.

I'd read Quran all my young life and could still recite my favorites surahs (verses), the Fatiha and Rahman by heart. But my first attempt to read and understand the entire 1,800-page tome during the month of Ramadan so overwhelmed me I knew there had to be a better way. Many Islamic instructions and stories I'd learned now came into question. Was it anything more than silly superstition, for instance, that required Muslims to keep the bathroom doors shut at all times to keep the jinn-devil-Satan from escaping? When I thought about it, I realized someone long ago decided some odors left behind in bathrooms are indeed offensive and should be trapped, which made sense. But to lay this down as official Islamic instruction seemed a bit much. Another teaching was that Muslims should honor spiders by not killing them in our homes because a spider once spun a web across a cave opening, thus protecting Prophet Muhammad from his enemies who saw the web and concluded that Prophet Muhammad couldn't have been inside.

Stevie Wonder's song said, *when you believe in things you don't understand, you suffer. Superstition ain't the way.* His song seemed to warn me against corner con-artist psychics and this foreign religion, Islam. So much of what I learned about Islam just didn't make sense anymore.

I'd been taught that the main fallacy of Christianity was that Christians worshipped Jesus Christ rather than the Supreme Being, which could not be personified or captured in any single image. But it seemed to me that imitating Prophet Muhammad and honoring everything he said and did amounted to the same kind of worship. I'd been taught that unity was the cornerstone of Islam, and further distinguished it from Christianity, which was divided into too many sects. But I'd recently learned there were also different sects of Muslims beyond the Sunni Muslims, who adhere strictly to the teachings of the Quran and Prophet Muhammad only; and Shia Muslims, who also follow Prophet Muhammad's successor, his son-in-law, Ali. Here, in America, there were also Ahmadayis Muslims, Nation of Islam Muslims, New Nation of Islam Muslims, United Nation of Islam Muslims and groups that splintered off from those. And even within a particular group of Muslims, sometimes the members couldn't decide on which way to pray. Should they face northeast or southeast? So much for unity. Come to think of it, wasn't that a form of worshipping a particular territory? I wondered.

Then there were so many contradictions. For instance, many of the Muslim men embracing Islam in the seventies for nationalist reasons quit their jobs, claiming they conscientiously objected to working for the vile, racist American government, which oppressed African Americans and exploited non-western peoples around the world. But they had their wives on welfare, subsisting on a meager unearned check from this same government. Many of the Muslim women embraced Islam as youthful acts of rebellion or out of sincere confusion and spiritual need.

I even had my doubts about the value of marriage, which I was told as a Muslim would be my greatest test as a human being. Allah prescribed marriage for all the believers, I was taught, and marriage was half a Muslim's duties, because protecting women and providing for them was half a Muslim man's religious duties. Keeping a husband happy and raising children was more than half a Muslim woman's duties. I wondered about the women who biologically couldn't have children. Would they be barred from paradise, having fallen short of their motherly duties? What about women who just didn't want to get married? If Allah had given some men professional desires—to become doctors and engineers and community developers, why wouldn't He have given women professional desires, too? And who said marriage had to be so hard, requiring so much sacrifice? It seemed to me like we were making life harder than it needed to be.

There had been too many rules and regulations governing everything I did. Beyond the five pillars of Islam: attesting belief that there is only one God and Muhammad is His last Messenger, praying five times a day, fasting during the month of Ramadan, giving charity, and making a pilgrimage to Mecca at least once in a lifetime to observe Hajj, there were too many other guidelines to learn and follow. I'd been taught, for instance, that as a Muslim I must wipe my behind with my left hand after using the bathroom and shake hands with only my right; and cast my eyes down rather than looking a man in the face when talking in the interest of "modesty." I'd also been taught to refrain from salat, daily prayers, during my menstrual cycle, a time when my body was too impure to stand before God—though some would claim this rule was to relieve women of this duty during her special time. I could not imagine that I could go to a god at the end of my life and say: "I said and did everything You said for me to do. Now let me into paradise." I knew better, or wanted to know better. And so I was off to seek out my own truths.

The house was dark behind me as I sat on the bottom of the wooden stairs in our four-story townhouse in Washington, D.C.'s Wylie Courts community. The white foyer light over my head was all the illumination I needed as I double-tied my cool, blue-and-beige "duck" boots, getting ready to leave for campus. All was quiet except for a few cars whizzing by on the rainy streets out front. In the six bedrooms upstairs, my parents and nine siblings were getting in a few more winks before they had to start their day. We'd all been up at 6:10 in the morning for Fajr, the first prayer of the day in our Muslim lives. I'd gone back to bed, too, but got up again at 7:30 to get out before the house came alive with the drama of my sisters and brothers fighting over the bathrooms, Ma yelling at somebody for not doing something, and Dad pleading with Ma to iron his gray uniform shirt for work so he could get to work on time for a change.

Excited about registering for classes at the University of the District of Columbia, the city-run college, I zipped my blue, puffy, long ski coat all the way up to my throat, hoisted my brown canvas book bag on my shoulder, and moved through the dark hall into the kitchen, lighted only by the soft blue light of daybreak spilling through the small kitchen window. I knocked lightly on the wall as I entered the kitchen, in case our mouse was out. A little knocking would scare her away. The red numbers on the stove clock showed 8:10. I figured I had enough time to walk the ten blocks to the subway station and save the eighty cents it would cost to take the bus there. Money was tight. I'd saved money from my summer job for books and transportation, and had to budget it wisely. Ma had taught me how to budget. Since my first summer job when I was fourteen, Ma had required me to bring her my one-hundred-twenty-dollar bi-monthly paycheck and a list of things I needed, such as toothpaste, deodorant, feminine hygiene products, laundry products for my own clothes, new underwear to replace torn pieces, things I wanted such as movie tickets, snacks, or a particular cereal, and a chart showing approximately how much I planned to spend on each. I also was required to contribute to household bills—one year up to eighty dollars a month! And required, after all that, to put aside something for savings. Of course I hated learning this lesson when Ma was teaching it, but now it came in handy.

Tipping quietly through the kitchen, I snatched open the fridge and got the sandwich I'd made the night before for my lunch. I also checked on the baked chicken and rice dish I'd made for dinner tonight to see if anyone had been pinching off it, and took out the six baby bottles of formula I'd prepared for Ma. I put them in a pot of water on the stove so all Ma had to do was turn it on to heat while she fixed breakfast for the others going to school. Getting the kids off to school had been my job for the last year or so since Ma had been pregnant with the twins, but now I had to get myself going again. I stuffed the sandwich and an apple in my book bag. The prayer schedule, written in Arabic, listing the exact times for prayer each day for the whole Muslim calendar year, fell off the fridge door when it slammed shut. I sighed and put it back next to Ma's schedule of everybody's household chores, then reached for the back door. The sight of my siblings' shoes piled up by the door rather than lined up neatly as I'd tried to keep them caught my attention, and I bent over to straighten them up. Ma liked this Arab custom of removing your shoes when entering a Muslim mosque or household because it helped keep our white tile floors clean, but to me, the custom was just a nuisance. It was a nuisance having to stop at the door and untie your shoes, a nuisance to remember to take them up to your room when you went, and a bigger nuisance to straighten them all when everyone else forgot what they were supposed to do.

"Dag. Ma need to be on their case like she used to be on mine," I mumbled silently. "If it was me, she'd've made me straighten up my shoes and everybody else's just to teach me a lesson."

I looked up at the clock: 8:12. I was pushing it. Pushing time. I left half the pile of shoes there and jetted out the door. The brisk January winds tugged at my umbrella as I charged up the wide-open alleyway taking the shortcut to the main H Street corridor in back of our house. Pushing past muddy, trash-strewn vacant lots and abandoned buildings on my way to the Union Station subway stop, I passed small knots of folks fending off the wind and rain at bus stops along the way. I was pressing a thirty-minute walk to the subway station. The train ride would be about twenty minutes. In less than an hour, I would be in another world. A world my mother had warned me about.

Out in the world, Ma had told me people lost their souls in the pursuit of worldly goals and material things. Satan was in charge out in the world. Racism, sexism, lying, cheating, lewdness, trickery would swallow me whole and quickly. That's why Allah had prescribed that Muslim women were to stay home and let men, the stronger of our species, go out and brave the world. Ma and I had argued fiercely about my decision to go to college rather than stay home and continue to help her take care of my younger siblings, which I'd been doing since I'd graduated the previous June. Most of my three sisters and five brothers were in school, but Ma needed my help tending to my eighteen-month-old sister, Abeena, and our infant twin brothers, Hakim and Halim. Ma had tried to convince me that my highest calling as a Muslim woman was domestic duty, but I had argued that homemaking was no longer a full-time job—or it wouldn't have been if she hadn't made it so by having so many kids. I argued that back in the Prophet Muhammad's time when Arab women didn't have washing machines, ready-made groceries, and public schools to cut their workloads in half, they probably needed to be home all day to get their housework done.

"Back then it took all day to pick some wheat and grind it to make bread for dinner," I'd argued sarcastically.

If Ma was already stressed, which she often was for a variety of reasons, my arguments might get me slapped. But sometimes she couldn't deny I was telling the truth.

One evening when I was sitting in the living room, complaining about my neck hurting, Ma thought she would seize the opportunity to explain yet another benefit of matrimony.

"If you had a husband, he could massage your neck for you," Ma said.

"That's what they make the new showerheads for," I responded at the time. This was before my first marriage that added stress to my life, and before my second marriage that finally proved that matrimony to the right man could be a blessing. At sixteen years old, I wasn't the least bit interested in getting married. Ma hated my comments condemning marriage. This particular time, she just sucked her teeth and went on about her business.

The subway was crowded with working folks reading newspapers, magazines, and books, or just holding on to the rail overhead. Some were more wet than others from the rain. A young man in a bulky orange ski coat and black skull cap took up a whole seat with his boom box, which was connected to headphones he wore. He bopped to his music. Up close, I could hear go-go master Chuck Brown's "I

Feel Like Bustin' Loose" blasting in the headphones. The white folks seemed especially afraid to ask him to move, but I thought he was downright rude and politely motioned him, with my dripping umbrella, for him to move his boom box. My older brother Darren was a tough guy, so their appearance didn't scare me like it did others who only saw young tough-looking men like this in police mug shots on the news. Resting my head on the window on the subway train, where bright fluorescent lights bounced off bright orange seats and orange-and-brown carpet, I thought about the arguments I was leaving behind as the train breezed in and out of dark tunnels, stopping at clean but bustling waiting stations. I was pretty sure I'd made the right decision to go to school. I remembered the first time I prayed about it. I'd asked Dad what I should do and he'd left the decision to me, not wanting to get in the middle of an argument between me and Ma.

"That's gonna hafta be between you and Allah," he had told me on his way up the stairs as I followed on his heels, waving my official school forms.

"But, Dad, I hafta get your signature, or Ma's since I'm not eighteen yet," I pleaded. "You do want your daughter to be educated, don't you?" I added.

"Sonsyrea, like I said, that's between you and your Creator."

He only called me by my full name when he was serious. I'd marched on up to my room on the third floor that evening and lay on my bed thinking.

"I'm going to school!" I said to myself. "Some kinda way, I'm going to college. They can't keep me in this house the rest of my life." I got up and marched over to the dresser where I'd tossed the financial aid forms and forged both my parents' names. Then I plopped back down on the bed. "I'm getting up outta here," I said. "I'm going to college."

I'd stayed locked in my room the rest of that evening, refusing even to join the family for Isha, our fifth and final daily prayer. Ma had sent my sisters and brothers up to get me, but I'd refused. And when she came banging on my door, demanding I come out immediately, I'd refused. After I was sure everyone was asleep, about 12:30, I'd quietly gone in the bathroom and performed wudu, our pre-prayer ablution, then tiptoed downstairs and unfolded the prayer rug for my private prayer. I recited the Fatiha and the other Arabic phrases as I bowed, then kneeled, then prostrated down to the floor, then stood to repeat the movements and recitations four times as required for the nighttime prayer. Then, after all that, I stayed on my knees and talked to Allah in my own words, explaining my dilemma.

"Oh Allah, Most Gracious, Most Merciful, I come before You now," I began. "Okay, God, I don't even talk like that. God, what am I supposed to do with my life? You know I wanted to be a reporter since junior high school. I have to go to college to become a reporter. Is it a sin that I don't want to spend my life at home taking care of babies? God. What should I do? I still got the number for the news anchor my principal introduced me to, I could still call her for help. God, what? Can I even get in the media? Some of my teachers said I'd need a back-up career plan because Blacks couldn't get hired in the main media, is that real? God? What am I gonna do? Oh Allah, please guide me. Guide me along the right path, the path of those on whom You have bestowed Your grace, not of those whose portion is wrath nor those who go astray."

I fell back into the English version of the Arabic prayer I'd recited for years, then stopped again.

"God, I don't even know who the righteous people are anymore. If Muslims are the righteous ones, why are we so poor?"

Imitating Arabs, who had the backing of the oil-rich land they lived on, had not made us any richer here in America. And hadn't the Arabs had African slaves just like the European-Americans?

"God, please show me what to do with my life. You gave me my talents with music and writing for a reason, right?"

Sirens from the trucks at the fire station across the street broke my concentration and I ended my prayer by washing the invisible blessings from my cupped hands over my face. I stood up, rolling the prayer rug to put it back in its place, and for the first time in my life, felt as if I'd been on a telephone line talking directly to God. I felt much lighter going back up to my room. The fire trucks roared down the street as I lay back on my bed, looking up at the ceiling, thinking.

I shoulda been praying my own way in my own words all the time, I thought. *Maybe I'd've had more answers by now.*

The ritual salat I'd learned when my family converted from the Nation of Islam to Orthodox Islam felt like nothing more than an empty religious rite I'd been taught and forced to do. I'd been excited about learning the Arabic at first because it was a new language and I enjoyed learning anything new. But all through my teen years reciting the Arabic prayers and going through the series of movements felt like nothing more than that—going through the motions. This was the first time I felt something personal, as if some invisible something spoke directly to me.

"I'm going to college," I told myself more resolutely. I smiled, looking up at the ceiling. "Yep. I'm going."

Six months later, here I was. On my way.

"Next stop, Van Ness," a woman's voice announced over the intercom. I hopped from my seat to the sliding doors and waited for them to open.

Chapter Twelve
Feeling Good

The city was awake by the time I emerged from the underground railway. Men and women marched toward or away from the subway wrapped in scarves and hats, swinging briefcases and purses or both. They looked hurried and serious, and I couldn't wait to become one of them—an important person with some important job to go to. Up and down this stretch of Connecticut Avenue, much cleaner than the H Street corridor I'd left behind, banks, real estate offices, stores, and restaurants were just beginning to come alive. I looked up at my college, the University of the District of Columbia, a complex of four- and five-story concrete buildings with thin slits for windows, and realized I had arrived. It was not idyllic like universities I'd seen in magazines where students stretched out on lush lawns, picnicking and studying between classes, but it was a college and I was happy to be here.

So, this is the real world, I thought as I proceeded toward the administration building where I was scheduled to meet my academic adviser this morning. Based on my entry exams, I'd been referred to the honors program. I was surprised and happy they hadn't held my high school grades against me. It wasn't that I wasn't smart or couldn't be. I'd been in programs for the academically gifted all my childhood until my senior year when I'd simply had too much to think about.

"Yes, may I help you?" a young woman asked from the front desk.

"I'm here to see Mrs. Jackson," I said proudly. I began peeling off my knitted gloves and coat.

"Are you a student here?" asked the young woman.

"Yes," I answered. "This is my first semester. I'm starting late, but..."

"Late? You look like you belong in junior high school." She laughed. Tall and lean, even sitting behind a desk, she wore her hair pulled back in a curly ponytail.

"I'm not as young as I look," I explained.

My hair was parted down the middle and neatly twisted into two large twists going back. My brown skin was smooth from eating healthy according to our Muslim diet, which in the Nation of Islam prohibited fried foods and as Orthodox Muslims limited us to only kosher chicken and beef, which cut down on preservatives and other toxins.

"How old are you?" the young woman continued.

"Sixteen," I said.

"You look twelve!" she said, laughing, surprised.

I was beginning to feel a little intimidated.

"How did you get to college so young? Were you skipped?"

"No, I wasn't skipped. I just started school early," I explained.

"You must have started real early," she said.

"I was three. I went to a private school where they gave us an early start."

"What school..."

Just then, a buxom woman, strutting in high heels, rushed in, her large purse swinging behind her. I was glad to get out of divulging my Muslim background. No one needed to know I'd been in the Nation of Islam and went to Muslim school in elementary.

"Good morning! Good morning!" the entering woman screeched.

She was polished, her red lipstick and nails carefully coordinated. Purple purse matching purple pumps.

"Mrs. Jackson, this is...what'd you say your name was?"

"Sonsyrea. Sonsyrea Tate," I answered, feeling shy in my new environment.

"She's here for the honors program," the woman behind the desk continued. "Can you believe she's only sixteen, and doesn't she look twelve?"

If they only knew. My Uncle Hussein had graduated from high school at the University of Islam when he was only fourteen, and he went on to George Washington University, a white college, and graduated as salutatorian of his class. He was my role model. Starting college at sixteen was nothing. But Uncle Hussein was sick now, looked like he was dying, so I tried not to think about him too much. I certainly couldn't talk about him without getting choked up.

"Are you sure you belong here," Mrs. Jackson said, smiling like I was some adorable little mascot.

At least I was feeling welcomed again, though.

"Yes, I got this letter saying I needed to see you before registering for classes," I said, turning the conversation back to the business at hand.

"And you didn't bring your mother with you?" She smiled. "I'm surprised she let you out of her sight."

"I came early so I can still beat the crowd at registration," I said, redirecting my adviser again. "I called last week and was told that registration can take three to four hours. I think if I get a head start..."

"Oh, look, she's so proficient," Mrs. Jackson said, still marveling. "Follow me, dear."

I followed her into her office where she sipped coffee as we discussed my interests and intentions.

"So you'd like to major in mass media?" she said, surveying the application she pulled from her file with my name on it. "You're sure about this?"

"Yes, ma'am. I plan to work in the media," I explained confidently.

"I wish more of our young people were so focused," she said.

"Some of our students leave here still not knowing what they want to do."

I'd been encouraged back in my Muslim school to identify my God-given talents, even if I was only supposed to use them for my family and Muslim community. That's when I'd decided to do something with my love for writing. The prayer I'd made before sending in my paperwork sealed it.

"I circled the classes I'd like to take," I said, leaning over Mrs. Jackson's desk.

"Oh you're going to do well here." She smiled. "I can see. You're going to do very well."

My favorite class that first semester was public speaking and most of our assignments were exercises in self-discovery—learning more about our interests and passions through persuasive speeches, for instance. For one assignment, we took an imaginary trip through the woods. Professor Legall, a short, tan woman with a short brown natural, a button nose, and round glasses that made her look like a cute owl, came from behind her desk at the front of the room and announced the assignment.

"Imagine that you're about to go on a hiking trip through the woods," our professor began. "Describe what kind of day it is."

"It's a warm, sunny, spring day," I wrote.

"Describe what you plan to wear and why," she continued.

"I plan to wear my old jeans and my rain boots in case it's still muddy from the rain over the weekend. And I'll wear long sleeves so the insects can't eat me alive. And..."

"You are going hiking alone or with friends. Tell whom you'll be traveling with and why," she continued.

"By myself. I like walking by myself so nobody can rush me or slow me down," I wrote.

I was enjoying this exercise. My answers were probably supposed to reveal more about me than I wanted known, so, I was careful to keep my answers short.

"On your journey through the woods, you find a cup," the professor continued. "Describe the cup. What do you do with it?"

"It's a broken china teacup," I wrote. "I pick it up and put it in the trash so the path won't get cluttered with more trash."

"There's a fork in the road. To the right, there's a paved dirt path, to the left the path is hardly visible through the forest. Which path do you take and why?"

I had to stop and think about this one. Since I was ten or so and my family converted to Orthodox Islam, I'd been reciting the prayer, the Fatiha, that says, "Guide me along the straight path, the path of those on whom Thou has bestowed Thou grace, not of those whose portion is wrath, nor those who go astray." But I was looking for new ground now, dissatisfied with the path I was on. Just last year, I'd read a book Uncle Hussein had given me about a fictitious, strangely ambitious bird named Jonathan Livingston Seagull. Jonathan had been dissatisfied with how most birds lived so he set off into new territory, spending his time perfecting his flying skills rather than scrounging days and nights for crumbs. Uncle Hussein had told me I was Jonathan and should live as Jonathan lived. As much as I tried not to think about Uncle Hussein, there he was, somehow, always in my thoughts. Jonathan flew far away from where the other birds stayed, I remembered.

"I take the road less traveled," I wrote, drawing from the title of another book I saw on Uncle Hussein's shelf. "If I came to the woods, I must have wanted an adventure, and I'll probably find more interesting things through the woods than on the path that's already been cleared," I wrote.

"Tell what you're thinking or feeling as you walk along the path you've chosen," Professor Legall continued.

"It's like it's just me and the sun and the trees and the wild grass and flowers and the insects all breathing together," I write. "It suddenly dawns on me that in the forest there are all kinds of trees and that they don't fight each other, trying to see which ones are the best or God's favorite. The oaks don't try to make the willows look bad and none of them try to invade the other's space and I wonder why people in different religions can't see this," I write.

But I really didn't want to think about religion since I wasn't home and didn't have to. I decided to keep my observations general.

"I think it's amazing that some flowers can be purple and some yellow or orange all on their own without any help from humans. I think it's amazing how they get all the water they need and whatever else they need to grow from nature without any help from humans. I think it's amazing the way the sun rays cut through the openings in the trees and still reach the littlest plants on the ground. I see tall trees that must be hundreds of years old and wonder why some of the other ones fell. I'm sort of scared that a snake might jump from under something, but also walking kinda softly because I don't want to step on any insects either. I wish..."

"You're at the end of your journey now," our professor continued. "How do you feel?"

"I feel like...I guess..."

It was much harder for me to touch a feeling than it was to explain a thought. In the Nation of Islam I'd been taught it was not good to be emotional. Life was logic. Think everything through. As an orthodox Muslim, I'd been taught that my opinions and interpretation—of Quran or Hadith for instance—did not count. Follow the letter of the law. Dress, eat, sleep, drink, do everything as the prophet Muhammad had done. Period. So, it was most difficult to know my own emotions and opinions without fear of the wrath of God coming on me.

"I feel good, I guess. I feel...I feel like this was a trip worth taking. I feel like I learned a lot about myself."

I scheduled my classes to keep me at school all day, and it was usually dark by the time I got home. As much as Ma tried to keep our home in order, scheduling our daily prayers, daily chores, weekend chores, and meals for the week in a desperate attempt to keep everything together, things were falling apart. I could tell. I could not bury my head in the sand like I saw the grown-ups doing all my life because the fact that we were standing on shaky ground became clearer than clear one evening in February. Denial was not an option anymore.

I wondered where my family could be as I approached the house this evening after school. The house was dark with a faint light flickering on the second and third floors. The front light usually was left on as long as anyone was still out, but that night the front was black, too, except for the lampposts in the court. I fumbled my keys and inserted the right one.

"Salaam-Alaikum!" I yelled into the dark, cold house.

"Wa-Laikum-Salaam," Ma called out from the kitchen. I saw a flickering light coming from her direction. "Come in here and get yourself a candle. The electricity is off tonight. So, we'll have to make do with these."

The house was unusually quiet and as I stepped into the kitchen, the flicker of a single slim candle on the countertop was all that illuminated the space between Ma and me. She stood next to the candle, head bent, scraping leftover food into dingy plastic containers. I'd never seen my house this dark before. Not even when I was the first to come downstairs and set up the prayer rugs in the morning had I found my house this dark. The darkness was descending on us and I knew it, felt it. It was a kind of darkness that manmade electricity and lights couldn't cut. Ma had paid the bill, which was wrong, overcharged by five-hundred-and-forty dollars. Ma had paid it to keep the lights on. She'd used part of the rent money to pay it, planning to catch up on the rent when the electric company straightened out its mess and refunded the difference. But she must not have paid it soon enough.

"What happened?" I demanded. I was unsympathetic in times like these. To me, things like this didn't just happen for no reason. They came after a while of not doing what you're supposed to do. Ma should've gone out and gotten a job to help out like her parents kept saying, then we would've had extra money saved in the bank.

Something had told me to call my grandparents two weeks ago when I found the pink notice to disconnect in the kitchen drawer. Dad had assured me he'd take care of it, but something had told me to call for backup. The only reason I hadn't was because Ma would've been embarrassed going to her parents for money again. When they gave her money they also gave her advice, and Ma hated advice.

"Ray-Ray, go on upstairs please and get yourself ready for tomorrow," she said, exasperated. I could hear sadness and defeat in her voice. She didn't face me to answer my question.

"I got some money saved up in my bank account," I offered flatly. "How much we owe?"

"Your father will take care of the bills," she said. "That is his responsibility."

That was Ma's problem, if you asked me. She was trying with her last breath to hold on to some ideal father-knows-best traditional family structure when everything was calling for change. The economy now was based on two-income families because women had wanted to and did work hard to get their own jobs to equalize their position in the family. But Ma didn't see things that way. She was stuck in an outdated way of doing things. Ma's own mother had worked as a nurse in hospitals, but Ma tried to be to Dad what his own mother, GrandWillie, who'd never worked outside the home, had been to her family.

I had other ideas, which I thought were simply more practical.

"If he doesn't take care of it tomorrow, give me the bill and I'll go pay it between classes," I said.

"Ray-Ray, just do what I *asked* you to do. Can you just do that?"

I took one of the three flashlights off the counter and proceeded up to my room.

"Pssst. Hey. Ray-Ray. Come 'mere," my brother Furard called from his room on the second floor.

I poked my head in his door and saw that neither he nor Atif were asleep. They each were trying to keep one of the twins under wool blankets in the bunk beds, trying to make the toddlers stay still as restless as they were. Atif created a light show on their wall using the flashlights for their room. The twins poked their arms and feet out from under the covers and tried to wiggle down to the floor.

"They gon' turn our phone and lights back on tomorrow?" Furard asked.

"The phone's off, too?" I asked.

"Um-hmm. Know what we had for dinner? Tuna fish and crackers and cold string beans!" Atif said playfully as if this were all a game, a joke that would be over in the morning.

"I got twenty dollars from my paper route. You want it to go pay the bills?" Furard asked.

"Hold on to your money," I told him.

I wanted my little sisters and brothers to have a carefree childhood, even if mine hadn't been. I wanted them to believe that our prayers would make a difference, even though I no longer believed it. I wanted them to feel safe in our household, although I felt it falling down around us. When I got to the top floor, Sakinah was sitting on a chair in front of the candle in the window in the hall, clutching a thin, brown plastic grocery bag stuffed with her clothes.

"What's up with you?" I asked, trying to treat my twelve-year-old sister like the woman she thought she was.

She simply rolled her eyes and said nothing.

"Where you think you going this late?" I continued.

"I ain't staying here in the dark!" she snapped.

"Where you think you going?"

"Somewhere! I got friends!"

I marched right back downstairs and plainly told Ma that her daughter was planning to sneak out again.

"Bring me her shoes," Ma said.

I wished she would go and slap Sakinah like she used to slap me. I'd been slapped for much less when I was my little sister's age. But Ma was getting more creative now. I went to the shoe rack next to the front door, but Sakinah's shoes weren't there. She and our oldest brother were the only ones careful to take their shoes to their rooms so you never could tell whether they were home or not.

"Ma said bring her your shoes," I told Sakinah.

"You snitch!" she hissed, turning to go to her room down the hall from mine. I aimed my flashlight in her face like I was the police. "You heard what she said."

She slammed her door and I could hear the lock click into place.

I was already under my covers when I heard Ma come up the stairs, the flashlight cutting a sharp path through the darkness. I knew the routine without opening my door to look. Ma would open Sakinah's door with a hanger, take her shoes, and leave without saying a word. Sakinah would lie still like she was asleep or dead. I curled up under

128

my covers, wishing Ma would turn the heat up, knowing she wouldn't because she wanted to keep the gas bill manageable. What would I tell my friends who tried to call me tonight? God, I hoped none of my classmates would call to ask about homework. My lifelong friends understood hard times, my new classmates probably wouldn't. I was glad I had some clothes already ironed. How could I get to the electric company on the bus? Nothing I could do about the phone. Maybe I could pay half of both bills and they'd turn our services back on.

The lights were still out when we woke up for prayer at dawn the next morning, but the living room was illuminated by several candles Ma lit. Dad led us through the rote recitation of Arabic, bending and prostrating our bodies only twice since the Fajr prayer only requires two rakats, as opposed to four for the afternoon prayer, Thor, and Asr, three for Magrib in the evening and four more for Isha at night. After salat I asked Dad if we would get the electricity back today and he said, "Inshallah," meaning "God willing." My younger siblings moped back up to their rooms, happy to get back to bed. Thoughts rushed me on my way up to my room.

"Inshallah? What does Allah have to do with it? I wish people would stop putting everything off on Allah. You refuse to use birth control, have more children than you know you can afford, then say whatever God wills! Refuse to go out and get a job like your own mother and father say you should to help your husband, then cry whatever is God's will."

By the time I reached my bedroom I was furious. I couldn't get back to sleep for thinking. I tossed and turned for the next hour, thinking.

God helps those who help themselves. Oh. Maybe that's just a Christian thing. I must've got that idea from Grandma and Granddaddy Thomas. Maybe Christians do know better. My Christian relatives aren't poor as the Muslims. In fact, I wondered why so many of my Christian relatives ended up with nice houses in the suburbs while so many of my Muslim relatives lived in public housing, depending on state benefits to survive. What were we doing so poor at a time like this? We should've had money saved up. The civil rights movement of the sixties, followed by President Carter's liberal administration in the late seventies, had afforded prosperity to many in the Black community. Some of my aunts and uncles had bought nice homes out in the suburbs and still had money left over for vacations outside the country.

Luckily, when we got up to get dressed for the day, the lights were back on. I checked the phone, but it was still dead. I decided I could live without a phone one more day. Maybe Dad had taken care of that, too, and it was just a matter of hours before it would be back on.

Between classes I checked to see if our phone was back on. The recorded message I kept getting irritated the hell out of me.

"We're sorry. The number you are trying to reach is temporarily out of order."

Absolutely embarrassing. When I returned home that evening, I had another surprise.

Chapter Thirteen
Spiritually Bankrupt

It was freezing in the house. Somehow I knew not to step out of my shoes at the door. If the air inside was this cold, I was sure our tile floor was freezing. As soon as I could close the door behind me, Furard walked past me carrying a pot of hot water up the stairs. Thank God the lights were back on, at least. I moved into the kitchen and found Ma huddled with the twins and Atif and Sakinah in front of the electric stove.

"You and Sakinah can share bath water tonight," Ma said matter-of-factly. There was no emotion in her voice, in her face. "She'll go first, so she can hurry and get under the covers. You can boil some more water if you have to."

I couldn't believe it.

"I'm supposed to wash my hair in a pot!" I said, standing in the kitchen doorway.

"Sonsyrea, do what I asked you to do!" Ma yelled back.

Something was very wrong, and I could see it in her face. Ma had always been stressed—since I could remember. She yelled at us so much, GrandWillie used to tell her to stop taking out what she was feeling on us. But something about this time was different. Like she was beyond a place of yelling and screaming for help. This time she was without wind. She was defeated. Down for the count.

"Go upstairs!" She sighed.

I was furious, but growing a bit sympathetic. I couldn't control my anger and I resented Ma for trying to stay calm. But, somehow I knew not to push her this time. I turned abruptly and left the kitchen.

"Did Ma tell you the police came and got Dad today?" Furard asked as I approached the second floor.

He was resting the hot pot on the windowsill while we talked.

"What?!"

"It was right before we went to school this morning. A bunch of policemen came busting in through the basement and the front door, and ran all around downstairs, then came up here and grabbed Dad out the bathroom," he said. Dad had been taking a shower when the police stormed in. He had left his nightshift at Capitol Hill Hospital, where he worked at a security job, early to come home and rest. The police snatched him out the shower, let him pull on some clothes, and marched him out the front door with his hands cuffed behind his back.

Furard seemed to be in a state of shock. That was his body standing there with me, and his mouth moved and his eyes blinked like normal, but he wasn't really there. He had retreated to somewhere deep inside.

I plopped down on the cold steps. The wind had just been knocked out of me. I was sixteen, and pretty much a surrogate mother to my younger siblings. I had failed to protect them from such an embarrassing moment, such a shameful experience. The neighbors would look at all of us differently now, and I was old enough to handle it, but them? What would they say when mean little kids teased them about their father going to jail? What would my friends' mothers say? Would Ms. Copeland tell me to stay away from their house, so my family's trouble doesn't follow me there? Ms. Copeland, my friend Chee-Chee's mother, was one of those people who made it out of the ghetto and didn't want ghetto behavior or ghetto people following her. She was the tenants' association president for our townhouse community and she helped enforce the rules that required all families come out on Saturday mornings to clean up the courtyards and sweep the sidewalks and pick up trash by the curbs. She was straight-up no-nonsense.

My siblings in junior high—Sakinah, Furard, Atif, and Tia—might be able to handle themselves, but Abena, in elementary, might not. Also, I was starting to wonder how Ma could take care of things with no job and Dad in jail. She couldn't go out and get a job now if she wanted to, having no work experience in more than fifteen years, and no college degree, I figured. I was mad as hell she hadn't gone out and gotten a job years ago like her parents said she should. They kept telling her, "Marvy (that's the nickname they called her), you need to go out and get a job like everybody else. Joe can't do it all by himself. Can't you see you're putting too much on him? You saw your mother go out here and work every day." My mother told us she resented having to cook and clean so much when she was young because both her parents worked. She had determined when she was young that she would become a homemaker. Now our home was breaking up. What would we do without Dad? First things first, I wanted to know how much the little ones had seen.

I was pretty sure my mother thought this was all the police's fault. Pretty sure she believed that police storming in like some damn Gestapo were overdoing it. Dad was no Al Capone. He had enough weed for himself and his friends. Why humiliate and incarcerate a man for using drugs instead of helping him to not need the drugs anymore? The whole damn society was out of order, as far as Ma could see. The government was there to oppress the masses, giving good jobs to a few, setting them up as examples of what's possible, knowing full well that everybody couldn't be in that middle- or upper-class category, even if they wanted. Ma often criticized "the mainstream." Sometimes her talking sounded like sour grapes. I had read in one of my first favorite books, *Aesop's Fables*, that when people find that the thing they want is out of their reach, they claim they didn't really want it because it's not so good after all. I thought Ma was stuck on some old-time sour grapes stuff. In the Nation of Islam she heard ministers degrade the American mainstream for all kinds of reasons, but the bottom line was, African Americans were legally denied access to the "mainstream," government jobs, government grants, bank business loans, the best public schools, hospitals, and stores, for centuries and learned to criticize that which we could not get. But time had changed things by the time I was growing up, and I didn't want to be stuck on the same old sour grapes. But it looked to me like Ma still feasted on them.

"Where was Tia and Atif an' 'nem when all this was happening?" I asked Furard.

"Ma was trying to keep them out the way. But the police were everywhere. They went through the living room and dining room, looking all around, messing up stuff like they was mad at something. What did Dad do?"

My head fell into my hands, my elbows resting on my knees. I was too hurt to cry. Everything inside of me froze. If I had tears, they were stuck, couldn't come out.

"They pushed him into the wall and put handcuffs on him," Furard said. "Then they pushed him out to their police car. Guess he won't be coming back, huh, Ray-Ray?"

Furard was so matter-of-fact about things. He was too unemotional to be so young, I thought, like he was numb. That was the damage I'd wanted the little kids to be spared. I'd seen kids shut down, down to the point where anger was the only emotion they could respond to, or further down to where they wouldn't feel anything at all. That was my first feeling of helplessness. I couldn't save my own siblings. That was when I decided I would not remain powerless the rest of my life. I would not sit on the sidelines of life and suffer things. I would make my way out in the world and somehow I'd be able to protect myself and my family someday.

A girl at my old Muslim school shut down after her father exploded one day, killed her mother, and hit my classmate in the head with a phone. Sometimes pressures build and people try to hold on to rules and regulations and ignore certain things they know and feel inside. Then it happens. Somebody, or something explodes. God! I didn't want my younger siblings caught up in this earthquake, but here we were. At sixteen, I was hardly an adult, but I knew what happened to children in these situations. Their lives get too cold, too confusing, too hard to figure out and they shut down completely or do the opposite and go crazy—unhinged. I think that's what happened with my older brother. He'd seen too much, so he was acting crazy now. Might as well. When your world doesn't make sense and you can't make sense of it, you might as well stop trying. You get crazy right along with it.

"Ray-Ray, they gon' keep Dad in jail?" Furard asked.

"He'll be back," I said.

With all the praying and fasting and charity-giving we'd done, Allah had to pull some magic trick out the bag for us. At least, that's what I needed to believe. That's what I needed my little brother to believe.

I went to bed dizzy and woke up feeling dazed when I heard Furard's voice calling the adhan, the Arabic call to prayer. The house was still cold and I dreaded the thought of splashing the ice water on my face, up my arms to my elbows and on my feet, making the obligatory ablution. But I did. Down in the living room, which Ma must've straightened after we went to bed, I lined up on a prayer rug with

Ma, Sakinah, and Tia behind Furard and Atif. Nobody knew where Darren was. Furard, being the senior male in the household at eleven, had to lead us in prayer. Ma couldn't lead her own sons in prayer because in Islam a female can't lead a male in prayer. Period. We went through the motions. Who knows, maybe Ma's heart still was sincere, but mine was full of doubt now. Doubt about our religion, our family values, about the power of Allah. What good was a God if He couldn't save you from yourself? I know there are laws and consequences, but doesn't the Quran say over and over again that Allah is the "oft forgiving" and "Most Merciful"? In fact we began each of our five daily prayers with "In the name of Allah, Most Gracious, Most Merciful." Now where was our mercy?

I could see my breath as I moved about my room and the bathroom up on the third floor. Ma had our one electric space heater in the hallway on the second floor with the kids' bedroom doors left open. Down on the first floor, she'd left the oven on with the oven door open all night, but that had only slightly softened the chill in the house. The chill cut down deeper than our bones. I slept in two pairs of socks and a pair of long johns under my flannel pajamas. I slept curled up in a knot to keep warm and to cradle myself.

I got dressed in my dark blue corduroys, a white wool turtleneck sweater, and two pairs of socks in my brown loafers. I carried my coat and books downstairs with me so I could leave as soon as I ate. Once I got downstairs, though, I suddenly wasn't hungry. The refrigerator was bare. We were down to a few meager essentials in the kitchen—oatmeal, eggs, one frozen chicken, and a bag of potatoes. And if Dad didn't get out of jail, Ma didn't have a job for us to fall back on.

So much for Allah, the Great Provider, I thought.

As I walked to the bus stop, I debated whether or not to call my grandparents. Ma would hate me for it because she'd tried so hard to prove to her parents that her every decision as an adult—from the man she chose to marry, to her decision to change religions, to her decision to have a lot of children and stay home to raise them—had not been one mistake after another. I was sure we all weren't mistakes.

Ma had been eighteen when she got pregnant with my older brother. Mistake number one. Her "good Christian" parents wouldn't have let her get an abortion, even if they could've afforded one, because that would've been a sin even in their eyes. And she couldn't have a child out of wedlock, so she and Dad had to get married. Mistake number two. Then she had me about a year and a half later. But I was no mistake. They were happily married now and had one baby boy to show for it. Having a cute little girl would've completed their perfect family picture.

For the first four years it was just me and Darren and our two young parents living in our own apartment, and that was the way it was supposed to be, according to the family pictures I saw in magazines and TV ads. Ma got pregnant a third time, but the twin girls were born dead. I felt disappointed when she came home without the babies I was expecting her to bring. In no time, Ma was pregnant again and it was a real blessing when Furard was born a healthy baby boy. We still were a small happy family, and after Dad's father died, we moved in with GrandWillie so Dad could be the man of the house to his mother and younger siblings. Then Ma got pregnant again and her parents and Dad's younger siblings began to question the logic of having a fourth child while not having our own place to live and surviving mostly off Dad's salary as a security guard, supplemented by what Ma made babysitting. Then a fifth was born, then a sixth, and the family—all except the Orthodox relatives who believed ten children was Allah's command—said my parents were irresponsible and foolish. Ma's life had been spiraling down ever since.

At least we got our own house by the time the seventh child, my sister, Abena, was born. The twins born the next year made eight and nine, and Ma's life was hardly in her control. And, no, she didn't particularly want her high-brow, finger-wagging parents to come to her rescue. But we needed them.

My head was anywhere but in my English class that morning. After class I called my grandparents.

"Hey, Grandma," I said, animating my voice up a pitch to camouflage the tension.

"Hi, baby. How you doing?" she piped back in her church-choir soprano voice.

"I'm okay."

"Are you sure? I tried to call your mother yesterday but the phone was disconnected. What's going on over there?"

"Um, yep, the phone got disconnected," I admitted. "And, uh, the gas got cut off. But the electricity's back on. So we did have some heat last night."

"Whaaaaat?"

"You know that little heater ya'll gave us. We finally used it last night. But it's not really enough. I'm scared the twins might catch a cold if we don't get the heat back on. We don't really need the phone..."

"Where are you?" she asked.

"At school."

"Aw, baby. It must be terrible for you, trying to concentrate on your school work with all this going on."

She only knew the half of it.

"Can you not tell my mother I called you?" I asked. "I don't want to get her madder than she already is."

"You don't worry about that," Grandma said. "You just concentrate on your school and let us handle the rest."

"Okay," I said, relieved. "Thanks, and tell Granddaddy I said 'hi.'"

"Okay, baby. You try not to worry."

I knew Granddaddy would be mad as hell when Grandma told him what was going on. He'd be disappointed that Dad wasn't taking care of his family sufficiently. But he'd be extra mad at my mother for not going out and getting a job to help carry the weight. Then he'd be mad at me for not calling them sooner. They both hated when I kept stuff from them. They said family members shouldn't keep hard times secret from other family. But I felt like I was betraying Ma when I let on that the life she ended up with was a mess. That was our little family secret and I'd've kept it, too, if it wasn't for the little ones at home. Dad came home a few days after the arrest, but it would be a long time before things got back to normal—if it ever could. His trial dragged on for more than two years before he was convicted and sentenced on charges of conspiracy to traffic illegal substances.

In the meantime, however, on this occasion, my grandparents came through with a check for us, but made it out to Dad, since he was the head of our household. Of course, they lectured Ma, and I was standing on the steps, out of sight listening. Ma never said anything to me about calling them.

Chapter Fourteen
Finding Favor, Finding Faith

The next two years of my life whizzed by as quickly as a subway ride. Very quickly, my academic lessons at school and personal dilemmas at home uncovered for me my strengths and weaknesses. Maybe it was weak to turn on your religion as soon as the real life challenges came. Maybe the whole point of fostering faith in a certain set of theories and practices was to see if you could hold on to them until your very last breath. I was not so faithful. Well, not where religion was concerned.

I believed there must be a Being, a Force in the world bigger than myself. But I wasn't sure there was a sure way to access it, wasn't even sure it was entirely outside of me. I was beginning to believe that this thing, this God, this Supreme Being, was just the sum total of all that existed. All the air, all the water, all the earth, all the living animals and insects in the world were somehow connected like spokes in a huge wheel. The wheel itself, made up of all us tiny particles was the thing we called God. Who had more power in this God? Christians, Muslims, Jews, Catholics or Buddhists? I now believed that whole dilemma was something men themselves had contrived. I was losing my faith in religion for sure, but maybe there was a God somewhere. For the most part, I tried not to think about it.

There was so much I could do with my life other than sitting in the house reading and learning about what somebody else discovered about life in general and God's purpose for my life in particular. The adults in my Muslim community had not yet evolved to understand that just because God or nature designed my body to carry embryos and give birth to babies that this must be my sole purpose for being on earth. Nor did it mean that I should begin having babies as soon as my body could produce them—which was the reason many of them believed they should marry us off at the onset of our menses. It did not mean that motherhood would be the only, least of all the highest, achievement I as a woman could aspire to.

These were the 1980s—way past the women's suffrage movement, just past the women's rights movement, but for various reasons men who wanted their wives' undivided attention remained stuck in a time zone.

For my part, by spring, I was interviewing for my first internship through a city-sponsored summer jobs program. A very tall, slender woman with her sharp nose pitched skyward asked me questions from behind her fortress of a desk.

"So, tell me about yourself," she said.

"I'm from a large family. Grew up here in Northeast. I graduated from Eastern High School and now I'm enrolled at UDC."

"I can see your credentials here on your resume, sweetie," she said smugly, in that tight little voice of hers. "Tell me about you the person."

"I'm the oldest girl in a family of ten, which taught me how to be responsible at a very early age..."

"Your mother has *ten* children?"

"My *parents* have ten," I said respectfully.

I knew what she was getting at. She thought I was some welfare kid from a house full of unruly kids running over our poor dope-addicted mother. I resented her type, middle-class Black folks who thought they were better than the rest of us.

She looked over the letters of recommendation I'd gotten from my adviser and said she was impressed. She said she usually didn't hire college students prior to their junior year because most of them don't know what they want to do with their life, but she'd give me a chance since I came so highly recommended. A few weeks later, I received the letter confirming my internship at WRC-AM all-talk radio station. But first, I was to report to the summer jobs program site for orientation.

Young people were hanging out all over the place when I arrived. Some of the girls and guys looked college or high school age, and with some you couldn't tell. I was a few minutes late, but orientation had not yet begun. I didn't recognize anyone I knew, so I took the nearest empty seat to the door to avoid having to parade past everyone. When the medium-height man with shiny brown skin and an expression like he had something sour in his mouth finally got up in front of us, the first thing out his sassy mouth was how pitiful we were for showing up late for orientation for a job.

"Your letter did not say nine a.m. *colored people's* time!" he fussed. "The first time I get a report of you showing up late for work, consider yourself fired. Don't even bother coming down here crying, talking 'bout 'Mr. Tyler, I missed the bus.' I won't hear it! Just go on home and wait for your little piece of check in the mail. Don't make sense, people bustin' their behinds to give you all opportunities we couldn't even dream of and you can't get here on time. I don't want any excuses! Let this be your warning!"

Then he introduced himself.

"For those of you who don't know me, I'm Mr. Tyler. I've been running this Vocational Exploration Program since we started two years ago."

He talked about what kinds of internships we'd all be working—at hospitals, in law offices, at radio and television stations, in government agencies and so forth, then handed us a "Code of Ethics" statement we had to review with him, then sign. There was a whole section on the dress code. We were to "dress for success," he said.

"I better not hear of any of my young ladies going to work in some little tight skirt halfway up your behind," he said theatrically. "That's the quickest way to get put out of the program! Your skirts should be here!" he said, chopping at a point on his leg just below his knee.

The fellas laughed and the girls mumbled.

"Mr. Tyler, that's not fair!" one of the brave girls hollered out. "I don't wear no granny dresses that long. How you gon' dictate what the girls wear and not the boys?"

A cunning look spread across Mr. Tyler's face. He pointed to the blackboard behind him and began his explanation in a calmer, though still sarcastic tone.

"Young people. You all listen up close to what I'm about to say. I see some of you are kind of confused about where you are. What do these letters stand for?"

He held his hand at the board until he got a response.

"Vocational Exploration Program," we said like a disjointed chorus.

"That's right. We are here to teach you about the wonderful world of work. Some of you young ladies don't know any better and it's not your fault. Your mamas didn't know any better. You saw your mamas strutting off to work in some little piece of a dress, then, soon as somebody says something to them, they want to run home crying about somebody harassing them!"

The guys cracked up, which gave Mr. Tyler just the extra push he needed.

"I know I'm talking 'bout some of your mamas, and if the shoe fits, wear it! In this program, our young ladies will go out dressed like decent young women!"

I felt like I was back in the Muslim community, the very thing I was trying so hard to get away from. But this wasn't quite as bad. I mean, at least here, we girls were given the opportunity to go out and earn our own money and learn about interesting and challenging jobs outside the home. But the idea of controlling what women wear still bothered me, so I was glad some of the girls here spoke up. I was glad they refused to be intimidated when Mr. Tyler and the guys tried to shut us down. This conversation could not have happened in my Nation of Islam community or in the Orthodox Muslim community. Once, when I was at a cookout, one of the senior brothers asked me why I wasn't wearing a veil and I respectfully explained that it was too hot. He then lectured me that it's going to be hotter than that in the hell fire where I surely was going for defying Allah's dress code. So, yes, this conversation was refreshing. At least the girls could be heard.

"Mr. Tyler, women should have a choice about what we wear. It's not our fault if men can't control themselves when they like what they see. Why should *we* have to suffer the consequences because they can't control *themselves!*"

Some of the boldest girls cheered her on, while the boys laughed and tried to shout in their two-cents' worth. I just watched and listened.

"That's how women get raped," some numbskull guy shouted from the back of the room.

"You idiot!" the girl leading the protest shot back. "What the length of a woman's dress got to do with a man thinking he's got the rights to put his hands on her! I wish some guy would try to grab me. I got something for alla ya'll!"

"He's just saying if you put yourself out there like that, you're setting yourself up," another guy added.

"I know *my* girl bet' not be out there looking like some tramp," another guy said. "Ya'll think that's what men want. We don't respect women dressed like that," he continued.

"Who said we're dressing for you to respect us," another girl jumped in. "What I need your respect for! You don't got nothin'! Who said we're dressing for *you* at all! What I look like trying to impress you? Wouldn't nobody be dressing for yo' ugly self."

The conversation had gotten loud and beyond Mr. Tyler's control for a moment. I rested my hands on my fists, my elbows propped on the desk attached to my seat, and followed the action back and forth across the room. I'd long since stopped wearing dresses and skirts of any kind, refusing to wear them down to my ankles. And rather than wear my shirts hanging loosely outside my pants, I bought only baggy pants to camouflage my womanness. Mr. Tyler banged on the blackboard to get our attention. As soon as the noise settled some, someone finally asked a question I wanted asked.

"Mr. Tyler! What if we don't want to wear skirts at all," one of the girls asked. "Can we wear a nice top and a pair of slacks?"

"In a professional environment, young ladies need to wear a dress or skirt," he insisted.

The same young woman who started the first protest jumped up again.

"That's sexist! I don't care what nobody says. That's sexist!"

"Aw, sit down, dyke!"

We all looked around to see who said that. Our budding feminist did look more like she was ready for the basketball court rather than a job, in T-shirt, jeans, and tennis shoes. But she was cute, with a long black ponytail. I wouldn'tve pegged her for gay. What I liked most about her was that she would not give up.

"Your mother, whoever said it!" she shot back.

Mr. Tyler raised his hands above his head this time to get our attention. We settled back down and he continued.

"Let's be clear here, young people. You always have a choice. Ladies, you have a choice. In this program you can do things the way we do them, or you can make the choice to excuse yourself from the program and go on about your business somewhere else. We have certain standards here."

Standards were changing. Women wore pants suits as often as they wore skirts to work in the early eighties, but Mr. Tyler taught us his old-fashioned ways.

"This is bull!" said our ringleader. She snatched up her purse and duffle bag and stormed right out of there.

"See you later and take care," Mr. Tyler shouted to her backside.

"She'll find out the hard way," he said, turning back to us. "You know a hard head makes a soft behind...Now, where were we? We have a lot of ground to cover today. Where were we?"

"Dress for success!" some guy shouted.

That weekend I went to a fabric store and bought materials to make myself some knee-length skirts. I was glad I knew how to sew since I didn't have money to go shopping at a nice retail shop, and thrift stores were out of the question. I'd learned to sew in Muslim Girl Training (MGT class) back when we were in the Nation of Islam. Then, I took home economics in junior high school just for an easy A. Both of my grandmothers sewed very well, and I'd learned a few tips watching GrandWillie make matching Muslim girl outfits for me and her, and watching Grandma Thomas make skirt suits for herself for church.

As soon as I returned from G Street Fabrics downtown and parted ways with my girlfriend Chee-Chee who'd gone with me, I went straight upstairs to the back room, which was used as our library, and dropped my bags there, ready to work. I pulled out the sewing board and sewing machine from the hall closet, snatched up the sewing kit full of pins, needles, and threads, and commenced to sew myself a working wardrobe for my new job. I locked myself in that back room, pretending not to hear the evening and night calls for prayer, pretending not to hear Ma calling me for dinner. I took a nap sometime after ten that night, got up a few hours later and kept going. I made three skirts and pullover tops that I could mix and match—one set light blue, one set tan, the other a nice blue-and-tan floral print. I was so proud of myself the next day, I didn't care what wrath I might face for ignoring Ma the night before.

Chapter Fifteen
Unbowed

At my job, I worked intensely, clipping newspaper and magazine articles for the producers at the all-talk, all-news radio station. But back home, Ma and I fought more and more about my priorities. It wasn't enough that on Sundays I cooked enough dinners to last through Wednesday, and that on Saturday mornings I did my part washing the walls, which we all had to do every week to keep our white walls white. After that I still had to clean the refrigerator, or mop some floors, whatever she had for me on the list posted on the fridge next to the prayer schedule. Through the summers I found time to take the little ones to the park some weekends. When they were back in school, I took them around the block to collect red and yellow leaves for their school projects, and when it snowed, showed them how to make angels in the snow. Ma said my priority as a young Muslim woman should be my family and since I wasn't married myself, this family was my priority. She and I argued and debated this same "priorities" issue for at least two years, and it all came to a head one day near the end of my sophomore year.

Ma stopped me on my way up to my room. She was in her bedroom changing Halim's diaper when she called out to tell me the bathroom on the second floor was still waiting for me to clean it. According to her schedule, this was my day to clean it. I insisted that I had cleaned it before I left for classes.

"I know you don't call that clean with that nasty ring still around the tub," she fussed.

"Dad left it like that," I snapped, proceeding past Ma up to my room. "Everybody's supposed to clean the tub after they use it. I don't see why I have to clean up behind a grown man." I was tired and so ready to fall in bed.

"You get back down here!" she yelled.

"Yes!?!" I said sharply, not budging from where I stood.

"Your father goes out there and works every day to pay the bills. He shouldn't have to worry about cleaning up around here..."

"When I was working and helping pay bills, I still had to do my cleaning," I said matter-of-factly, controlling my anger.

True, Ma had watched her own mother do most of the housework, even though she worked and paid half the household bills. And true, our religion dictated that we, as Muslim women, maintain the traditional roles of women as homemakers, baby-makers, the ones to raise and teach the children first and foremost. Dad had never learned to clean house, never even learned to iron his own clothes. His mother had cleaned behind him and his seven siblings and had done his laundry the whole while he was in school. Since he got married right out of school, he had a new wife to take over these tasks. Ma had been doing this since my older brother was born. But as far as I was concerned times had changed and I was changing with them. Somebody in our family needed to.

"We have a certain order in this household," she said through clenched teeth. "Everybody has a role to play and everybody has to do their part."

She placed Halim on his feet, then lifted Hakim up out of the crib to change his diaper. Halim ran to me and I dropped my book bag and picked him up for a big squeeze.

"When you don't do your part, it makes my job harder because the younger ones are watching you and they try to do like you," Ma continued.

I blew gurgle sounds in Halim's skinny, little chicken neck, tickling him until he wiggled out of my arms and ran down the hall to his big brothers' room.

"Can't you ask Dad to clean the tub behind himself like everybody else?" I persisted, still trying to keep my attitude and anger in check out of respect.

"Did you hear what I just said! That's not your father's job!" she said, losing patience.

"Well, school is *my* job!" I snapped. It really was too late for this mess. I'd had a long, very busy day. She was getting on my nerves— and apparently, I on hers.

"No! That was your choice!" she shot back. "Your first responsibility is to your family!"

"My first responsibility is to *myself!*" I didn't know where that came from, but it did come out my mouth. Then there was more. "I'm not tying myself to nobody's house just because some man fourteen-hundred years ago said I should!"

She set Hakim on his feet and a few pieces of laundry fell from the huge pile on her bed to be folded.

"You think you know better than Allah now!" she fumed. "Allah gave us the Quran to live by, not some man fourteen-hundred years ago, as you say. You been to college a couple of years, and now you think you know better than the Supreme Being who created you!"

"No Supreme Being wrote the Quran! Men wrote it!" I said, whispering angrily half under my breath so the little ones wouldn't hear.

Ma was furious now. Any other day she would've slapped me clean across my face, but her actions were more measured this evening for some reason. She stepped in my face, taking me on toe-to-toe.

"I suggest you take yourself downstairs right this minute and make up your salats," she said in a voice harder than I'd heard before.

I stepped back one step and reached for my book bag so I could retreat to my room.

"I made 'em," I lied, hardening my voice.

A mother knows a child's lies. The next thing I knew, Ma grabbed my arm and was dragging me down the stairs. My book bag fell and tumbled over the banister, dumping the books out. The kids came out to see what was all the commotion. Ma dragged me over to the prayer corner where we kept the prayer rugs rolled up.

"You too high and mighty to bow down now!" she hissed.

From the stairs, all my little sisters and brothers were watching. I snatched my arm from Ma's grip and crossed my arms in front of me, staring at her with the meanest eyes I had. My face was burning and hot water streamed down my cheeks. My chest heaved as I tried to catch my breath and regain some composure.

"I said I already did!" I hissed back.

She picked up a prayer rug and hit me across the arms with it, the frilly strings on the end grazing my chin.

"Take it!" she yelled.

I held my position.

"You can't *make* me pray!" I said through my teeth, keeping my jaws closed tight.

Ma used to say that Prophet Muhammad said it was the parents' responsibility to teach their kids to pray, and to enforce regular salats, using punishment when necessary. But I was no longer a child and Ma could not make me pretend to believe in something I was finding more dubious by the day.

"Ya'll go back to your rooms!" Ma shouted up to the kids. They scrammed.

Ma unfurled the prayer rug, a small, dark-green-and-gold rug of Persian decorations. I stepped back from it, but Ma grabbed me by the back of my neck and tried to push me down to the rug. I stumbled but wouldn't fall. She lunged to push my back, but I slipped from her reach and fell on the couch.

"You stay there!" she said, pointing.

I really could've kicked her at this point. I was so mad, I could've thrown my foot in the air to kick my own mother. This fight was not about salat and she knew it. It wasn't even about our religion really. It was about things changing. About the past meeting the future head on. We both knew things were changing in our household, in our lives, in our hearts. Ma was trying hard to hold on to something familiar, formulated and formal. I was reaching for something new and better. Deep inside we both were anxious. Ma had to sense she was losing ground, and that's a frightful thing. And deep in my heart, beneath my surface bravado about stepping out into the world, I was scared to death. Maybe some part of me wanted Ma to hold me back where I knew I'd be safe at least. But the better part of me knew I had to go on. It was too bad she'd stepped into my personal battle and I into hers. No, this was really not about our religion at all. This was about having our comfort zones—and the fear of losing it.

My sister Sakinah bounced down the stairs and Ma snapped at her. "Didn't I say go back to your rooms!"

Sakinah was unfazed.

"You didn't tell *me* that. This my first time coming down here," she said sassily. "I just came to get some water." And she bounced on into the kitchen. Ma was too tired to fight with her and let her go.

I sat on the couch fuming and Ma turned the light out on me and went back up to her room.

"You *better* not move 'till I come down here and *tell* you to move," she said before disappearing.

I sat there in the dark thinking.

"Ray-Ray, what happened?" Sakinah asked from the doorway

between the kitchen and the living room-dining area where I sat.

"Nothing."

"Ma beat you up? That's what Atif said."

"No."

My little sisters especially, thought I let Ma get away with too much and by the time they were eight and nine they were already planning to be different from me. They had already insisted on wearing the same skimpy clothes they saw the other girls in the neighborhood wear and would throw a serious fit, screaming and carrying on in protest when Ma confronted them. They talked back to Ma often and Ma acted like she was too tired to deal with them, as though if she could somehow make an example out of me, they'd fall in line. But they resented my acquiescing, and didn't notice my silent protests.

Enrolling myself in college was a form of protest. But they couldn't know it and I couldn't explain it to them. They simply saw what they saw. Sakinah was so bad she got kicked out of the Muslim school when she was eleven. The Muslim school was different from when I was enrolled. By the time she got there, Elijah Muhammad's son had taken over the Nation of Islam and changed it so much it was all the adults could do to keep up with the changes, let alone keep up with the kids. Sakinah and her partner in crime, our cousin Asiyah, who was Sakinah's age, refused to keep their headpieces on and rolled up their long skirts right in front of their teachers. One of the brothers told them they made the walls of the temple bleed, and sent them home with a letter saying they couldn't return. Ma was not up to fighting to get her back in.

"What she do, slap you?" Sakinah asked, looking at my face, tight from anger.

"No," I said in a muffled voice.

"You okay?"

"Yeah."

"Want me to stay in here with you?"

I shook my head. The knot in my throat was tightening again. Upstairs I could hear Tia and Atif blaming each other for who left the twins unattended long enough for Halim to fall off the top of the bunk bed in the boys' room. In the girls' room, Ma was fussing at Abena for not putting her laundry away, and somebody was running a bath.

Darkness is a good place for thinking.

How she gonna make somebody pray? I thought. *I pray when I need to pray.*

I didn't feel like praying anymore, mostly because all the praying I'd done for my Uncle Hussein in the last two years failed to bring him back from his death bed. Uncle Hussein had prayed his whole life, and when he was a teenager GrandWillie didn't even have to remind him to make up the salats he missed while out at work. I used to marvel at him coming in from work and going right up to the bathroom to make wudu for salat. Even when I greeted him eagerly at the front door with a whole new set of questions about life or some subject at school, he told me he'd get back to me right after he made up his salats. I'd admired that and planned to be just like him. But by the time he was twenty-four and I was sixteen, his legs began to weaken and collapse on him some days. He still made his salats, though. Then he was diagnosed with multiple sclerosis and within months was bound to a wheelchair. And he pulled his wheelchair up to a prayer rug in the living room at GrandWillie's and still prostrated his body as best he could. In less than two years he was flat on his back in a hospital bed in GrandWillie's living room and still clutched his zikr beads, his meditating beads, to count the number of times he could chant Allah's name and attributes. I'd grown increasingly furious watching his decline. I couldn't stand to see him in so much pain, and what was worse, I couldn't understand why this was happening.

One day when I left his bedside after a very brief visit, my inner voice screamed out to Allah.

"Is this the best you can do! This is how you reward your best servants!"

I kicked cans and rocks on my way home that evening, then at home fought with Ma over why I shouldn't have to wash the dishes since I'd cooked dinner for that day in advance. I wasn't really fighting over the dishes that day, though. I was angry and deeply irritated but couldn't make Ma understand. She'd explained to me that Uncle Hussein's illness was his "test" from Allah and that when Allah saw fit to take his soul from the piece of clay that was his body, his soul would most likely go on to paradise because Uncle Hussein had been such a devout Muslim. That was not good enough. My "Fruit of Islam, F.O.I." soldier, my role model, my love, my uncle had crumbled right before my eyes. In the Nation of Islam, the F.O.I. were the brothers strong and disciplined enough to provide our security at the temples. Uncle Hussein had been an F.O.I. leader. Now, he was weak and dying. His brown pupils that used to shine down confidence on me were now glazed and fluttered in fear and pain.

Growing up, Uncle Hussein was a short, dark-skinned, round-faced, ready-with-a-smile boy who protected me around the neighborhood and delivered me safely to school in the mornings. When he was a teenager, he was cool and confident, sporting cowboy boots—which other boys in our neighborhood didn't wear—and stiffly creased jeans with starched shirts or very expensive, very colorful sweaters. He escorted me to the few high school dances I was allowed to attend only because he went with me. As an older teen, he donned gold-framed glasses like his idol, Mahatma Ghandi, and introduced me to Eastern philosophers and allowed me to listen to his German tapes as he studied the language. Now, this disease was melting him down to nothing.

His body had shriveled down to wrinkled skin wrapped around scrawny bones, and he shook violently. After a while he needed a brace to hold his head still. His fingers were twisted so, he could no longer even feed himself. It was difficult for him to steady his head enough to drink from a straw I held to his mouth. It was devastating to learn that earnest prayers could go unanswered—or worse, that the answer could be no. All this flooded my mind as I sat there in the dark thinking. I felt the burning tears stream down my face again, and curled myself up in a knot on the couch.

Upstairs, the kids got quiet after a while. And I thought some more. The scent of musk incense wafted down from where Ma had lighted a few sticks in the hallways. I hated it. It was the scent of some foreign country, with a foreign religion that was imposed on me, and I hated it.

I'm leaving this place, I thought. I kicked the prayer rug away from me. *I know how to pray in my heart and I don't need to make some big production out of it.*

I was still thinking about all this when Dad came in and flicked on the lights.

"Sonsyrea, what's your problem?" he asked. "Why're you sitting in here in the dark?"

"Ma made me sit here because she wouldn't believe I already made my salats," I said with burning, pleading, angry eyes that had to be good and red by now.

"Go on upstairs," he said, leaning on the wall to take off his shoes.

"I haven't eaten," I said in a flat voice.

"Then get some dinner," he said.

I ate pieces of leftover baked chicken cold and skipped everything else because I didn't feel like taking the time to warm anything. I wanted to eat enough just to kill the hunger pangs, just enough to be able to get to sleep. Sleep was my only escape besides school these days.

Chapter Sixteen
It Becomes You

Away from home and away from my neighborhood, I managed to keep my Muslim background a secret. I hadn't worn the traditional Muslim women's outfits since junior high, and had modified my clothes so much that you couldn't tell anything but that for some reason my clothes always looked big on me. I looked more preppy than anything else, donning khakis and sweaters with loafers like the girls in *Seventeen* magazine's special Campus Fashions edition. Never mind that they were all white and I was enrolled at a ninety-percent Black school. This was a timeless look, a classic look, so it fit me just fine.

Ma had taught me how to buy "classic clothing" rather than trendy fashions that would go out of style before I might outgrow them. She said that was the way rich people shopped and that's one of the ways they held on to their money—by not spending it on new clothes every year. I didn't know any rich people personally to confirm this, but I knew it was how Ma's middle-class parents had shopped, and that gave the idea enough credibility.

With money from my summer job, I bought two wool plaid pleated preppy-looking skirts with matching sweaters to mix and match for my junior year at the university. The first few times I wore anything cut above my ankles out on the streets, I felt half naked, and hoped Allah would forgive me. But I was used to it now. I still wore my hair in a conservative French roll in the back and judging from the way people related to me, I must have still looked like a goody-two-shoes.

I was walking across campus one spring afternoon when a tall, medium-brown guy in a tan trench coat, fedora and black wing-tip shoes approached me with a flier announcing a lecture by Minister Louis Farrakhan on campus.

"No thanks," I said politely.

"Aw, sister, at least come and hear the teachings for yourself," he insisted, equally polite. "I guarantee..."

I shook my head, still walking past him, but he followed, still pushing the flier toward me.

"C'mon, sister, I guarantee you won't be disappointed. If the Honorable Minister Farrakhan doesn't open your eyes to the absolute truth, you can find me right back out here and I'll give you your money back. That's how sure I am that once you hear the truth, you'll be so..."

"How long have you been in the Nation?"

"Three years, sister."

"I grew up in it."

A smile spread across his face.

"Sister! As-Salaam-Alaikum!"

He stood back to survey me again. He was right the first time. I wasn't dressed like a Muslim.

"Wa-Laikum-Salaam. But I'm not in the Nation anymore," I explained.

"My beloved. You left the Nation of Islam? I'm so sorry to hear that. But you can come on back. That's probably exactly why I ran into you today, sister. You're like the prodigal daughter. It's time for you to come on back home."

Now I smiled, but it was more a smirk. He couldn't be serious. I shook my head.

"How long have you been wandering?"

"I'm not wandering anywhere. My family followed Elijah Muhammad's son into Orthodox Islam when he took over."

The brother backed off. The rift between Louis Farrakhan and Warith Deen Muhammad had been nasty and public. Their followers did not mix or mingle and each side sharply criticized the other. Nation of Islam members berated former members for embracing the traditions of Arabs who denounced Nation of Islam theology as heresy, and former Nation of Islam Muslims who converted to Sunni Islam condemned those who lined up behind Farrakhan to rebuild the old Nation of Islam as people stuck in the past. I did not realize at that time that at least three other Nation of Islam splinter groups had formed, all claiming to be the real "original N.O.I." But Farrakhan had, by far, the largest following and was continuing to build it, in part, by lecturing at colleges and prisons across the country.

"So, you're a follower of Warith Deen?" he asked.

"I'm not a follower of anybody," I said proudly.

He smiled again. The afternoon sun washed over us, and a gentle breeze tugged at my pant legs. Students passed us coming and going across the concrete plaza. Then there was a wolfing sound and we both turned to see a train of young men dressed identically in black sweatshirts with gold inscription, black jeans, and black combat boots chucking to the center of the plaza.

"A-fy-eeeeeeeee!" one of them shouted.

The others whooped or wolfed some strange animal sound. The leader broke into an arm-waving, thigh-slapping, foot-stomping routine and the others followed him. Students gathered to watch them—a line of good-looking guys, different shades of brown, various heights, moving in unison. They looked so intense, their faces twisted into tight grins.

"I pledge my soul...!" *Stompedy-stomp-stomp.* "To the..." *Slapety-tap-tap-tap.* "The Black and Gold!" *Stomp-stomp-clap-slap-stompedy-stomp-stomp.*

As they sang in unison and performed this rhythmic routine, I was drawn back to my days at the Temple, back to watching my uncles perform elaborate drills as part of their F.O.I. drill team.

"Aw, man! We used to do that!" I told the bow-tied brother excitedly. "I mean sort of like that. We had the best drill teams in the city. Wiped the public schools out every time!"

"I know, sister. And we're trying to get that back. That's why we need our prodigal children to come on home."

I shook my head.

"Been there. Done that," I said.

Everyone wants to belong to something, I realized. But at what price?

"Sister, you know what the Holy Quran says about those who turn their back on their faith. Woe to those who..."

"Faith and doctrine are two different things."

"What do you mean?"

"I mean my faith is in God, not in a religion, not in a book. Religions are just tools to control the masses. You've heard the term 'opiate of the people,' haven't you."

"Ah, sister. That's that western, European foolishness got you all mixed up. You know, returning to Islam is just returning to your roots," he said. "Our people in Africa were Muslims."

"Our people in Africa were lured into Islam," I told him, drawing on a bit of history I'd gleaned from a video at the library. The video was produced by Muslims and by their own account, Islam was spread in Africa by discounting the wisdom and worshipping practices the Africans already had.

"The Muslims went in Africa and did the same thing the Christians had done. They went over there telling Africans their ways of worship was devil worship, that by honoring the sun and the trees they were praying to false gods. Africans already knew we humans have some kind of connection to all living things, but these Christians and Muslims, with their own agendas, went in and changed all that."

He looked puzzled, like I was telling him something he'd not heard, not thought of, but something maybe worth looking into at least.

"I grew up Muslim. Got all kinds of Christians in my family, and of course everybody thinks they're right and that all the others are going to hell. That's why I don't put my faith in religion. I mean, I make salat sometimes, more so out of force of habit or out of respect for family tradition, but I sure don't confuse these little rituals with my connection to God."

He shook his head as if he was confused now.

"My sister! How did you get so far lost! You really need to come see the Minister. You need to come and get the truth!"

"I'm telling you, I *had* the truth. Let me give you a little tip so you don't get strung out like some other people I've seen devastated when they find out the truth changes every ten or twenty years," I said. "As soon as you get it down pat, something'll happen, and along comes a whole new truth. People want to make like there's some magic prescription for living, like you can say ten Hail Mary's or make five salats and curry favor with God. God is like the air, he—if God is a he. God just is."

I was off on a tangent now.

"God is like the very air we breathe. Some people would control the air if they could. Some people want to put it under a microscope and examine it, then tell you you've got to pay them some money to find out what they saw, or you have to behave this certain way to access it. God just is."

"Now, see, that's your opinion," the bow-tied brother countered. "That's the problem. Everybody's got an opinion, and some people think their opinions are true facts. But what the Honorable Minister Louis Farrakhan is teaching is not his opinions. He's teaching you the facts."

"I know. It's his understanding, his interpretation of what's real, and what's right. That'll change, too. Watch. I'm tryna tell you. I been through it already. What he's saying now, let the political winds change, he's gon' change. He's gon' say what he needs to say when he needs to say it. Right now, he's tryna build up an organization for himself again. He's gon' tell ya'll what you want to hear—that all your problems are caused by the bogey man in the closet, the white man, Mr. Ron, or his evil twin, the Jews. That's our oldest cry. It's what's familiar. Farrakhan can come along like a Pied Piper playing that same ole tune. Give you a few fresh examples, make you think nothing's changed except maybe gotten worse, and here you are—out here handing out flyers so people can come pay their five dollars to get in, get stirred up enough to buy a coupla tapes of more of his speeches, maybe join his Nation and give up some free labor and help him buy a bunch of nice stuff for himself."

Come to think of it, I couldn't remember us hating the Jews when I was in the Nation of Islam. This was new race-baiting for Farrakhan. In the Nation of Islam under the leadership of Elijah Muhammad, we opposed white people across the board, not singling out Jews. That would've been too much to put on this brother trying to pull me into a Farrakhan lecture now.

He shook his head and reached into the black book bag hanging from his shoulder.

"Let me show you something right here. It's right here in black and white..."

"Actually, I got a class I need to be getting to right now. I'm already late," I said. "Even those books you got. You think that's like writing on the stone, right? Stones crumble, too. Watch."

I couldn't fully appreciate what the brother was doing. He believed in this all-black Nation of Islam and was working hard to help build it up. He did not see himself as exploited, manipulated, taken advantage of by Louis Farrakhan. I believed Farrakhan was working for his own glory, exploiting people who believed him, using them to buy himself a mansion in Chicago, fancy cars, bodyguards, a chauffeur, and expensive goods and vacations for his family.

My family had helped to build the Nation of Islam temples and businesses with charity we could barely afford to give. I still resented that. Elijah Muhammad had us buying him a damn airplane and my family could barely keep gas in the used car we'd bought. We'd paid dues for building temples, dues for building an all-black national hospital. We had sold *Muhammad Speaks* newspapers and fish and profited little, and I resented the hell out of the Nation of Islam's officials who got all the benefits from our labor and charity. Black-on-black exploitation is what it looked like to me. My grandmother and uncles didn't feel the same as I did. They appreciated the lessons they had learned in the Nation of Islam, lessons, which they had gotten nowhere else—lessons in Black pride long before that notion took on in the Black community as a whole. The men gained practical lessons working in the Nation's restaurants, and a few of my uncles were able to take those skills and get jobs cooking and build their own catering services specializing in natural, healthy foods.

This brother recruiting for Farrakhan now might never become resentful. He might appreciate building something for a man who looked, felt, and spoke like him.

"Take this and at least think about it," he said, handing me the flier he had offered on his first approach.

I accepted the flier and dropped it in the trash on my way into the building. On my way up on the elevator I thought about the word *return.*

If I was going to return to anything, to any religion, that is, it would be to Christianity, the religion of my grandparents and great-grandparents, just for the sake of tradition, and I would be careful not to confuse what I was doing culturally with some divine mandate from God, I thought.

I thought about my growing resentment toward Islam as I'd known it and realized the main thing I disliked was that it changed every decade or so. At least in America it did. It was as if it was being created and re-created as we went along. I needed a religion that would remain the same when everything else changed, something solid to hold on to in a confusing, ever-changing world. If your religion is confusing and unstable, you're in trouble. The very name of my religious organization changed three times before I was fifteen.

We started out as the Nation of Islam, then after Elijah Muhammad's death our organization evolved and was renamed the World Community of Al-Islam in the West. We were told to consider ourselves Bililian Muslims, after the darkest Muslim that followed the original prophet of Islam in Mecca. (Before then, we'd been taught not to associate with the Muslims of middle-eastern orthodoxy because our Nation of Islam version of Islam was different, and, for us, better than their ancient, foreign religion.) Elijah Muhammad's son, Warith Deen Muhammad, who led our organization and re-named it the World Community of Al-Islam in the West, changed the name of our organization again. He now said we would call ourselves the American Muslim Mission.

As we changed customs and practices to align ourselves with the world-wide Orthodox Muslim community, Warith Deen Muhammad said we would no longer all follow a central leader because Arab Orthodox Muslims did not do that and we were modeling ourselves after them. Each imam, Muslim minister, in each city would be responsible for his own sheep, and we all would follow the ways of the prophet Muhammad as did orthodox Muslims the world over.

The name of our place of worship changed from "temple" to "mosque" to "masjid." This was all too much change for me at a time when I was trying to establish some roots and build a foundation for my life. Christianity was appealing to me because even though people left it, I knew it didn't change. It would remain the same when and if you needed to go back to it. I resented the swift changes in our religion because to me it meant nothing was solid, nothing was real.

By the time I was nineteen, I held one truth to be true: Maybe there was a God. Which of His religions were true, and which of His rules really needed to be followed, I wasn't sure. When I was a little girl, I'd been taught that the same God that put the sun, moon, and stars in the sky would punish me if I ate any of the foods off our How-to-Eat-to-Live forbidden foods list, which included white potatoes, white bread, and white rice. But by the time I was ten and we were "evolving" from our Nation of Islam race-based theology toward a "universal brotherhood" kind of Orthodox Islam, I was learning God's orthodox laws did not prohibit all those foods and I was mad I'd missed out on some goodies. At thirteen or so I'd been forced to believe that if I didn't wear my Muslim-girl head-pieces and long clothes, I would incur the wrath of the same God who created beautiful heavens for the devout and pits of hell for the disobedient. Then when I was seventeen or so, the women in our loosely structured orthodox community decided they no longer needed to don the Middle-Eastern garbs. Those outfits had more to do with maintaining a culture than a connection to one's spiritual Supreme Being, they reasoned. The "truth" changed again to suit people's convenience and comfort.

By the time the elevator doors opened, I had to snap back to reality. My thoughts had taken me someplace else. I went on to English class and tried to pay attention to the discussion on Mark Twain's works.

When I left my last class Friday evening, I walked toward the gymnasium to see if a crowd was already gathering for Farrakhan's appearance. I was not surprised to see students lined up for at least a mile, zigzagging from the gymnasium where Farrakhan was scheduled to speak. Reagonomics had poor folks scared, had poor Black folks terrified. Students were eager to hear somebody's "truth" about what was really going on beyond the bits and pieces reported in the news. They wanted to know what they were dealing with and how better to deal. Farrakhan seemed to have the answers.

Here was an apparently proud, independent, uncompromising, bold, downright arrogant Black man. And, yes, some of his programs and ideas had worked. People in the Black community had witnessed for at least five decades how Nation of Islam teachings could help Black men get off drugs and get their families back together. Those of us who'd actually been on the inside and knew more than what the Nation of Islam propaganda perpetuated also knew the quick-fix solutions were just that more often than not. But Farrakhan gave his admirers courage and a sense of pride—and ideas and information to ponder that they were not getting from any other source. I got in line to go in, just in case he had something new to offer. Halfway through his fiery, very passionate lecture, I realized it was nothing new to me and I left.

Chapter Seventeen
A Courageous Woman

I was glad I had someplace else to go other than home after classes. I was working a new internship in the same building where I'd worked the previous summer. When the snooty woman from personnel told me I'd be assigned to work for a producer named Aisha Karimah, I thought I was in for a special treat, working for a Muslim woman. I had not known any professional African-American Muslim women except teachers, nurses and secretaries. To find one who had ventured into a position usually held by men, would be nice. When I arrived in her office and found her dressed in regular slacks and a blouse, I began to wonder whether she was in fact a Muslim.

"Ms. Karimah, are you a Muslim?" I asked.

"Oh, no. Don't let the name fool you, honey. I just wanted to choose a name for myself 'cause I didn't like the name Fanny. I mean, what *is* a Fanny? I saw a lot of people going into Islam changing their names to something they liked, and I just figured I could change my name, too, if I wanted," she explained, laughing. "People want to make a big deal out of it, though. And, honey…," she went on, "don't even get to talkin' 'bout my hair. These people, especially white folks, think it's some kind of militant statement that I cut all my hair off. It's convenient is what it is. I don't have to fool with it every morning. That's all. Ain't about no statement."

"So, if you liked what the Muslims were doing, why didn't you become one?" I asked, collecting supplies from a box in front of her desk.

"Oh, honey. That just wasn't for me. That's some ole foreign something or other. I'll stick with the religion my mama gave me, even if I did change my name."

I enjoyed talking with her in the office. She was six-foot-something, with broad shoulders and dangly arms like a basketball player, and simply awesome, if you asked me. Her skin was the color of butterscotch, her hair cut in a short natural like Ms. Legall's, and her feet were long and slightly skewed out to the sides, but the main thing that stood out about her was her laugh. Ms. Karimah, which I kept calling her because I couldn't get used to calling a woman my mother's age by her first name with no proper title, laughed loud and often—the world be damned. She didn't try to squeeze her big self into anybody's small idea of how a lady was supposed to act. She cussed and fussed better than some of the men on the job and wasn't the least bit apologetic about being a woman—or about being Black for that matter.

Some of the African Americans squeezed up in corporate outfits seemed always to be apologizing for themselves and for the sorry race they were unfortunate enough to be born into. But not Ms. Karimah. I stood behind her in the control booth when the half-hour public affairs show she produced was being shot and marveled at her camaraderie with the white boys. They all had oversized cups of coffee in their reach, and several dragged on cigarette after cigarette. During commercials they laughed and joked about somebody's little dick or somebody's alternative sexual preference. Not every thought or word carried the weight of life and death here and I loved it.

At home, I shared my excitement with my younger siblings. Our household was calm for a stretch of several whole months, and that was good. We enjoyed our dinners together and watched TV together afterward. When the news came on, I pointed out the people I worked with on the show, then enthusiastically pointed out my name at the end of the credit roll. They squealed with excitement.

"Sonsyrea Tate, that's you! Tate! That's our name!"

Furard was most excited of all.

"How'd you get our name on there?" he asked.

I tried to explain, but ended up promising to take him to work with me one day to show him.

A few months later, I ended up taking Atif with me instead because Aisha—I finally got used to calling her that—had invited him to appear on the show to discuss children's reading habits. It was National Reading is Fundamental Month, and when discussing what approaches we might take to celebrating it on our show, I suggested bringing on some kids who'd won prizes for reading the most books at their school. I told them how excited Atif had been when he received an award certificate and a fifty-dollar gift certificate to a bookstore, and Aisha asked if he could be on the show.

"I'd love to show these crackers that our kids read, too," she said.

It was mid-July when I took Atif to the station. The sticky heat was already dripping from the backs of our knees as we walked from the Van Ness subway station uphill toward the studios at 9:30 in the morning. The gnats, flies, and butterflies whizzed by as fresh and enthusiastic as we were. The stately trees up here dripped luscious green ambiance and shade. In our neighborhood, we had mostly baby trees in cute little tree boxes. Our baby trees could not compare to the big grandparent trees up here. I loved trees and knew they loved me wherever I went—in my part of town or anyone else's. You could tell these houses, made of red brick or white stones or a combination of both, were old. And you could tell their occupants had to be rich. I was going to have me one of these houses one day. These houses were retired behind carpets of manicured lawns and sharply shaped shrubs and walkways made from brick or stone.

"We still in D.C., Ray-Ray?" Atif asked.

"Yep. This is still D.C. You don't remember when Ma used to bring us up here to the zoo? The zoo's not that far. And my school's not that far either. It's right down the street. I walk up that hill every day. Ma used to bring us up here for picnics, too. You remember that park where we got in the water and walked across on the rocks? That's up here."

He shrugged his shoulders. "We came all the way up here to go to the park? I don't remember that. We got our own playground right up the street."

I didn't bother to explain that Ma thought the grass was greener up here.

"You come all the way up here? Every day?" he asked.

"Yep."

Institutions for higher learning and outlets for mass communication, or any big business for that matter, just were not located in our part of the city.

"Yep. I take the bus and the subway, then walk about seven blocks," I explained.

"Dag!"

Seemed like I was doing too much to get away from our little world back home.

"It's not that far," I told him. "You could get used to it."

"I'm glad my school ain't this far."

"*Isn't*, Atif," I corrected. "You gotta use the right English up here, especially when the cameras go on, a'ight?"

"You mean be fake."

"No. I mean act like you know," I said.

Atif cracked that crooked grin of his.

"I'm just gon' be myself," he said confidently. "I'ma act normal."

"You *better* act like you know," I insisted.

I looked down and was tickled at the sight of him in the little outfit I'd put him in. Atif hated collars and ties, but I had him in a long-sleeve, light-blue oxford shirt, dark-blue pants, and tan suede dirty bucks this morning. This was the only dress-up outfit he had. Ever since I started working summer jobs when I was fourteen, I made sure he had a good pair of slacks, a dress shirt, and a sport coat in his closet in case of emergencies. That's one thing I'd gotten from both of my grandmothers. Even though Ma had insisted I wear Muslim clothes—long dresses, or long shirts over my pants, and some rag on my head—Granny made sure I had regular shorter dresses we kept at her house. Though, out of respect for my religion, my emergency dresses were still cut two or three inches below my knees. I wore them to church when I visited with Granny and Granddad or went to one of their Mason or Eastern Star banquets. GrandWillie had made sure I kept a Nation of Islam-styled outfit to wear to the temple with her after Ma called herself converting to Orthodox Islam.

I looked at Atif with his round stomach poking out from the McDonald's breakfast I'd treated him to, trying to balance his stack of books under his arm while we walked, and couldn't help but smile at my child, my child. Atif's big brown eight-year-old eyes were round as saucers. They beamed with playfulness and innocent curiosity born not out of a need, or a desperation to understand the world quickly enough to save it. His eyes weren't worried like mine, or anxious like Furard's. Furard and I had tried to shield our younger sisters and brothers from much of what we knew and saw. Somebody in our household deserved to be kids, and Furard and I, without discussing it, had decided we would be the surrogate parents so the youngest kids could enjoy being kids.

"I'm not gon' be able to see myself on TV, Ray-Ray. I just thought about that," he said as we entered the studio. "Look at these big cameras, Ray-Ray!"

"Yep. Wait till you see those big lights come on." I was holding his hand now and pointing like a tour guide. "Wanna go see the radio station real quick?"

"They got a radio station in here, too?"

"Yep."

As we walked along the corridor I smiled and greeted everyone we passed with a cheerful "Good morning," which was not a custom in our neighborhood. I proudly introduced my little brother to the few people I knew well enough.

"You don't know none of the white people, Ray-Ray?" Atif asked.

"I just don't remember their names," I told him.

The rush of all these white faces in my presence came on as a blur initially. I couldn't distinguish one from the other, but after a few weeks on the job, I began to remember details—the white woman with black hair or the one with brown hair or red hair or blonde hair. I began to remember the names of the ones who spoke. Finally, I would begin to see their faces, then match their faces with their names.

We ran into one of the cameramen I knew pretty well from his long chats with Aisha in her office. Ortez Timberlake was Aisha's height, but add about two-hundred pounds. Today, as usual, he was strutting about like he owned the place, chilling in his sagging jeans, oversized black T-shirt, and tan hiking boots.

"S'up, Tate? Who dat?"

"This my little brother, Atif. He's gon' be on the show we're taping today. Talkin' about getting more books to inner-city kids."

"My man," Ortez said, reaching to shake Atif's hand.

Atif was impressed. He'd hardly glanced up at the few brothers we passed in suits, hardly noticed the white guys at all, but he studied

Ortez, who was more his kinda guy. Ortez wasn't afraid to represent our styles and speak our language, even in the white man's world. Ortez wasn't like most African Americans in large corporations—suffering from TWMD, The White Man's Delusions—those few Blacks picked for middle-class professional jobs were in all ways better than blacks who had not been chosen. TWMD, left many African Americans feeling, and looking, schizophrenic, living double lives, speaking double languages on a daily basis as they tried to fulfill standards set by whites at work, while maintaining the less formal language and interactions at home.

Atif looked down at the corny clothes I'd dressed him in and scraped the bottom of his right foot over his left. I'd even polished his shoes. Corny stuff. He yanked at his shirt tucked too tight and neat in his pants, pulled it up as much as he could without taking it all the way out. Cut his eyes at me.

Ortez suggested we get some footage of Atif heading into his classroom with his backpack stuffed with books. Atif was a star at his school for that day. Two weeks later my sister and brothers and I waited in front of the nineteen-inch TV in the living room to watch Atif's debut. No doubt his classmates and teachers around the neighborhood would tune in too. At least I hoped they would. I'd mentioned to everybody I'd talked to in passing that he'd be on Saturday morning at eight o'clock. As much as folks in our parts complained that "they" never put Black people on the news unless it was for something negative, I was sure they'd be happy for this shot of good news. And maybe after they saw Atif on the show and noticed some Black-looking names in the credits at the end, they'd tune in more often.

Ma had long since taught me that there was a conspiracy in the media. White men supposedly held long meetings about how to control the images of Black people and make sure they only showed the bad and the ugly—poor test scores, welfare fraud, corrupt officials, arrests of Black men, drug raids of people's homes in the projects. Of course, by the time I was in my teens, I figured she was wrong. And to prove her wrong, I was studying and working to become a part of the elusive media. It did not occur to me at that time that I'd wound up working with a woman who believed some of what Ma believed, a woman who was trying to teach me some of the same things about the media that Ma had tried to teach me.

In our living room, we waited for the other guests for today's taping to finish their segments so Atif could sit in the large, plush, rust-colored chair on the set.

"Why they got all these other people on my show?" Atif asked, as a tall white guy on screen gave an ice-sculpting demonstration for the cameras.

"You're coming up next," I assured him. "Watch, they 'bout to tease you."

"Why they gon' do that?"

"No. Tease means they 'bout to say you're coming up next so people will stay tuned."

"Oh. That's a'ight then."

That's exactly what happened in the next few seconds. A clip of Atif bouncing into his classroom zoomed across the screen as the host, Mr. Fred Thomas, said, "Next, meet a young man who loves books more than he does basketball."

"Ma! Turn to channel four real quick! He 'bout to come on!" I shouted up the stairs to Ma's closed door.

Dad wasn't home. His shoes weren't lined up near the door with the rest of ours. But this was Saturday morning. He likely was at his job or out with the Muslim brothers involved in some collective effort to provide for their families. For instance, some Saturday mornings they bought fresh produce and meats in bulk wholesale to save money.

"Shhhh, shhh! Here I come," Atif said.

We stared intently.

"Atif, you shoulda…"

"Shhhhh!" he hushed Sakinah.

The host, Mr. Thomas, tall and dignified even sitting in his cushioned armchair on the set, spoke of city-wide efforts to conquer illiteracy. I'd done some of the research, and was overjoyed to hear him speak so eloquently using information I'd provided. His diction was perfect, and his tone smooth and commanding. I did not think he was "talking white" as kids in my high school might say. He reminded me of Frederick Douglass, who I imagined must have sounded the same way when he read his famous essays. Atif sat up in his chair as I'd instructed. He looked good.

"I like books because they're fun," he said. "The charact… charac…the characters make you laugh."

"Boy! You did good!" Furard shouted.

"Shhhhhh!" Atif insisted.

"Tell us about some of your favorite books…," Mr. Thomas asked, and Atif listed them.

"And what are some of your other hobbies? What else do you enjoy doing?"

"I play with my friends sometimes, but I mostly like to do my puzzles."

Yes! We'd rehearsed these answers, and even if he didn't appear as natural as he really is, I was happy. The phone rang, and I ran to the kitchen to answer it. It was Grandma.

"Hi, baby!" She beamed. "Tell Atif he did very well. Your Granddad and I watched him and he should be very proud of himself."

"You wanna speak to him? He's right here."

"No, no. We're running out the door. Got a prison ministry this morning. We're supposed to be at the church by nine, but we didn't want to miss our grandson."

"Okay. I'll tell him."

When I went back into the living room, Atif was strutting around with his arms up like a wrestler, as if he'd just triumphed in a match.

"Oh, you ain't all that," we joked.

As much as I loved my grandmothers and respected their backgrounds, I was happy to be going into a line of work they had not dared dream of pursuing. I sensed they were happy, too, and proud. The career fields open to me had not been open to them. Ma might have been more encouraging, but she was still trying to figure out her place in the world. She was still defining who she was supposed to be or could become as I was setting out on such a pursuit. I guess that's what happens with young parents sometimes. They end up growing up *with* their kids rather than ahead of them. I think in some ways I was showing Ma what was possible, who she could become, what possibilities she might consider. I know I was showing her the world wasn't so bad as she'd feared. I also was trying to prove to her that she did not have to confine herself to out-dated traditional roles.

Chapter Eighteen
Just Survive

I was washing the downstairs walls with Sakinah and Furard one Saturday morning when we saw Dad and one of the Muslim brothers pull up in a black pickup truck. Dad and "the Muslim brothers," as I'd come to group them all in my mind, worked together trying to make ends meet for their large families. Most of them had between four and twelve children, and tried often to pool their monies from their vending stands, from their jobs, and from their wives' public assistance. Saturday mornings—and this lasted six to eight months or so—they'd co-opt and buy fresh produce wholesale to save on grocery store prices. They bought enough for the seven or so families in our small circle of Muslim families, and to sell around the neighborhoods where we lived in the public housing, or low-income neighborhoods.

"Go get the other boys," Dad told me as I held open the door for him to bring in the large box I'd watched him pull off the truck.

Dad hadn't noticed Furard washing walls right there in the kitchen. When Dad was busy, intent on making something happen, he couldn't see past what his hands were attached to at the moment.

"Furard's right here," I said.

"Oh good. Go get your brothers, and ya'll help Brother Adam bring the rest of those boxes in."

Atif could come down from upstairs to help, but Darren was nowhere to be found. I could no longer keep up with his schedule. He had a job cooking at a senior citizens home where Uncle Sharrief was the head chef, and some weekends he had to get up early to go there. But some Saturday mornings he wasn't home to help clean because he partied all night and crashed at a friend's house. Dad pulled off his shoes and took them with him to the basement steps.

"I'll get the bags to help bag," I called out after him.

"Ray-Ray, you go upstairs and help your ma out. We can take care of this," he said.

I hated that. I was good enough to wash the greens and cook, but not good enough to help weigh the greens, bag them, and go knocking door-to-door around the neighborhood selling them? Domestic skills were not the only skills I wanted. Dad couldn't understand that, though. There was not enough to do inside the house to develop my mind and spirit the way I wanted.

I moved away from the door and let it shut, even though I saw Brother Adam approaching with his arms full. I went back to washing the walls in the living room and paid the brothers going in and out the door no mind. I retreated to my bedroom when I finished and stretched out on the bed with one of my Khalil Gibran books. I could read Gibran for hours, and often I did. Here was a man from the Middle East who thought as I thought about so many things.

"And an old priest said, "Speak to us of religion." And he said, "Have I spoken this day of aught else? Is not religion all deeds and all reflection, and that which is neither deed nor reflection, but a wonder and a surprise ever springing in the soul, even while the hands hew the stone or tend the bloom? Who can separate his faith from his actions, or his beliefs from his occupation? Who can spread his hours before him saying this is for God and this is for myself; this is for my soul and this is for my body? All hours are wings that beat through space for self to self. He who wears his morality but as his best garment is but naked."

I would read these passages over and over again, enjoying the poetry that it was, and further enjoying the confirmation. I knew religion wasn't an outfit you wore or a memorized prayer you recited at certain times each day. And here was a man from Lebanon who knew it and said so publicly. I read "The Prophet" several times.

Ms. Karimah had become my new "mother" for insight and advice as I proceeded into the professional arena; and Gibran I adopted as my new "dad" for spiritual guidance as I ventured beyond Islam.

One evening, I heard Sakinah outside with a few of her girlfriends playing an old patty-cake hand-tapping game for big girls.

Rockin' Robin. Tweet. Tweet. Tweet.

Your muva's in the kitchen cooking rice,

Fatha's round the corner shootin' dice,

Brotha's in jail, raisin hell,

Sistah's in the basement selling pussy for sale,

Rockin' Robin. Tweet. Tweet. Tweet.

Same game I used to play. You do it louder and faster each time till somebody can't keep up. Then you bust out laughing and start over.

Muva's in the kitchen cookin' rice!

Fatha's round the corner shootin' dice!"

But now I couldn't stand it because it was coming too close to true in our own family. It was fine when it was just a joke of stereotypes we could enjoy in the privacy of our own neighborhood, but now that some of it was seeming true, I didn't want to hear it.

Eggs and vegetables were not all Dad and his friends were selling out of our basement. After his arrest, it seemed like what had been done in the dark for so long was about to come out in the light.

"Sakinah!" I hollered out the window. She looked up. "It's time to come in!"

She took off running out of sight, laughing with her girlfriend Dinky.

As I was pulling my shade back down, I saw the girls my age coming up in the front courtyard to hang out around the tree box. They played the dozens and laughed like crazy. I heard them teasing my friend Chee-Chee about getting beat up by the Wylie Street girls.

"Yeah, I should kick your ass for standing there like a punk while I got jumped," she shot back. "Punk!"

At that point, I had to get up to see who she was talking to. I drew the shade in my window just enough for me to peek through with my chin resting on the windowsill.

"Pumpkin, ole big-ass self. Standing there crying while I'm getting my butt kicked."

There were seven girls sitting around the tree box having a good time. Pumpkin was the one with her booty jutted out a whole foot behind her. She got teased for that a lot growing up. But as we grew into teenagers, the boys realized what she had was a treasure, and began to treat her differently. They wanted to push up on her now. And if they still wanted to fight her, it wasn't because they didn't like her for reasons they couldn't explain; it was because they liked her so much they wanted her all for themselves, and could only hope to keep her away from other guys by making her scared as hell to talk to any others. Pumpkin had a boyfriend named Pete, who everybody knew beat on her. Pete's cousins were the ones who jumped Chee-Chee, and that was the real reason Pumpkin had left Chee-Chee fighting off three girls by herself. Pumpkin couldn't go against her peoples and her boyfriend's peeps were her peeps, too. We all knew it, but it wasn't right.

"Ain't nobody gon' be getting caught up in your mess," Pumpkin shouted back at Chee-Chee. "You be running your damn mouf. Then when you get caught up, you expectin' somebody else to get in it."

These girls had been fighting each other, and fighting the girls in nearby neighborhoods since we were younger. Now, as they grew into young women, it seemed like fighting was all they knew. They got into fights on their summer jobs at school and recreation centers around the neighborhood. That was another reason I wanted a job outside of the neighborhood. I'd not gotten into a single fight with any of the girls and the two times I might've fought one because I'd heard she was talking about me behind my back or disrespecting me right there in my face, I let it go. Wasn't worth it to get my face all scratched up or cut up. I'd pretend the slights didn't bother me.

My training at the Muslim school had taught me how to let stuff slide. Rather than getting emotional, I'd been thought to step back and think a thing through. Fight only when absolutely necessary, and then fight like hell to the bitter end. I'd taken a self-defense class in Muslim Girl Training, way back when I was eight or so. I'd learned how to kick and punch, but had never had to use the skills because of my thinking through situations instead.

I'd been lucky that being in a tight Muslim community, I never had to fight. My Muslim girlfriends and I never came to blows because we needed each other too much for survival. All our mothers had too many babies, giving us too much work, and we'd had to counsel each other through. So, we never got into arguments or fights. That was one good thing I could say about my Muslim background.

The boys around our way were beginning to notice me, but I'd already decided I didn't want to get mixed up with any of them. They noticed that I wasn't wild like the other girls, that I carried books all the time or my little black case with some mysterious instrument inside. Some of them really went for that.

One particular night, Mitchell, a tall, slender, penny-colored guy with a bad case of acne, came to my window Romeo-style. I heard him asking the girls nearby if I'd been out earlier.

"You know her muva ain't lettin her out the house," I heard one of the girls say. "I know she can't breathe up in there. I'on't know how she can stand it."

"You think she up there now? Ain't no lights on," he asked.

"Yeah, she up there. Probly peepin' like she always do."

He glided over to the front of my house, moving slow and cool as he did, a baseball cap turned crooked. He wore regular jeans and a T-shirt, nothing fancy. Mitchell was a few years older than the rest of us. He had to be at least twenty, which to my seventeen-year-old mind seemed too old to even try. He whispered up to my window.

"Pssst. Ray-Ray? Hey! Pst!"

My parents' window was right beneath mine, but if he saw the living room and basement lights on and their bedroom light out, he could pretty much figure out the rest. He began singing what happened to be one of my favorite hits from The Whispers.

"You say you love me, ladaaaaaay. Girl, I hope you do. Only you can sa-eeeve my life because you. Kiss me, drive me crazy..."

"You corny muthafucka!" one of the girls shouted.

He continued until he saw my hand reach out to shut the window, then pull down the shade. The girls burst out laughing.

"Ya'll don't know nothing 'bout that. Ya'll girls don't have no class," he said.

I was beginning to reject the whole notion of me being some little princess up in a tower. For reasons I couldn't quite put my finger on, it already struck me as a farce. Some things I already knew. For instance, my mother's fairytale fantasy—that she could stay home and play house while her husband went out and made the living— was a farce. Ma's life was a struggle whether she wanted to admit it or not, and I figured if I'd have to struggle, it would be for something else. I stretched out on my small bed looking out into the night until the house got quiet and the girls were gone, and I could daydream about the different kind of life I would have in the future.

Let's see. What will I be doing five years from now, I thought, my eyes closed as I began to imagine. *Sure won't be tied down to a house full of kids. Rather than spending my life changing diapers, I could be the one to find a cure for cancer or something. Okay, Ray-Ray, you're not trying to become a doctor. Couldn't do math if your life depended on it.*

I enjoyed these conversations with myself. My thoughts were my best friends, my constant companions. I could entertain them, and they entertained me even when I couldn't hang out with my friends in the neighborhood. Conversations with myself were like dances sometimes, but sometimes my thoughts could dance circles around me and leave me exhausted and dazed.

I wasn't allowed to receive phone calls from boys, and dating or having a guy visit me was out of the question. Ma had some fantasy idea that some guy would tell my father he liked me and my father would make this guy swear by some honorable intentions. Then we would visit in my home under supervision, then his parents would meet my parents, then we'd get engaged, and I wondered what planet Ma was visiting from. She had all these ideas based on how she thought rich folks lived. In our poor neighborhood, life simply was not so nice and neat. Ma thought I could live by these high-brow ideas even though she had not. One boy had wanted to take me to my high school prom, but I was so embarrassed by Ma's interrogation of him, I changed my mind. Sitting with the guy on the couch, she'd asked him questions about his family's background, his mother, his father, their religion, his thoughts on religion, his thoughts on marriage, and I was thinking, *I just wanted to go to the prom. I wasn't trying to marry the boy. I just wanted to go to the prom!*

Neither Ma nor I could've predicted that in two short years, I'd run off with the ex-convict who lived next door.

Chapter Nineteen
Through the Fire

I was sitting on the front steps under the soft glow of the late afternoon sun one day, snapping the ends off green beans from Grandma's garden, when my next-door neighbor, Ron, bounced up the courtyard toward me. He was wearing the same red, white, and blue nylon Nike sweatsuit I'd seen him in the day before, and the same white crocheted kufi he wore day in and day out. But he had the zip-off sleeves removed from the jacket today, showing off the smooth, round bulges at the tops of his arms. Grinning like a Cheshire cat, he looked wily. His walk was hasty, his torso leaning forward, long arms and knocking knees beating a path in front of him. He was kinda cute, though. *Too damn hyper, but cute,* I thought. The courtyard was empty except for a few children playing on the gym equipment, a good shout away from where I was sitting.

"Salaam-Alaikum," he said, smiling all over the place as he approached. "Fresh string beans, huh? Most of these girls can't even open a can, but look at sho'ty."

"Hey, Ron." I smiled back at him, moving over since he was determined to squeeze himself in the space next to me.

The steps weren't that wide, but I made room for him. It was kinda nice having a cool guy finally notice me, even nicer to have his full attention for a moment.

"Dawud," he insisted.

His mother and sisters still called him Ron, and he still looked and acted like his same old self to me, so I called him by the name he had before he'd gone to jail, declared himself Muslim and adopted a new Arabic name.

"Oh, I forgot," I lied.

"Yeah, Dawud is the name of the King! David. The imam at Lorton gave it to me," he said proudly.

"Okay, Da-wud," I obliged.

Before we could get any further, I heard the door swing open behind us.

"Sonsyrea, come on in. It's time for salat," Dad said firmly. He stood there waiting for Ron to leave or me to move, something.

"As-Salaam-Alaikum, Brother Yusef," Ron said, standing up to face Dad.

"Wa-Laikum-Salaam, Ron," Dad said, looking at him sternly. "If you want Darren, you know you can knock on the basement door around back."

There was an awkward pause between them. Ron nervously adjusted the kufi on his head.

"Oh. Uh. I just stopped to see what Sonsyrea was doing here," he explained, trying to lose his nervousness in a smile.

I picked up the brown bag of green beans and the plastic white bowl I'd been dropping the snapped ones in as Dad held the door open for me to go in. Behind me, I heard Ron still stuttering.

"Oh, uh, Brother Yusef, I was on my way in to make Mahgrib myself when I came up here and saw Sonsyrea. Can I make it with ya'll?"

No Muslim man could decline another's offer to pray together, however skeptical he might be. Dad had his doubts about Ron because a couple of years ago, when Ron first arrived at his mother's new house next door to ours from a juvenile detention center where he'd been for three years prior, he gave Darren a gun. Darren was seventeen at the time. I'd just turned fifteen.

One night when Darren came home late and found me watching TV in his room—which he didn't like me to do unless I'd agreed to do his chores that day—he pretended to get upset and started digging around in his closet saying he was gon' fix me once and for all.

"A'ight. You won't stay out my room. I'ma fix your ass," he said, digging like a madman under a pile of clothes on the closet floor. "Bus' a cap in your ass. That'll keep you outta here."

He turned from the closet pointing a black revolver at me. My eyes popped and my mouth dropped open.

"I'ma tell!" I said in a low voice, losing my breath.

"Shut up!" he snapped between clenched teeth in a smooth low voice, mocking a cowboy or gangster. "Or I'll bus' a cap in your ass right now."

I stood frozen, terrified. I'd never seen a gun in real life. I mean, I'd seen them in display cases at the FBI Building on field trips with my schools over the years. But I'd never seen one in the hands of anybody I knew. Darren opened the revolver, turned the gun so I could see there was a bullet in it, closed the revolver, spun the chamber. Then, with a sly smirk on his face, he continued his gangster role.

"I think I'ma hafta kill you," he snarled, jokingly.

I could tell by the red, glassy look in his eyes that he was high on something. Probably marijuana laced with PCP, "love boat," the party drug of choice at the time. I doubted plain marijuana would've made him so wild. He pointed it at my foot and pulled the trigger. I yelled and ran downstairs.

"Maaaaaaa! Maaaaaa! Darren got a gun!" I said, catching my breath in the doorway to our parents' bedroom.

Without any questions, Ma yelled for Darren. She knew her son—and she knew me.

Darren came down the stairs as smoothly as if nothing happened.

"I was just playin' with her," he said, laughing. "I had my hand in my pocket like this, saying I had a gun. I was just playing."

I looked at him in disbelief.

"Ma! He had a real gun. He pointed it at me, right in my face!"

"Darren, go bring whatever it was that you had," Ma demanded.

"It wasn't nothing," he insisted. "I had my hand in my pocket like this."

"Ma, he's lying! It was a black gun! A real one!" She could see the terror in my face.

"Ray-Ray, you know I was just playing with you," he said, hoping the glare he shot at me when Ma looked away might scare me.

"Ma, it was real," I insisted. "Make him stay right here. I'll go up and get it."

"Darren, have a seat," she told him.

"Ma, you know how she is. Scared of everything. I was just playing."

"Sit down," she insisted.

He sat on the stairs and tried to clip my foot as I rushed past him. I searched the closet under the clothes, on the top shelves in all the shoe boxes, checked the insides of his designer tennis shoes that he'd bought with money from his afterschool job when he couldn't steal them. I checked under the bed, behind the TV. Checked in all the dresser drawers and couldn't find it. I went back downstairs and was about to go back to Ma to tell her when I looked down at Darren's feet in his dirty socks and got another idea. I went to my room, dumped my dirty laundry out the garbage bag I used as a laundry bag, returned to Darren's room and collected all his shoes so he couldn't leave the house before Dad got home and made him come clean. I put the bag of shoes under my bed, then returned to Ma to tell her I couldn't find the gun.

"I don't know where he hid it, but he does have one," I insisted.

Darren couldn't keep from grinning.

"Told you I was playin'," he said.

"And I've told you about playing too much," Ma said. "Both of you go on back to your rooms. And Darren, you're in for the night."

It was so unfair that usually he was allowed to stay out till midnight because he was a boy. He was only a year and a half older than me, and, I was a year ahead of him in school. I thought that should count for something. But because I was a girl, I had to come in by nine, even when I was hanging out at a girlfriend's house. I knew Darren might leave as soon as Ma closed her door because the worst punishment she could give him was a right jab across his chin, which she was prone to do. Darren was immune to that by now. He looked at me as he got up to return to his room and it was all he could do to keep from bursting out laughing.

More determined to keep him in, I marched downstairs to see if he had any other pairs of shoes he could use to leave the house. I picked up his shoes from the rows at the front door and hid them in the basement behind the couch. Found another pair in the basement and hid them behind the couch, too. I returned to my room, locked the door, and stretched out on my bed, looking up at the ceiling, smiling at my cleverness.

The clock on my dresser was reading 1:30 a.m. when I was awakened by Darren's ranting at my door.

"Ray-Ray, I know you took 'em! Give my shoes!" he hollered, banging on the door.

"I 'on't got your shoes!" I yelled back.

He yanked on the doorknob and kicked at the door, but knew better than to kick too hard and wake Ma. We were the only ones on the third floor. Ma had said this was the teenage floor. We had our own bathroom to squabble over, and the other bedroom up here was used as our family library.

"You know I'ma get you back," he fumed.

"You betta get away from my door!"

He yanked at the knob some more, then kicked the door one final time.

The next morning when we all arrived in the living room for our morning prayer, Darren and I each rushed Dad with our side of the story. He said he didn't want to hear it right now, that we should be getting in the frame of mind to make salat. Ma came in from the kitchen fussing at Furard for not putting the trash out the night before. Sakinah, Atif, and Tia were busy setting up the prayer rugs. After salat, Dad approached Darren first.

"Boy, if I find out you brought a gun in this house, your behind is mine," he said matter-of-factly.

"Dad, it's in here," I insisted. "I wouldn't make something like that up."

"If so, it'll show up again," he said.

I wasn't known to lie, but I was known to scare very easily and overreact.

"And what'd I tell you about teasing your sister?" Dad continued. Darren shrugged.

"She can't take a little joke," he said. "She ain't tell you she went in my room and took all my shoes. Yeah. She ain't tell you what *she* did."

"Sonsyrea, go get that boy's shoes," Dad said without a second thought.

Just then Furard called out from the back door.

"Here it go!" he said. "It's right here behind the trash can!"

We all rushed to see. Dad picked the gun up and glanced over to Darren.

"Ya'll go on back to bed," he said to me and the other kids.

"Yusef, I'll let you deal with him," Ma said. "I'm tired. If it was up to me, I'd let him go on out there. Let him live out on the streets until the police finally pick him up since that's where he wants to be so bad. I can't waste any more of my energy. I got these other kids to raise, and he's making it harder."

"I'll handle it, Munira," Dad said.

I was still standing there.

"Didn't I tell ya'll to go on back to bed!" Dad shouted at me.

Dad never raised his voice. That was the big difference between him and Ma. Dad never lost his cool, and hardly showed any emotion except when playing his horn. Anytime he raised his voice at somebody, it was time to scram.

I left, but didn't go far. I waited till Ma closed her door and crouched on the steps to hear Dad fussing at Darren.

"Ron gave it to me," Darren finally admitted. "I told him a guy at school threatened Ray-Ray with a knife. So, he gave me the gun."

"Did you think about what would've happened if you shot the boy and killed him!" Dad fumed. "I swear! What goes through that head of yours? You think you can handle somebody's death on your hands! I know you *think* you're tough like these guys on the streets, but you don't really wanna know. You think you slick. Think 'cause you out-slick your mamma, think 'cause you can pull one over on me, *think* you a real hustler. Maybe I shoulda let the police keep you the last time like your mamma said. You one of these dudes with a real hard head. You know what a hard head gon' get you?"

Darren didn't try to get a word in. He knew when Dad finally blew up, it was time to chill out. Dad was usually quiet and patient. We never heard him yell or fuss, so getting a lecture out of him meant he was finally touched. Usually he was preoccupied with too many thoughts—his job, his band, his many hustles that included selling bulk groceries around the neighborhood and selling drugs to make ends meet. He didn't want to be an all-out dope dealer, but providing enough weed to keep his band high and keep their out-of-pocket costs down seemed a sensible thing to do. None of it made sense to me. It was all a contradiction. Two of Dad's brothers had been to jail for bank robbery. Breaking the law to make ends meet didn't make sense to me. I listened to Dad lecture Darren, but I wondered if

Dad could make Darren do right. Darren and I both knew that Dad's drug dealing was illegal. How could he tell Darren anything?

"The jails are full of smart guys like you! And even if the cops didn't get you, your conscience would!" Dad said. "What? You think you gon' shoot somebody like you do on the video games and they gon' get back up and keep on living. Come back to fight you again?!"

There was a long silence before Dad spoke again.

"Go get him," Dad said.

"Huh?"

Darren sounded humbled.

"You heard me. I didn't stutter," Dad said. "I said go get Ron."

"They're not up yet," Darren muttered.

"Hustlers never sleep. They can't. They got to sleep with one eye open."

"His mother might come to the door."

"Oh, you don't care 'bout nobody's mother. You a tough guy."

"Ray-Ray got my shoes."

"You don't need shoes, boy. Your feet don't cut like the rest of us. What? You might bleed? Nah. Hustlers don't bleed."

The new day had broken in when Darren returned with Ron just moments later.

"Ah, sorry, Mr. Tate," I heard Ron stammering. "I ain't mean no disrespect. I was just tryin' to help the young brother out…"

"If that's the best help you can give a young brother, then you need to go on 'bout your business and stay away from here," Dad told him.

"Mr. Tate, I'm sorry. I thought…he said…he said his sister was in trouble, and I just knew what I would do if it was *my* sister…"

"Like I said, if that's the best you can come up with, don't come around here."

I pressed my lips to my knees to keep from laughing. That's what Darren's stupid butt gets.

"Ya'll already made Fajr? Can I make Fajr with ya'll?" Ron asked, seeing us in the living room about to make prayer.

Fake! I thought. *He ain't bit more thinking 'bout no prayer.*

Ron joined us for prayer on a regular basis, then suddenly stopped. He disappeared for several weeks.

One Saturday morning when I checked our mailbox in the central unit that stood front and center in our courtyard I was surprised to find a letter from Ron with a P.O. box as the return address. Curiously, I tore it open quickly and read it as I walked back to the house, the other pieces of mail tucked under my arm.

"My Dear Sweet Sonsyrea: I hope this missive reaches you in a state of peace, as that is all I wish for you. I pray that Allah continues to bless you and your family and keep you safe. As for me, you have probably guessed by now that they got me caught up in this wretched penal system again..."

I thought, *Oh, puh-lease. What you done now?*

"But I am certain that by Allah's mercy, I will be released soon. In the meantime, I do hope that you will find it in your beautiful heart to write to me and come visit. You can come with my mother and sisters inshallah. My visiting days are Thursdays, six to nine, and Saturdays, nine to twelve. I hope to see you soon."

I refolded the letter and put it back in the envelope. This was a beautiful, sunny Saturday morning, with glorious yellow-white sunshine beaming off the gray concrete, and a soft gentle breeze. The July humidity had yet to rise for this particular day. No way was I about to waste a moment of it writing a letter to a jailbird. Behind me, a car began honking and I turned to see if someone was honking for my attention. It was Ron's mother's black Firebird.

"Ray-Ray! What you doin' today? You wanna ride out with us? We're going to see Ron!" She hollered all this across the courtyard.

Ron's mother was the opposite of Ma, even in looks. Ma was short, light-skinned and quiet-looking, and plain. Ron's mother, Liz Bates, or Ms. Liz, as we called her, was tall, dark-skinned, loud and always done up in makeup and skinny braids weaved down her back. If the two of them had slipped into hell together, Ma would've been repentant, humble, and prayerful. Ms. Liz would've put burgers on a grill, conjured up some beer, and thrown a party. While I mostly admired women with professional achievements or at the very least moral standing like Ma, I also had a little respect for women like Ms. Liz who survived by sheer wit and will because that was all they had. Not every woman could be a brain surgeon, not every woman a saint. But we could all survive.

"Come here for a minute," Ms. Liz yelled.

Looking closer, I could see the car was full of women. As much as I didn't want to waste time with her ghetto behind, I had to show some respect because she was an adult and somebody's mother.

"Yes?" I said, leaning into the window.

Ron's sisters barely spoke to me usually, but they were excited about going to see their main man this morning.

"Ron said you gon' be his wife," his sister Saundra teased.

I pretended not to hear her.

"Ron wants you to come visit him," his mother said. "He told us not to tell you he was locked up until after he had a chance to write and tell you what was up, but he said you shoulda got his letter sometime last week. I didn't want to knock on your door 'cause you know how your mother is always trying to keep you in and everything. But let me know when you wanna go."

"I, uh, you know, I stay pretty busy. But tell him I said hi," I stammered.

Back in my room, I looked at the letter again and was reminded about the men in my family who had been to jail. I'd never been to a jail to visit them and wasn't about to go to visit this guy I barely knew.

Even when I was a little girl and two of my uncles, who'd been raised in the Nation of Islam but turned to crime in their teens, went in and out of jail, I was never taken to visit them. GrandWillie had said it was their choice to do things that would get them taken away from home, so no, we didn't need to run behind them. Let them take their punishment like men. Plus, it was downright embarrassing to have sons arrested for petty crimes—trying to rob banks and selling dope.

Uncles Edward and Avon knew better. From the time they were boys, they had attended Fruit of Islam training, men's training in the Nation of Islam, and Sunday service. But when they got old enough to get away from home a little, they got into all kinds of trouble and tried to justify it saying they were just trying to take back some of what the white man had taken from Blacks for so many years. That explained the bank robbery attempts. The dope thing they justified as giving their people unlicensed "medicine," claiming the only reason these feel-good substances were illegal was because the government had not found a way to control the distribution.

Uncle Avon went one step further to say that the white man spent mega money and major time in laboratories concocting substances they knew would be addictive, particularly to African Americans. He was standing on the front porch at GrandWillie's house explaining it to me one day.

"They said, 'I'm gonna make this drug so strong, so powerful, you won't be able to say no,'" he told me.

I said nothing, as usual holding in my thoughts.

"They created this thing, then planted it in our neighborhoods, one, to make some of our best and brightest minds crazy, and, two, to make criminals out of us. See, you sell it, you're a criminal. You use it, get addicted to it like they planned, and, again, you're a criminal."

Finally I spoke up.

"Well, if you know that's the plan, that's all the more reason to stay away from it in the first place," I said.

"Baby girl, it's not that simple," he continued. "See, they make it so you can't get a decent job doing the right thing. Then they send somebody your way with this opportunity to make some money, and you just trying to feed your family, so you gotta make some money. And you think, I'm just goin' do it a little while, long enough to save up some cash and take care of this and that, then, boom! Before you know it, you all caught up in the game, caught up in the system."

He really believed this, but because my younger uncles worked hard cooking and cleaning in kitchens, I knew Uncle Avon's way wasn't the only way, wasn't even the best way. But to hear him tell it, his younger brothers were spared falling into the street traps because he had walked that road for them. They could be all the more determined not to get caught up because they had seen what had happened to him.

By now though, all these excuses sounded trifling and trumped up. I dropped the letter in the box that held other loose papers on my dresser and sorted through the rest of the mail before taking it to Ma.

I all but forgot about Ron while he was gone. So many other things were happening.

Chapter Twenty
Choose Church or Crack

Mind-altering devices don't always come in the form of a powder or pill, and I was about to find this out.

Dad got put on leave from his job as a security officer at work after they learned of his arrest and pending trial. His mood swings became particularly drastic, going from somber in the mornings when he might've been at work, to erratic in the evenings and on weekends when he and the other brothers worked one of their enterprising ventures.

Whether he was bagging groceries to sell on weekends or rehearsing his band to do a few fund-raising performances at community centers, it was as if Dad was determined to prove he could make it on his own, without depending on some white man's penny-ante job. We were all on edge between his mood swings. Not that he was violent or prone to strike any of us. He never had. It was just that he was not himself, and we weren't sure what to expect. Finally, Ma explained to us during dinner one night that Dad would be gone for several weeks. She'd taken him to enroll in a drug rehab program outside the city.

That night I lay awake thinking about what was happening to my family. It was so horrible that my younger siblings had to see Dad taken out of the house in handcuffs. Now this. Did our parents know what kind of stain these events put on our family's reputation? I had been so proud to be a Tate. We had been one of the few "whole" families in the neighborhood. If I was no longer "Shorty Tate," a reference to Dad and my uncles who'd also been fine examples of clean-cut Black men, then who was I? How could this be happening to my family? Hadn't we prayed enough? We'd fasted during the month of Ramadan since I was a little girl and prayed together as a family daily—not once a week, but up to five times daily. Didn't that count for something? I knew some of the brothers did little things like selling nickel bags of weed, but doesn't a man's good deeds outweigh his bad? Would Allah send Dad home to keep the family together? All my life I'd been taught that the family was the nucleus of a community from which strong societies grew and then strong nations. All my life I'd bought into the ideal of a traditional family. God, what was happening now?

Two weeks later, I arrived home from work just in time to pile into the family station wagon to go out for our group session at the rehab facility. The revitalization efforts along the commercial strip around the corner from where we lived weren't progressing fast enough. Too many buildings still were boarded up. Too much trash was still strewn about. And there were still too many sunken faces and broken spirits littering our neighborhood.

Sitting in the front seat next to Ma, I looked straight ahead as we traveled through our neighborhood. I hated the sights all around. I was no happier passing through upper Northwest on our way out to Virginia, though. Who got to live in those huge, fancy houses with manicured lawns? What kind of work did they do? What kinds of families lived there? Whole families, I was sure. Probably professional moms and dads like the ones I saw in sitcoms and commercials, like the ones I worked with. My family seemed all out of sorts.

We drove past the city limits, exited onto the interstate, and drove a good distance through a countryside. I noticed the budding trees and flowers and wondered how pink and purple flowers grew in the woods all by themselves without any tending. Seasons changed and they grew and it was as simple as that. Nobody watered the woods. Nobody fed plant food to the plants out there, but every spring they came to life again. I was reminded of something Aunt Kemba used to say when I visited her home in the hard-core projects. She would point to a dandelion growing through a crack in the cement and tell me and her daughters we would grow up beautiful despite our surroundings. Her husband wrote a song titled "Lotus Lady" about beautiful flowers growing from the ghetto soil.

They said they wanted us to be little ladies, and I believe they did, but I was quickly coming to realize that I might not be able to depend on a man to take care of me for the rest of my life, even if I wanted to. Ma had gone from her father's home straight to her husband's and expected me to do the same. But that wasn't what I wanted for myself. GrandWillie had gone from her father's house straight to her husband's house. He died when she was in her mid-forties, but she remained in that house until her death. I realized Ma had been holding onto Dad for dear life, and that our whole illusion of a happy home hinged on his return from drug rehab. All these thoughts raced through my mind as I stared out the window, not talking to anyone. I'd even tuned out the noise the younger ones were making in the back until Ma finally screamed.

"Don't ask me any more questions! Just wait and see!"

Then I turned around to settle them down.

"Ya'll quit playing. Can't you see Ma's stressed," I told them, pulling Halim's leg out from under him, making him sit straight.

If we could keep the family together long enough for the twins to grow up in a stable home, I'd be happy.

"Ya'll chill out back there," I insisted. "Darren, can't you keep them…"

"He sleep," Furard told me. Darren was in the far back knocked out.

"Wake that boy up!" Ma yelled.

Sakinah, who was back there with him, gladly proceeded to shake
him awake.

Atif and Furard let the twins out of their seatbelts and set them
loose outside the car. Before we knew it, they were racing to a faraway
tree. Those two were in a world all their own. They could laugh and
joke and run and play regardless of what was going on around them.

"Atif and Sakinah, you two can keep an eye on the twins while we
go in to this meeting," Ma told them. It was late in June; it would
be daylight for a couple more hours.

"Furard should stay with them," I suggested. I thought he should
be spared, too. But he insisted on joining the grown-ups.

We proceeded up some wooden stairs, across a wooden porch. The
fresh air, the natural beauty all around was not lost on me. Darren
stepped on my heel and pretended it was an accident. I elbowed
him hard as I could.

"Damn, girl!" he shouted, before catching himself.

"Don't make me pop you in your mouth," Ma told him. "You wanna
act stupid?"

"It was an accident," he conceded.

"Do it again," she threatened.

"I said sorry," he said.

Ma flung open the door and we were greeted by a cheerful white
woman in her forties who guided us to the living room area where
the group already was in session. My eyes focused on the people
sitting in the circle of wooden chairs and I was at once shocked and
tickled. There were only two Black men in the bunch. It was a large
group of thirty-five or so, and you really couldn't tell where one
family ended and the other began, but what struck me was that the

majority of the people were white. They had drug problems, too? I'd thought drug abuse was a Black problem caused by the white man. I'd thought black men took drugs mostly to numb the pain of the white man's oppression—the pain of not getting the jobs that could afford their families the kinds of luxuries they saw white folks enjoying on TV, the pain of promotions denied no matter how hard they tried, the pain of the past even—of slavery and its legacy that lasted generations in the form of self-hatred and poverty. Now, what were the white guys in here for? Suddenly, I was interested.

The woman who escorted us in began setting up chairs for us next to Dad. We'd missed the introductions and my mind was only half focused as Dad introduced each one of us. I was half-dazed, surveying the others in their faded, torn jeans, dingy T-shirts, stringy hair, clean khakis or oxford shirts. One young white girl looked out of her mind with attitude toward her parents. Her eyes were dark and she had purple streaks in her hair, sporting punk-rock fashion. She looked zombie-like, disconnected from reality. But why? I wondered. What problems could white people possibly have—especially white kids? All they have to do is go to school, come home to cookies and milk, and get whatever they needed from their parents. Well, that's what I thought. Maybe that girl's ideal little world had fallen apart, too. I was snapped out of my wanderings when the conversation landed on us. What my older brother was saying was so absolutely stupid I had to cut him off.

"I'm sayin', everybody got an addiction," he said, expounding on his street smarts. "I don't see why we all here harping on this one man's affliction. Half your congressmen are alcoholics! That's a drug. Don't nobody see nothin' wrong with that. But let a Black man try to get his drug of choice and you want to criminalize him…"

"We do not *all* have addictions," I snapped. "And alcoholism *is* a problem. Some of these people are here for just that…"

"Aw, shut up," he said, waving his hand to dismiss my comments. "You got an addiction, too. How long can you go without a cup of water?"

He couldn't be serious, I thought.

"That's a habit! That's not an addiction!" I said.

"Habit, addiction, it's all the same…"

The group guide cut in to get us back on track.

"Mr. Tate, you look like you have something to say," she said to Dad.

"Yeah. Well, I just want to say I really don't appreciate my family sitting here talking about what all I didn't do for my family. I've always taken care of my family. There were times when I worked three and four jobs to be the man of that household, and I really don't appreciate my family turning on me like this when things get a little hard."

None of us had said anything about Dad failing our family. I'd thought it many times, but never said it. Ma never said anything to me about Dad failing us. I didn't know why Dad thought we had been talking about him behind his back. We certainly didn't expose our feelings openly in the meeting. Many years later I understood that a person's own guilt can make him hear things even when people around him aren't talking.

At the group therapy session, Ma appeared frozen emotionally. She would be in tears if she wasn't sitting there holding herself together so tightly.

"I know," Darren added. "This man been providing for us all these years, now soon as the cops bring a little heat, the women go runnin' scared."

Ma was gon' whup his butt later, I was sure. Whup his butt or send him packing. I zoned out again until the session was over. Dad was so upset, he marched out of the living room and straight up the stairs without saying good-bye.

Outside the center, I called the little ones back to the car. We were all silent except for Atif, who wanted to know what he'd missed.

"A bunch of weak people feeling sorry for themselves," Furard said.

I was surprised. I felt the same, but I was surprised Furard had picked that up, too.

"Your brother's goin' be right back here with them at the rate he's goin'," Ma said.

"Ya'll trippin'," Darren said.

"I'm 'bout two seconds off your tail," Ma hissed. "I suggest you keep your mouth shut the rest of the night."

Back home, I got the twins ready for bed while Ma led the others through salat and Quran study. She'd read them a passage, then talk about what it means and ask them questions. I'd tried to read the whole Quran the summer before starting college, but it proved way too much to digest in one month.

It is prescribed that we each read the Quran in its entirety during the month of Ramadan, which fell during the summer that particular year. I'd fasted and read as much as I could in the evenings when I got in from work, but the reading filled me with more confusion and more questions than before. I couldn't digest much of it and thought I must be evil or lacking the special blessing of understanding only granted by Allah. Then I read a passage that said Allah grants understanding in degrees. At that point, I began to realize that I couldn't sit down and read a book to understand all the answers to life's questions at one time. And why had we tried? My family, and the other Muslim families in our unstructured community, had jumped into Islam head first, gobbling up all the practices, information, and ideas from as many books as possible. And guess who got the stomachache? Guess who was about to vomit, spiritually speaking? Me.

Just a few weeks ago one of my neighbors who also had recently converted to Islam and came to our house for direction—God help her—came to me one night telling me Allah told her to sacrifice her babies. As I bathed the twins this evening, I remembered that night as if it was just now happening. I was sitting on the living room couch when my neighbor, a young, very thin, beautiful, medium-brown-skinned woman with long jet-black Indian-wavy hair, ran in through the back door, which we kept unlocked until bedtime. Her eyes looked crazed and she grabbed me by my shoulders.

"Ray-Ray, Allah wants me to sacrifice my babies," she said, trembling, and near tears. "I don't know what to do. I don't want to kill my own children. But that's what Allah just told me to do."

"Where are they!" I demanded, standing up and gripping both of her arms. I knew I needed to remain calm. "Where are they right now? Are they okay? Are they in the house?"

She broke out in a gut-wrenching cry.

"I don't want to do it," she cried. "I can't kill my own children. I was giving Junior a bath and Alicia was crying and screaming from her crib in the other room and I have been thinking about this for the last few days and I don't want to do it, but Allah said. Just like when Allah told Abraham to sacrifice his only son..."

"Is Junior still in the tub? Did you leave him in the tub?"

I was trying hard not to panic. Her son was my baby brothers' age. I steadied her arms, her hands still gripping my shoulders, looked her in the eyes, and told her to let me go check on the children.

"I'm gon' tell my mother to come and talk to you while I go check on the kids, okay?"

She turned me loose and fell back on the couch, wailing a painful sound into the air.

"Allah! I didn't want to kill my babies. I'm sorry, Allah..."

I snatched my shoes up from near the front door and ran to the basement, where Ma was putting a fresh load in the washing machine. I told her everything as I slipped on my shoes and ran out the back door without tying them. I ran to my neighbor's house and was relieved to find her mother there. I proceeded to tell her everything, but before I could finish she took off running upstairs, screaming the children's names. She came back down with both of the lively little ones in her arms, both of them looking more shocked by their Grandma than anything. She called her son up from the basement and, loading the tots into his arms, began ranting and raving about having had enough of this nonsense and how she was going to call St. E's, as in Saint Elizabeths Hospital for crazy people, the nut house.

"I'm sorry for scaring you like that, I just..."

"It's not your fault, Ray-Ray. That girl needs some help. She got mental problems and this foolishness is going to stop right now! I told her 'bout getting all mixed up in that religion mess. I'm not goin' have her putting my grandbabies at risk like this..."

I didn't understand mental illness or what triggered crazy moments. I had almost snapped like my neighbor the month when I tried to read and digest the whole Quran. I felt like one more piece of information or one more burst of inspiration at that moment would have tipped me over the edge. I wondered if my neighbor had snapped due to an overdose of religion. I'd seen people snap and do crazy stuff in the name of religion before.

I was glad the babies had not been sacrificed due to their mother's delusions. That's when I realized it was entirely possible to get too much of a good thing, too fast and in that way religion could be as poisonous as anything else. For some reason, that incident crossed my mind while I was bathing the twins.

God, please protect them from the madness going on in this house, I prayed in my mind.

I allowed the twins to play with their boats and animals in the bubble bath for a while, then toweled each one off and took them to the room they shared with Atif to put on their pajamas.

"Ray-Ray, we didn't have dessert," Halim piped.

"Oh yeah, Ma said we could have our dessert when we got home," his twin added.

"Ya'll gotta get into your jammies. I think it's too late for dessert," I told them. "If you eat this late, you might get nightmares."

"Get what?"

"Nightmares. You know, when you see monsters and ugly things in your dreams at night."

"We don't believe in no monsters, Ray-Ray," Hakim said.

"Monsters are like Santa Claus. There ain't no such thing," added Halim.

"Well, just in case," I told them. "If Ma says yes, you can have a little bit."

I hadn't told anyone, and wouldn't for years to come, but once when I was standing next to Dad making salat, just he and I together, I looked up and there was a monstrous shadow in Dad's place. It was as if I were standing next to what the Quran described as a jiin, a devil, an evil spirit. I'd never known Dad to be anything but a mild-mannered man. I resented his addiction and what it was doing to our family, and maybe that's what I was seeing standing next to me—not him, but his horrible addiction. The spirit of what he had become or was becoming stood where my father had been. It frightened me stiff and I'd rushed up to the bathroom without embracing him after the prayer. After that, I'd prayed privately in my heart and in my head, in the privacy of my bedroom, that God please protect our family from any satanic forces, regardless of who might bring it into the house.

I bounced down the stairs with one of the twins in my arms and one swinging from my back, taking them for some dessert I'd promised. When I set them down, they pulled stools up to the counter and climbed up as I put red Jell-O in small blue plastic bowls for them. While they slurped and played with the Jell-O, I began washing the dinner dishes. The phone rang and I snatched it up.

"Tates' residence," I said, answering the way we always did.

"As-Salaam-Alaikum," GrandWillie said, sounding serious.

"Wa-Laikum-Salaam."

"Where's your ma?"

Whenever GrandWillie sounded that sharp, things had to be serious.

"She just went upstairs. Uncle Hussein doing any better?" I ventured.

"Naw."

"Uh, is he doing worse?"

"Yes."

"Oh. I'ma come spend some time with him tomorrow. I got classes in the morning, but I can take off early from work."

"You do what you have to do, Sonsyrea. I'm taking care of your uncle. You just concentrate on your schooling."

"I know. But I'ma come see him."

"Get your mother on the phone."

"Okay. Hold on...Maaaaaaaaaaa!" I called upstairs. "GrandWillie!"

I pretended to hang up the phone, but kept the receiver to my ear with my hand over the mouthpiece.

"Hang up the phone, Ray-Ray."

Ma didn't miss a beat. I hung up the phone but crept to the top of the steps to listen by her bedroom door.

"If he doesn't stay this time, he'll be incarcerated," I heard Ma say. "Yes, I know all that. But Yusef has got to start taking some responsibility for his actions. I've got a family to raise now, and I've done all I can do...Um-hmm. I'll see...Yes, but how long is he going to use that as an excuse...He can't keep saying one thing and doing another...He's putting us all in jeopardy here. There are children in this household. Yusef can't keep hiding behind all these excuses... I think I've been quite tolerant..."

Dad left the rehab center before completing his treatment. Ma refused to go pick him up, but he found a way home. I was afraid he would end up in jail since he still had drug charges pending. If he completed his treatment, he could go to court and claim that he had been selling drugs to feed his habit. I learned this from overhearing bits and pieces of grown-folks' conversations. Dad's lawyer would have a harder time using that defense since Dad didn't finish the treatment program.

Chapter Twenty-One
Hold on a Minute

D ad couldn't go to jail at the same time his brother, my role model, was dying. I lay across the bed with this and a thousand similar thoughts racing through my mind one night as I heard the neighborhood girls outside carrying on. Then, down the hall from my room, I heard what sounded like small rocks pelting the windowpane in Darren's room. I went to investigate, and sure enough, there was our snaggle-toothed next-door neighbor, Ron, Darren's ace, tossing rocks up at the window. I didn't even know he'd gotten out of jail. I hollered down at him, assuming he was trying to get Darren.

"He ain't here."

"I know," Ron said in a loud whisper. "He's over my house with Kim. Meet me out here at ten o'clock. Right here by the tree box, a'ight?"

I shook my head.

"Why not?"

"I can't come out that late," I said.

"Just wait till your muva goes to sleep," he insisted.

Again, I shook my head. He backed up, stretching his arms out, head cocked to the side like this charm was supposed to make a difference. I pulled down the shade and returned to my room. These guys seemed to get a kick out of calling up to my window, as if they had their own Romeo-and-Juliet kind of fantasy in mind.

Back in my room, I turned on my radio as I curled up on my bed. I was changing channels on my way to the "Quiet Storm" station, when I heard one of Uncle Hussein's favorite Doobie Brothers' tunes.

"*Minute by minute by minute by minute, I'll be holding on...*," they crooned.

I had to go see my uncle. I didn't want to see him the way he was. I wanted to remember the way he used to be. But I had to visit him again. The last time I visited him was in the hospital a couple of weeks ago. He'd hardly been able to hold his head up long enough to drink. God, I wanted to shake that memory. Uncle Hussein used to give me piggyback rides. How could he be all shriveled up under some blankets?

After Uncle Hussein's song went off, I got up to turn to the R&B station for the evening "Quiet Storm" of love ballads, trying to be someplace else. I had a bunch of uncles and loved them all, but was especially close to the two youngest ones, Uncle Hussein and his younger brother, Uncle Wallace. They used to protect me and make the boys show me respect. They made sure I understood the importance of self-respect, too.

If one of my uncles had seen Calvin singing to me at my front window, or Ron throwing rocks to get my attention out back, they would've told them to be a man and knock on the door to ask for me. But they weren't there to keep the boys away now—and, in a way, I was glad. Now I would get to see and know what the other girls saw and knew. I'd get to live a little, maybe. But first there would be some more dying.

Uncle Wallace was numbed by his brother's sickness. I could tell by the way he dropped in a chair after carrying Uncle Hussein back down to the bed in the living room after giving him a bath. Uncle Wallace had to carry his big brother like a baby in his arms and it was probably as hurtful for him to do as it was for me to watch him do it. When I sat next to Uncle Hussein, it was as if only my body was sitting in the chair. My eyes stayed glued to the TV, but I couldn't tell you what was on it. My thoughts rode on the wind that came in through the front window, lifting the light-green sheer curtains in the air and gliding out the back window, barely ruffling the white blinds back there. I had to go see him again.

I dozed off to sleep and dreamed I saw Uncle Hussein on a train racing through the countryside. There was snow all around on the trees and grass, and I stood by the tracks waving. He looked happy, waving back from his seat on the train. I heard the take-off whistle and jumped up out of my sleep. I felt cold even though this was the middle of summer and the central air was not on. Outside my window, the fire trucks hummed loudly as they pulled back into their slots behind the raised doors. Maybe that's all my dream was about, me waking up feeling cold and seeing the fire trucks. They're sort of like trains, right? They're both loud and fast.

Since I was up, I decided to get everybody else up for prayer. It had been hard to get everybody up and together for prayer since Dad went away to drug rehab. I wasn't sure why I was so willing to go through these motions except that it was a habit now and when all else fails, that's what you fall back on—some kind of habit. Darren hadn't come home, Sakinah had her door locked, so it was just me, Atif, Furard, and Ma. Furard had to lead since he was the oldest male there. Ma and I prostrated behind him, following his lead.

I had instinctively risen to pray, and wanted my siblings to pray, too. At the end of salat, during duwah, the time for us each to make our private prayers in our own words, I wasn't sure what to pray. Pray for Dad to come home? Was that the best thing? Pray for Uncle Hussein to live? He was in a lot of pain the last time I saw him, and all our prayers together hadn't made him better. Pray for him to die? Unthinkable. I sat there on my knees with my hands cupped in front of me next to Ma, just wondering what to pray for. Pray that God's will be done? I didn't like the idea of leaving everything up to fate. If we had no control of things, why pray at all? I got up and folded the prayer rug. I went back upstairs to my bedroom, feeling no better than before I prayed.

Later that day, I arrived at GrandWillie's house just in time to make the evening prayer with her. We made salat upstairs in her small bedroom rather than down in the living room where the family used to pray together. Uncle Hussein's hospital bed and medical equipment took up the living room now. After salat I sat next to Uncle Hussein, who was withering away like a grape off the vine. If our prayers were some connection to God, it seemed like God had cut us off without justification. Beneath white sheets and a light blue blanket, Uncle Hussein shook violently. The multiple sclerosis had attacked his nervous system and he shook all the time. His health had declined rapidly since he agreed to medical experimentation at a national medical health center, apparently deciding he'd contributed to medicine one way or another. When we were growing up, he talked about becoming a doctor, but shortly after finishing under-graduate college, he was diagnosed with this hereditary disease. We'd celebrated his twenty-third birthday in the hospital just a few months ago, and now he clearly was dying. He suffered to breathe through the tubes in his nostrils and his body had melted down to thin, frail, twisted limbs beyond his control. He struggled to communicate. He could hardly talk, but would point to his cup or the TV or for me to put my hand in his. I felt so awkward, so weak. This sadness, this depression, this anger and confusion moved me way beyond tears. I couldn't even cry.

We sat in the dark once the sun went down. Only the flicker of the TV light illuminated the room. GrandWillie had retreated to her room for a brief nap since she would be up through the night tending to Uncle Hussein when he hollered out in pain. Even my favorite TV show, *Fame*, did nothing for me this evening. I watched the screen as I sat there filling up with anger for another hour or so. Then, once Uncle Hussein dozed off to sleep, I moved quietly up the stairs to tell GrandWillie I was leaving.

"It's dark out, Ray-Ray. Is Furard or Darren going to meet you halfway?"

"I'll be okay," I told her.

My safety was the least of my worries at this moment. The idea of dying somehow set me free. It wasn't a happy kind of freedom yet, and wouldn't be for a few more years. But here was an introduction to freedom. I could die at any time and for any reason, so what was the point in trying to follow all the rules for living? But what is death? As a young girl in the Nation of Islam I was taught that there was no life after death, that once you died your life was over. Then, as a teen studying orthodox Islam, I learned the concept of eternal life after death, and that was the idea I needed at this moment, so that's what I clung to. Then I thought further and realized that just maybe there was no such a thing as death, that I would live forever—period. Another book Uncle Hussein introduced me to, a collection of poems by Khalil Gibran, had suggested as much.

Death didn't terrify me, but watching Uncle Hussein suffer infuriated me. It wasn't fair. I tried to think this thing through. Uncle Hussein was the respectful one, the responsible one, the promising one. He was off to the races, and wham! It was as if he'd been hit by a moving train, as if he'd been tied to the track or something and couldn't get off when he saw the train coming. He'd done so much with his life to inspire others and seemed destined to do so much more, then, wham! He'd stayed on the honor roll all through school and graduated from high school at fourteen as valedictorian. He'd enrolled in the city college that I was now enrolled in, then transferred to the prestigious George Washington University on scholarship and graduated from there as salutatorian. All this had inspired me to excel. Beyond that, he worked part-time jobs and internships and bought me things. Then, wham! Goddamn, this was so unfair! No amount of philosophy, no amount of Islam, no prescription of prayers could change that. I cursed up at God, I really did. In my heart and in my mind I told Him that if this was the best He could do for His most righteous people then I was going to the other side. As I walked home that night, I thought if someone tried to attack me, mistaking me for the four-foot-eleven little woman they saw, they'd be in for a shock. I felt like I could kill anybody at that moment. I had enough anger in me to do it.

At home, Ma was in the kitchen washing dishes and I thought that was nice for a change.

"GrandWillie said she told you to call down here for one of your brothers," Ma said as I walked in.

"I can take care of myself," I said.

Didn't she realize my role model was dying?

"That's not the point, Miss Independent," she said. "We have certain precautions for our…"

"Whatever."

I pushed past her.

"Sonsyrea, you…"

Whenever she used my whole name, she was serious, but tonight, I didn't care.

"I made my salats, yeah, yeah…," I said, going up the stairs.

"You better watch your attitude."

I slammed the door behind me, turned on the radio, and dropped my book bag to the floor. I sat on the edge of my bed looking out the window, resting my chin on the windowsill. A tear fell. Then another, and another. There were too many questions now. Why Uncle Hussein? Why now? What's the use in trying? Let's see, we prayed, we fasted, we gave charity even though we needed charity ourselves. I went down the list of the five pillars of faith in Islam. We'd done everything but the last. None of us had made the pilgrimage to Mecca. But, hell, who could afford it? The five prayers a day, I'd been taught, was like some sort of spiritual bath that washed away all your sins every few hours. It was beginning to seem like silly nonsense to me. There was no science to it. An average of five prayers a day for the better part of twenty-three years equaled what? Multiply that times the number of family members praying for the better part of three generations and what do you get?

In school I'd taken a logic course, and now I was thinking certain actions must lead to certain consequences. Crime equals punishment and sex without birth control equals five babies you can't afford. And a lack of education or formal training or at the very least an enthusiasm for work equals no job or a low-paying one. Life could be better if we got back to good ole common sense. Strip away all the religious nonsense. One plus one equals what? That was becoming more real to me than a lot of the religious ideas I'd learned growing up.

Of course, Ma said I was looking at it all wrong. GrandWillie said the same.

"Allah says we'll all be tested," Ma tried to explain once.

"Ain't no prize," I sneered back.

"For all you know this may have been Hussein's last test before going on to paradise. We don't know what his test was with that illness, but for all we know, if he passes, when he dies, inshallah, he'll go on to paradise."

I heard her but I didn't hear. The words would stick enough for me to remember them years later, but for the moment they had no impact, didn't make me feel any better. GrandWillie's wisdom didn't help either.

"Look at the bright side," she'd told me. "Look at all he was able to accomplish before he got sick."

I thought of all the more he could do, all the more he deserved to do. Not that I thought I could play God and decide who deserved to live or die. But, for as long as I'd bought into the ideas of doing good to be in God's grace and shunning evil to avoid His wrath, I'd believed that good deeds should amount to something, yes, a long, healthy, and prosperous life. Things were not adding up. I was outraged, no, enraged. I had questions, so many questions about everything I'd ever been taught. I cried a lot in my room, but held cucumbers to my eyes before going to sleep so I wouldn't wake up with puffy eyes. I cried and asked God for answers. Then Uncle Hussein died and a good part of me died with him.

At his funeral I was there but not there. His body was wrapped in a sheet and put in a closed casket as per Muslim custom. No viewing of the body, and that was just as well because I didn't need to see him this way.

For the next few weeks, my body walked to the bus stop and sat on the subway and sat up in class. At home, I stayed in my room even more, fought with Ma even more, prayed even less. Then Dad learned there was a warrant out for his arrest because he had violated his probation by leaving the drug rehab without completing the treatment program. Dad turned himself in.

Another night Ron tossed rocks up to the back window to get my attention. This time I agreed to meet him later that night after everybody else had gone to bed.

I was glad to escape the madness by going to school and work six days a week. I worked at the campus radio station as a newscaster and talk show host for a few semesters, and the older guys there adopted me as their little sister. Gary and Dawud, another young man who had adopted the same name Ron adopted, especially saw themselves as my protectors and my wise old men. We'd sit around in the station's lounge and talk politics and bullshit for hours in the evenings. A guy named Kevin, who was more serious about developing his talent and less excited about all the ladies across campus hearing his name on the air, liked me romantically, even gave me the most expensive birthday present I'd gotten from a guy—a fifty-dollar gift-certificate to Hats in the Belfry, a hat shop in an expensive part of the city. Kevin was shy and quiet like me, and I didn't know until years later that what we also had in common was a lot of responsibilities at home caring for siblings and parents. Kevin was different from the other guys, too, because he didn't party with their fraternities and didn't sit around bragging about which girls he made come when and where.

Kevin escorted me home one night when I left the radio station late. We laughed and talked while riding an old bus into my neighborhood, enjoying each other's company so much that neither of us even bothered to comment on the drastic differences between the part of the city where our campus was located and the part where I lived.

Campus was located on Wisconsin Avenue, where the streets were lined with beautiful trees, the sidewalks and courtyards were very clean, and the university buildings were made of whitish-gray cement, adding to the pristine look. Being there was proof positive that there was a different world from the one I returned to daily. When Kevin and I got off the bus at Thirteenth and H streets Northeast, we had to ease past dirty, drunken men and women. Trash littered the streets and stood out even in the dark. There were trees here, too, but the dilapidated storefronts—burned out during race riots after the assassination of Dr. Martin Luther King, Jr. twenty years earlier—made the neighborhood look grungy. People looked helpless and beat down along H Street.

Kevin got off the bus to walk me all the way to my front door and I was glad until a guy bumped into us—on purpose.

"Man, give me your wallet," he said.

"Hey, man. I'm just trying to walk the young lady home. I…"

He pushed Kevin against a wall and took his wallet. We didn't see a gun, but assumed he had one. I felt bad for bringing Kevin to my neighborhood.

"That's so messed up," I said.

"I'm not gon' worry about it. At least nobody got hurt."

I cried that night and wasn't sure why. Nobody had gotten hurt physically, but I felt sad. We had been violated. I didn't want to think of Kevin as a punk, but he'd failed to protect me, and I'd put him in harm's way. The men in the Nation of Islam protected us, at least that's how it seemed when I was a little girl. My dad and uncles protected us—at first. Now, Dad was gone.

Chapter Twenty-Two
Our Own Space

My girlfriend Chee-Chee called over the weekend and asked if she could move in with me because she and her mother had a falling-out. Sure, I told her. She'd have to pay half of everything, and we would have to work out some kind of arrangements to have privacy with our boyfriends, but sure, she could move in. Chee-Chee and I had been buddies since high school. Laughing at her sliding down a mud-slick hill on our way to school one morning bonded us as much as the time she took my place in a fight. Chee-Chee was only two years older than me, but somehow she took on the responsibility of protecting me and trying to teach me to stand up for myself and fight back. She thought I allowed too many things to get me down, not just people, but also circumstances.

"Girl, quit your whining!" she'd say. "I can't stand people to be whining all the time like the whole world's out to get 'em. Do something about it or shut up!"

"Maybe I just need to talk. That's what friends are *supposed* to be for," I'd say. I hated her response.

"Don't be calling me up for no damn pity party!" she'd say with finality. "I'm sorry. You ain't bringing me down with you!"

At that point, I usually slammed the phone in her ear and knew I wouldn't hear from her for a week or so. When she called needing a place to stay, it would've been the perfect time to get back at her, if I was petty. Would've been the perfect time to emphasize that yes, friends do need each other to get through rough spots. But she would've told me to go to hell, that she didn't need my place to stay if she had to hear my mouth. Her independent spirit and powerful attitude sliced me up or down depending on the circumstances. Sure, I wanted her brand of confidence and her courage, but I only wanted it walking next to me. I didn't necessarily want to earn those badges the way she'd earned them. I didn't want to actually fight to know I could win or flex my muscles to know they existed. Fighting and flexing, according to my religious training were so, so…unlady-like. But Chee-Chee was unbound by such conditioning. She simply was who she was, and simply did what had to be done.

I'd told her to ask her boyfriend to help her move, because although I was an emerging feminist, there still were things I thought should be left to the men—like moving heavy boxes. But Chee-Chee, whose mother had raised her and four other girls single-handedly, wouldn't concede to needing any man for anything—well, except that one thing.

We'd planned to start moving early Saturday morning and she was all packed when I arrived. We loaded her belongings, stuffed in large trash bags and whatever boxes she could find, into my small red Hyundai and made four trips moving her things into my apartment.

"Don't drop it, Ray-Ray!" she shouted as we hauled a large box up two flights of stairs. "You act like it's heavy or something!"

"Stop trying to go so fast!" I shouted back. "You think you're Superman!"

We fussed and laughed all day moving her things.

"Here, girl. See if you can handle this little bag," she said sarcastically.

"I don't know, that might break a nail, too," I shot back.

"Ya'll prissy girls a trip. And you, Miss Wanna Be Prissy."

Chee-Chee was five feet four, with rich mahogany skin and double-D cups that had been a source of embarrassment ever since she was in junior high. While my sensitivities had caused me to withdraw from other children, hers had prompted the opposite reaction. She'd become extroverted, screaming and cursing folks out. Our friendship turned out to be a perfect match. We could find a balance between us even if we didn't understand that's what was happening.

We finished unpacking her most important things and storing the rest out on the closed-in back porch, then looked around to see how we could improve on the place. The curtains and rods I'd bought weeks ago still lay under the window waiting for one of my brothers to come and help me put them up. But Chee-Chee wanted them up and out of her way.

"Furard's coming by to put them up," I told her. "He said he'd get over here as soon as he can. You know he's always busy."

"Girl, give me the hammer," she said.

"I don't have a hammer," I told her. Sometimes she got on my nerves with that superman complex of hers.

"Well, give me one of them shoes you got with them clunky ole heels."

"What shoes?"

"Them brown flicked-looking ones you wear to try to make yourself taller."

I had to laugh with her. Bantering was what we did best. I went to my closet and retrieved said shoe.

"You better not break my heel," I told her. I wanted to see her put those rods up with my shoe. The woman was genius all right. I had to give it to her. *Bang! Bang! Bang!* "Hand me another nail," she ordered.

"You go, girl!" I said.

"That's the difference between me and you," she said. "You'll wait around for somebody to do something for you."

"Not!" I defended myself. I was very independent. I just wasn't wrenching my back moving heavy stuff if I didn't have to.

Who did she think she was talking to anyway? I worked for *every-thing* I got. Nobody gave me *anything*. When she was chilling at home under her mother's roof, cursing supervisors out because she knew she didn't really need the job, I was working to pay my rent because I knew I couldn't live at home for free. Ma had even charged me eighty dollars a month out of my summer job checks when I was still in high school. Me wait around for somebody to give me something? What a joke. I put the rest of the nails on the window ledge so she could reach them, then went into the kitchen to put something on for dinner.

"I got leftover Hamburger Helper," I yelled. "Or leftover chicken and rice."

It had been hard getting used to cooking for two rather than eight, and cooking for one since my husband was out of the picture meant I'd have even more left over.

"What else you got to go with it?" she yelled back.

"To go with what? The meat or the chicken?" I asked.

"Either or. You got any bread?"

"Nope."

"Something to drink?"

"Nope."

"Well. Damn. girl, how you gon' fix somebody some dinner?" she said. "Run me back down to my mother's house."

Bang. Bang. Bang. And the curtains were up. The clock on the living room wall showed it was after eight, but the summer sun was just beginning to set. Chee-Chee called her mother's house, then, satisfied that no one answered, hurried back into her shoes.

"Come on, Ray-Ray. Hurry up," she insisted.

We were back at her mother's in no time. I wondered why her mother hadn't made her surrender her key earlier. I stood by the door, thinking she would just go in and grab a couple of sodas and wrap up a few slices of bread.

"How you gon' just take your mother's soap powder?" I asked as she began going through her mom's kitchen like it was a free grocery store. All she knew was that she needed what she needed. "Her food, Chee-Chee! How you gon' take her food. You can't take the whole loaf of bread!"

"Girl, shut up," she said.

"A whole pack of hot dogs!"

I wasn't raised like that.

"Would you shut up! I know what I'm doing! She don't need all this stuff. My mother buys stuff to be buying it."

We left with two grocery bags full.

"Let's stop at the liquor store," she said.

In our neighborhood there was one every half-mile or so.

"I'm broke," I told her.

"I got you. What kind you want?"

"Black cherry."

She came back with two wine coolers for herself and two for me. That would be enough for us. We weren't really party girls—not yet anyway. We were just stepping out on our own. We'd have to crawl before we could trot.

"Heeeeey!" I yelled to a car full of guys next to us at a stoplight.

"Hey. Where ya'll heading?" the one in the passenger's seat up front responded. There were three of them, but we only needed two.

"Wherever ya'll tryin' to go!" I shot back. They all smiled.

"Okay, pull over," the driver said.

"No. We'll follow you wherever *you* tryin' to take us," I said. I was getting good at this flirting thing. You can say I was a quick study. I knew how to smile just so, not too wide. Only a crack of a smile. Knew how to work my eyes to say what the rest of me would never cash in on.

"Cool! Follow us!" the passenger said, too excited for his own good. *Men are so stupid*, I thought.

"We could be ax murderers or something!" I told Chee-Chee, laughing.

"Girl, you are *crazy*."

"Watch this!" I said, pulling up bumper to bumper behind them at the next light.

"Girl, you better watch yourself. *They* could be murderers!" she said. In some ways she was out the box, and in other ways, I was.

At the next corner, I made a right turn from the far left lane, speeding in the opposite direction from the car full of guys.

"You know what, Ray-Ray? That was simple!" Chee-Chee said. "That was some simple stuff. Don't be doing that simple stuff when you got me in your car."

"Girl, calm down. I'm just having a little fun," I told her.

I'd missed this sort of craziness when I was in my teens. I figured better to be zany in my early twenties than not at all.

Chapter Twenty-Three
Girls Night Out

Chee-Chee and I took a Greyhound bus to Norfolk to visit one of my two best friends who grew up Muslim with me. Shawn was enrolled at Norfolk State University, and had a dorm room on campus. She'd told me about the drinking binges she went on with her friends, and I couldn't wait to get to Norfolk to party wild with her. She had gotten a late start on partying, too, having grown up under the strict confines of our Muslim families. Seemed like we went straight from the bus station to the club, but we did stop at the dorm to change from our jeans to clubbing gear.

We could hear the music from the parking lot when we arrived at The Big Apple nightclub in Norfolk. As we walked in, I got a tingle from something pulsing in the air. I suddenly felt overdressed in the light-peach cotton-knit straight dress that hung two inches below my knees. The cream-colored stockings and brown pumps suddenly felt too churchified or something. Luckily, my girl Shawn was wearing the exact same outfit, except her dress was off-white. You couldn't tell Chee-Chee she wasn't working it in her oversized black-and-white striped sweater and white jeans. She was leading our little train with a bounce in her step.

Flashing red and yellow lights spun overhead, cutting through the smoky, dark room jam-packed with hyper college-age girls and guys flirting, dancing, drinking, talking, and exchanging phone numbers written on corners torn from napkins, the back of their drinks receipt, or any little piece of paper they could find. My girls and I eased our way into the scene as smooth as butter soaking into warm toast.

"'Scuse me…'scuse us…'scuse me," I mumbled as we pushed our way into the crowd like a three-woman train, one hand clutching the shoulder in front. "'Scuse me…."

I felt a large, sweaty palm on top of mine and turned to see a light-skinned, freckle-faced boy, half-smiling, motioning with his head for me to go with him. I shook my head and stayed moving with my girls, pushing our way straight to the bar, which of course was crowded. We tried peering over shoulders or through cracks, raising our hands for the bartender to notice, then I finally squeezed into a small opening and my girls eased in beside me.

"Whoah, Shorty! Chill out!" grumbled the guy whose feet I stepped on.

"Sorry," I said, without slowing down. I got the bartender's attention, finally. "Is it still Happy Hour?!" I yelled.

She nodded.

"Two rum and Cokes!" I said.

"House?!" she asked.

"What that mean?" I asked Shawn.

"Bacardi brand or no-name," Shawn explained.

"Green!" Chee-Chee laughed, pushing my shoulder. "Miss Muffet."

I figured "house" must be cheaper, so that's what I ordered. The bartender couldn'tve been much older than me. Probably in school, I figured. What a cool job! And she was handling her business! Looked tough enough to hit a guy if he tried to skip on a bill. Her hair was cut down to a natural nothing, close like a dude's, and she wore three sets of tiny gold hoops in her ears. Shawn and Chee-Chee ordered strawberry daiquiris. I eased the short glass up to my lips, trying to look cooler than them, and gulped down half a drink in two swallows. I felt like I was looking cool, sort of. I was bopping my head on the up beat, looking around, keeping my eyes open for the next guy who might ask me to dance. Then my song cued up and I lost my cool.

So what if the lyrics were misogynistic; a song about a guy just wanting to "do" a girl, then kick her out. Ma used to forbid us to listen to those kinds of songs in the house, always scolding us about "that junk we were filling our heads with." She said the things you "programmed your mind for" would make you behave a certain way. Ma was so wrong. People listened to music for the beats, just to feel something down in their bones. Like right now, I didn't care about the words to this song. The beat was strong, and that was all that mattered. I actually liked the words, too, but only because they rhymed so well and were rapped so forcefully.

"Heeeey!" I shouted, clapping my hands high above my head, moving toward the dance floor. I stopped at the edge, thinking I had to wait for a partner to go on, still grooving with myself. I noticed some girls pulling a guy they'd picked onto the dance floor, but that wasn't the way it was supposed to be. So I waited, moving my hips around sexily, my hands in half fists rhythmically moving at my sides. Bopping my head and smoothly looking around and behind me, trying to catch some guy, any guy's, eye.

When I say leave I wanna hear her say left. And if I say was it good? She better say best!

A guy I hadn't even noticed came up to me from the side and slipped his forefinger into my half-folded palm, taking my hand, leading me onto the dance floor. I followed his broad shoulders, clad in a soft-green sports coat, grooving out into the center of the crowd. He moved fluidly, and even from the back he looked distinguished in this crowd because he was wearing a nice sports coat and slacks, not khakis or jeans like the college guys or whole suits like the young professionals there to impress the college girls. From the back

I could see he had that fine, silky black hair like a foreigner. When he finally danced around facing me, my heart jumped. Had to be from Pakistan or somewhere. Rich copper skin, thick, jet-black eyebrows and mustache. Gold-frame glasses. Not too tall for me either, though usually I preferred to look way up at a guy. He was only seven or so inches taller than me. I danced away from him to get my rhythm back, and he reached for my hand. I threw my hands over my head, waving them wildly.

This far from home, in the middle of a thick crowd in a dark night-club, I didn't have to be who I was supposed to be. I could be myself—even if I was still finding out who that was. I looked this brother dead in the eye—which I wasn't supposed to do. As a Muslim girl, I'd been taught it was a sin to look a man in the eye. We were always supposed to lower our gaze. But I could do so much with my eyes, and, come to think of it, the men who wrote our Holy books probably knew this much and that's why they tried to suppress such a subtle little act. I locked pupils with my dance partner just long enough for him to know I was paying attention, then turned my back to him so he could know he could lose my attention.

"Heeey!" I shouted again.

This was *my* dance really, and I needed a partner only because that looked better. Dancing a circle around my partner, I slid my hand playfully around his neck, tracing the tips of my fingers in his sweat. Brother was fine, but I kept a straight face.

He reached for my waist and I turned my back so I could move in closer. I pushed my behind into his pelvis and, next thing I knew, we were doing the Rock, an old dance I hadn't done since junior high when I had to sneak to go to the day-time dances at my school. I liked rocking in this man's groin, side to side, moving as one. My drink—or the music or the lights or the electricity in the air—had me feeling less tense now and I was loving it. I looked up and saw Shawn dancing her basic two-step with some guy, careful not to smile too much. Shawn had deep dimples she knew guys loved, but didn't offer them up to every guy. I motioned my hand to my mouth as if I had a drink in it, asking her about my drinks I'd left at the bar. She mouthed that Chee-Chee was watching them. I turned back facing my dance partner and slipped a new move on him when Salt-N-Pepa's "Shake Your Thang" cued up.

It's my THANG and I'll shake it the way that I feel. With a little seduction and sex appeal.

We ladies were waving our hands in the air and squealing. Must've been some sorors in the house. The flashing lights grooved me. And, no she didn't have on fishnet black pantyhose with that teeny red skirt! Shawn and I both caught this scene and laughed. Red pumps! That stuff went out with Prince's Purple Revolution back in the early eighties!

My partner was smiling. He definitely was no college student. I sensed some maturity here. Young men my age didn't smile, it was too uncool, un-everything. I smiled back slightly, keeping my cool in check. And my feet were starting to hurt in those heels.

When the lights dimmed and the music mellowed, my partner pulled me in for a slow dance, but I took his hand and pulled him off the dance floor, noticing a crowd forming at the bar again. Ray, Goodman & Brown's "You Must Be a Special Lady" was playing, and my partner wanted to dance. I shook my head gently. When we got back to the bar, Chee-Chee was still keeping an eye on the drinks, still sipping from her same first daiquiri. I gulped down the rest of my first drink and snatched up the other one. Chee-Chee turned up her nose at my dance partner.

"Can I buy you a drink?" he asked me, trying to stay close as others pushed past, coming and going.

"I already got two," I told him. Never mind that the ice had melted in them. Chee-Chee nudged me.

"What?!" I snapped at her.

"Girl, let that man buy you a drink," she said sternly in my ear, the music still blasting overhead. I shook my head.

Must be a special lady, and a very exciting girl. Must be a special lady, 'Cause you got me sittin' on top of the world.

I sipped my warm drink and found space to lean back on the bar to take in the sights. Shawn was nestled in her partner's arms on the dance floor, but she still looked stiff. Her light-brown hair had been nicely coiffed when we arrived, but now it was falling. It looked better falling actually, looked more natural. The fly women in the house wore the shiny, hard, stiff 'dos gelled and waved back from their foreheads and coiffed up high in spiral curls or loopy ones. Some of the 'dos were dyed platinum, red or purple "plum." The more sophisticated ladies wore short, tapered cuts.

Shawn and I still sported our homemade 'dos, which made us look more like some old presidents' wives than anything else. Coolness just doesn't come overnight. Our Muslim-girl modesty had yet to wear off, but we were working on it. Girls in the club wore low-cut, cleavage-celebrating, form-fitting dresses or painted-on designer jeans with high heels, and gaudy-gold door-knocker earrings dangling all over the place. Guys sported khakis or designer jeans and shiny silk or oxford cotton shirts opened down their chests to show off layers of gold chains. In a corner near the entrance, groups of guys or girls, and a few couples posed for photos against a painted backdrop featuring a sparkling black luxury Mercedes-Benz.

"You look nice," my dance partner said into my ear.

"Thank you."

I wondered if I looked as out of place as Shawn. Even if I hadn't known her, I would've spotted her in the crowd. Looked like she was straight out of somebody's Catholic school or something. There's a certain look of innocence not easily washed away with a few drinks.

Her dress was too plain, too shapeless. She looked so, I don't know, pure-bred or something. I was sure I didn't look *that* innocent. At least I hoped not.

My girls and I danced and took pictures and laughed all night. We'd stopped buying drinks after Happy Hour and didn't accept any others. As the night went on, I thought little of the fact that I danced with the same partner all night. I liked him. He seemed steady and easy-going, self-assured, and smooth, but not in the slick player kind of way. His name was Gary. He was thirty-eight, divorced, had no kids, and was in the Navy. I'd given him about as much information about myself, except I left out the part about being married. It was a stupid marriage anyway, a stupid thing I'd done. I'd stopped going to visit my so-called husband in jail, telling him I was too busy or too tired, and as soon as I mustered up the courage, I would stop accepting his collect calls, too. I'd already decided I was getting divorced, so no need to tell Gary I was technically married. I told him I was twenty-two, about to graduate from college, and worked at a newspaper in Washington but was in town for the weekend visiting my girlfriend who went to Norfolk State.

We partied till the white lights came on and the music stopped. As we all pushed our way out the door with the crowd, Gary asked me in my ear if I wanted to go for something to eat. I shook my head and turned to tell him I wanted to stay with my girls.

"They can come, too," he said. "I have a two-seater, but they can meet us there."

I reached behind me for his hand, while tapping Chee-Chee in front of me.

"Gary wants to take us out to breakfast," I told her.

She flexed her shoulder, trying to throw my hand off. She wasn't thrilled about my new friend, I could tell. I tapped her again.

"Did you hear me?"

"Ray-Ray, we don't know this man," she said.

Not entirely true. By now, I'd also learned that he'd been divorced two whole years, left the house to his wife, was living on base until he found himself an apartment, and he liked my bright eyes and pretty smile.

We made our way out into the open parking lot where others were milling about, apparently making plans to extend the night, too.

"No offense, but can I see some ID?" Shawn demanded. "A driver's license, your military card...?"

I sighed, a little irritated.

"He said you can follow us," I explained.

"You're riding with him!" she snapped. "Ray-Ray, you don't know that man!"

They were trippin'. I'd survived Ron. I could survive anything. But I didn't feel at all threatened by this guy. In fact, I felt safer with him, as if he were my own oasis even if only for a night.

"We should stay together," Shawn insisted.

"I'll tell you ladies what," Gary cut in calmly. "There's a pancake house right out Military Road..."

"We know where it is," Shawn said.

"Why don't I meet you there," he concluded. "You don't mind if I walk you to your car, do you?"

I took his arm and he and I walked behind my friends. I stumbled over a rock or crack in the pavement and almost fell into Chee-Chee. I wasn't drunk, though. That's for sure. My two drinks had long since worn off. I was still feeling good and silly though. Must've been the music or this man I'd met. I wanted to kiss this man so bad. That's why I wanted to ride with him and meet my girlfriends there.

"You okay?" he asked, breaking my fall. I nodded and giggled. He held my hand all the way till he sank me in the backseat of Shawn's two-door Toyota. "See you in a bit," he said, closing the door after Chee-Chee got in the front.

"Ray-Ray, you musta lost the little bit of sense you had!" Chee-Chee screeched.

"Quit lunchin'!" I shot back.

"You lunchin'! How you gon' leave the club with some guy you just met! Stupid! Old man, too. Man look old enough to be your father!"

"No, he doesn't!" I argued, not at all angry. "Brother was fine!"

"He did look kinda old, Ray," Shawn said.

I lay across the backseat.

"Wake me up when we get there," I said.

"Wake your drunk behind up!" Chee-Chee shouted.

She turned up the radio to blasting Madonna's "Lucky Star" kicked in my ear.

Star light, star bright. First star I see tonight.

"You listen to that white music?" Chee-Chee shouted to Shawn.

White music, I thought to myself. *What is* white *music?* I'd had so much nonsense about "black this" and "white that" pumped in my head back in the Nation of Islam, I'd started tuning into white music on the radio as soon as my uncle, who'd also been raised in the Nation of Islam, showed me where it was. Something about dwelling on the differences made us want to find common ground, and you could find such a place inside a song. Music was music to me. It made you happy or made you sad.

"Girl, my car got a mind of its own," Shawn told Chee-Chee. "Hit a bump and I get a whole different station."

They laughed. No way was I going to rest for a few minutes, as much as I needed to.

"Could you turn that mess down!" I shouted to Chee-Chee.

Shawn and I never cursed or yelled at each other because growing up in our Muslim community, we always greeted each other with the Arabic words "Peace to you," and with that kind of intro, how can you jump and curse somebody out? I meant no harm to Chee-Chee, and I was sure she meant none to me, even without either of us stating this. It was just the way we talked to each other, ever since we first met and instantly started hanging out together when I was thirteen and she fifteen, right when we were both just learning to curse right and practicing on each other. We teased each other all the time. Sometimes I took the first jab, sometimes she did.

"You need to wake your drunk ass up!" she snapped back.

She started dancing and rocking so the back of her seat hit my knees.

"Won't ya'll cool out!" Shawn demanded. "It's too late for that mess!"

We all were kinda irritable and tired now, but had to party on.

"What time is it, lush?" Chee-Chee asked in a quieter tone since Shawn turned the radio off. My watch said 3:55, which meant it was 3:45. I kept it ten minutes fast trying to trick myself into getting places on time—not that it worked.

"Time for your mother to leave that boat alone," I said, jokingly referring to the latest street drug of choice, "Love Boat," which had claimed many of the fathers and a few mothers in our neighborhood.

"Oh you know LaVern got a can of whup-ass for you." She laughed.

"Keep on talkin'," she said. "Tryna jone. Can't fight your way out a wet paper bag and you tryna jone."

Shawn pulled into the parking lot of the International House of Pancakes and we saw Gary getting out of his silver T-Bird.

"Brother-man is fine!" I said, anxious for my friends to get out the front of this two-door contraption so I could get out, too.

We were eating and laughing, having a good time in our sticky booth when Chee-Chee realized the sun was coming up and suggested we head back to Shawn's dorm room in case Shawn's mother called early in the morning, as she was known to do. Gary asked if he could keep in touch with me and I told him I had a pen out in the car. Actually, I had a few pens and business cards and a reporter's notepad in my purse, but I wanted to get him out to the car for a kiss.

"I got a pen for you right here, Boo," Chee-Chee said. Shawn nudged her. "What? You need a pen? I got a pen," Chee-Chee continued.

"I'm going out to the car for a minute," I said sternly, rolling my eyes at her.

Gary was trying not to laugh. Shawn was finishing up her pancakes and I could feel Chee-Chee's eyes boring a hole in our backs as Gary and I left the restaurant.

Oh man, could he kiss! My heart beat faster and my booty throbbed. If I could've pulled him deeper down my throat, I would've. But he pulled away. I opened Shawn's car, climbed in the backseat and motioned him to join me.

"Your buddies'll be looking for you any minute," he said politely.

I felt embarrassed. He was rejecting me? He reached for my hand to pull me out of the backseat, but I climbed out on my own. He shoved his hands in his pockets.

"Does that mean I can't call you?" he asked.

I reached in my purse and handed him a business card.

"Aren't you gonna write your home number on the back?" he said in that ever-suave voice of his.

Who did he think he was, some kinda foreign Billy Dee? I fumbled in my purse for a pen and wrote it for him.

"Gimme yours, too," I said flatly.

"You know I live on base. I don't have a phone," he said.

"You got a work number, don't you?" I insisted. My silliness was gone now. All my buzz—from the evening, from his scent, from his smoothness—had worn off now.

"Yeah. But I'm on the ship, and it's hard to reach me. I'll call you," he said. "Promise."

"That's not right, Gary. I just gave you *both* my numbers."

I couldn't believe it. I thought we'd had a great time together, now he was pulling back.

"You can write it right here," I said, giving him the back of another one of my business cards.

He scribbled his name and two numbers on the back, handed it to me, and must've noticed the sad look on my face. He grabbed my face and kissed me on the forehead.

"I had a great time," he said, pulling me into a bear hug. "You are really good company."

"Yeah. Let's keep in touch," I said sarcastically, pushing away from him.

As he predicted, my girlfriends showed up within minutes.

"Nice meeting you ladies," he said, turning to get in his car.

Chee-Chee climbed into the backseat and was waiting to pounce on me when I got in the front.

"Hot-ass!" she snapped. "Throwing yourself at some old-ass man!"

"Leave me the hell alone!" I snapped back.

"Hold-up, hold-up. I s-mell something back here!" she teased. "What was ya'll doing back here?"

"Your muva!" I quipped.

She leaned forward and tried to hit me. I turned around and threw up my dukes like a prizefighter.

"I keep telling you 'bout puttin' them little dick beaters up at people. Somebody gon' snatch 'em off for you."

I reached back and tried to slap her.

"Would ya'll quit it!" Shawn said exasperated.

I leaned my seat back and watched the streaks of red and orange break the day. How long ago had it been since Shawn and I woke up with our families about this time for our early morning prayer? How long since we'd been awakened by the sing-song of our father's or brother's voice calling us to worship Allah, the Most Gracious,

Most Merciful? Come to think of it, perhaps Allah had been merciful that night. I'd read news articles about young women leaving nightclubs with strangers, only to be found later dead and partially clad. But those articles hadn't registered with me once I was under the influence of alcohol and flashing lights and music and sex in the air and the smoothest man in the world dancing at my hips. It occurred to me that crazy doesn't always look crazy and this man could've been a killer for all I knew. My girls were right. They say God looks out for babies and fools and, clearly, I'd proven I was still a little of each.

I closed my eyes and rested my head.

"Thank you, Allah," I said in the quiet of my heart. "Thank you, thank you, thank you."

Chapter Twenty-Four
Flowers at the Office

Monday morning, back at the office, Margo called me to the receptionist's desk to pick up a package that had her giggling all over herself. A few of my co-workers smiled knowingly at me as they passed my desk. I finished typing notes from my notepad for a feature article I was working on.

"Sonsyrea, I don't think you want to leave this sitting up here too long, deary," Margo said in a singsong. She was so pleasant.

I figured a public relations person had probably hand-delivered something for a story they were pitching, but what's the big deal? I rushed up to the front desk so I could get back to my work.

"Yes, ma'am," I said, approaching Margo around the huge bouquet partly blocking her view. She was giddy with excitement, but Margo was always happy about something.

"These are for you!" she piped.

"What?" I said, waiting for her to hand me a package.

"These," she said, sliding a glass vase with a dozen long-stem yellow roses, adorned with white babies'-breath to me.

I had no idea what this was about. I tore open the card and was shocked to see the words: "Thanks for a wonderful time. Stay sweet." Signed: Gary. My whole self went limp as a cooked noodle. I could've cried I was so delighted. But I quickly composed myself.

"Thanks," I said politely, pulling my present to me.

"That's all?" Margo asked. "Who's the thoughtful gentleman?"

"Somebody I just met," I explained.

"Looks like you made quite an impression."

Back at my desk, the guys on my team, Len and Bobby and Sean, and even Kathleen, got all excited.

"Whoaaaaaaah, Sonsyrea! Must've had soooome weekend," Sean said.

Bobby made a fist and slid his arm forward and back in a gesture the guys used to indicate screwing.

"How was *your* weekend, *Miiiiiss* Tate," Len teased.

I shook my head.

"Sonsyrea, when they say practice safe sex, they don't mean practice all the time," Bobby joked.

All I could do was shake my head and try to keep from laughing.

"Do tell, do tell," Len insisted. They were like big brothers to me.

"Nothing happened," I said shyly. "I went out clubbing with my girls, and this guy took us out to breakfast. That's all."

"And what happened after you ditched your friends?" Bobby asked.

"Sonsyrea wouldn't do that," Kathleen said.

"The hell she wouldn't!" Sean said. "Nice girls need it, too. Obviously."

Our boss, John the jerk, returned from lunch and busted the whole groove.

"Sonsyrea, I need that story by three," he said nastily.

"I'm almost finished," I said meekly.

The guys grunted and went back to their terminals.

"What a dickhead," Sean mumbled.

I was sure John heard him but pretended not to.

I was so happy scooping my flowers into my arm at the end of the day I could've floated out the door with them. I fished around in my purse and found the card with Gary's number on it. Called both numbers throughout the afternoon and when someone finally answered, I left a simple message: "Thanks for the beautiful flowers."

I'd really wanted to talk to him though. It was too bad I couldn't reach Shawn because she was in class, and I couldn't reach Chee-Chee because she'd taken her preschool kids on a field trip. I couldn't wait to get home to tell them.

At home, I cleared all the old mail and other collected papers off my dining room table so my beautiful flowers could stand alone.

"Thank you, God," I said out loud.

My anger with God about all that had gone wrong despite my and my family's efforts to try to do right subsided in times like these. In times like these, I felt there really was a God, and this God really was good. I almost felt like taking out my prayer rug and making Magrib, the evening prayer I'd been trained to perform. But the prayer that was already being prayed effortlessly in my heart felt more sincere.

The phone rang.

"Hello. This is the operator calling collect for…Ronald…Bates. Will you accept the call?"

I hung up without answering and again I heard myself talking to God.

"Oh, Allah, please give me the strength to get completely all the way away from this man."

The phone rang again with the same voice and message. I hung up. An hour later, it rang again. Same thing. I only picked up because I was hoping it was Gary. I called Chee-Chee and she was surprisingly happy for me.

"For real?" she said, her defenses finally down. "That was nice of him. He didn't have to do it. That was really nice."

"I told you I know how to pick 'em," I joked.

"Naw. God protected your silly ass," she said.

I knew it was true. If God was testing me to see if I would stick to my home training, I was testing Him to see how far His grace and mercy could go. I didn't hear from Gary again, and couldn't reach him, but that didn't bother me at all. Over the next several months, I went to clubs alone and even brought home a guy once or twice. The first guy, Sam, turned out to be a proud Morehouse Man. He was tall and slender as I preferred, a pretty-boy-type, clean-shaven, and well-groomed down to his hands. I'd allowed him to buy me a few drinks, then allowed him to follow me back to my apartment, then invited him back to my bedroom. I lit some candles and turned the radio to WHUR's "Quiet Storm," but nothing worked to get me in sync with this brother's body. He was too jerky, too hyper or anxious or something. This tryst was so bad I found myself talking to God as I closed the door behind him.

"That one doesn't count," I told God.

When Sam called to come over the next evening, I was downright rude.

"You didn't satisfy me *last* night," I said.

"What you mean?"

"I mean, it ain't worth the trouble," I said.

"Forget you then," he shot back.

"You tried," I said confidently. "Sorry-ass." I slammed the phone down. If I'd had a gun, I would have blown smoke from the tip of it, satisfied to have knocked one down.

If I'd once worn an invisible halo, an image I admit I did project at one time, it was now cocked to the side, sliding off my head. I picked up men off the street, in the park, at the bank, anywhere, but so what? Like the song said: it's my thang, and I'll shake it the way that I feel.

I became so happy and full of life, as I noticed the seasons changing quickly. Spring blossomed to summer, summer faded to autumn, then winter stepped forward naked and bare. I had a boyfriend, as opposed to a series of weekend flings, by December. I'd met a country boy named Juan when he was visiting his uncle, who was Chee-Chee's mother's boyfriend. Juan was fun-loving, laughing loudly with his uncle when I first met him. He was not very tall, but slender and brown-skinned, the same complexion and tone as me. His brown kinky hair was cut in a high-top fade, too high for any city guy, but Juan was cool just because he was so relaxed and fun-loving. I'd seen him in Chee-Chee's front yard one day near the end of the summer. We'd flirted, exchanged numbers. I'd gone to visit him at his parents' house where he lived in Charlotte and for Christmas, he came to spend the weekend with me. I took him to my grandparents' house for dinner and as we were leaving my self-righteous Uncle Lloyd, asked, "So where is the young man staying?" Trying to show off in front of everybody. I hesitated to answer only because my grandparents and mother were looking.

"You know I have a sleeper couch," I said respectfully.

"Sonsyrea, you know what the Quran says about men and women being together alone," he said. "Satan'll be right there with you. You're inviting temptation is what you're doing."

My little sisters and brothers snickered. I couldn't stand him! He irritated the hell out of me with that bull. He'd been divorced twice, barely took care of his daughter from his first marriage, but he acted like he was holier-than-thou because he maintained his prayers and followed the book. The man barely kept a job, claiming he couldn't hold down a steady job because no employer would allow him time out of the day to make his salats or Fridays off to attend Juma. I thought he was just trifling. Holy and trifling. When Juan and I got back to my apartment, I blasted my Salt-N-Pepa song, "None of Your Business," and rocked Juan up against the wall.

If I wanna take a guy home with me tonight
It's none of your business

I realized my actions were hardly Islamic, barely lady-like even by

American standards. I had a new theme for my life, and Salt-N-Pepa were rapping it cleverly.

Even while dancing with Juan I realized I was getting bored with him. On Christmas day when I opened his gift and found a tawdry little teddy bear, I threw a fit and called it quits. He must've expected it, probably even planned it. Of course he got the sleeper couch that night, and the next morning I let him call a cab back to the bus station.

My sex habit was getting worse even by my girlfriends' standards. I was flexing my freedom by getting laid as often as I could. It was the sexual healing Marvin Gaye sang about, I figured. My mother would have lectured me for singing it, me being a young un-married woman, but I was grown and on my own now. I enjoyed partying with my girls now that I was out from under Ron's spell. They had hated the times when they came to pick me up to go to a club as planned only to arrive and find that Ron had called collect and fucked up my whole mood. Those times, I would tell them I had a headache or was too tired from work, but the truth was a call from Ron could drain me. There ought to be a law against men calling collect to curse women out. There ought to be a law against women being silly enough to accept those calls time after time because of some unreasonable guilt or unreasonable wish to console the un-consolable. Finally, I got out from under Ron's spell.

Shawn was home on winter break and she and I made plans to party on New Year's night. Chee-Chee planned to ring in the new year at her new church. When my date arrived to pick up Shawn and me for a New Year's Eve party, she and I were already stupid drunk and laughing about our glassy eyes in the instant photos we'd taken. This time, we both wore leather skirts. She wore a long, tight one with a long split up the back. I wore a mini black one with silky black stockings. We both had our hair teased out cool this time, and could barely keep our eyes open for the camera my neighbor from across the hall, Marla, used to snap photos of us. My date, Joe, whom I'd met through a friend at school, escorted us to and from the party, having only a couple of beers during the night while Shawn and I stayed toasted.

By the time Shawn returned home for spring break, my behavior had gotten downright scandalous, but little did she know. I was dating a Howard student who was so obnoxious I could stand him only long enough to reach my peak. He was loud, arrogant, and old-fashioned in his views of women, but he was a good screw, so when he called I went to pick him up, or screwed him in his dorm room. The few times he asked about going to dinner, I was like, "Oh, hell no. Who's sitting across a table with you for a whole hour?" Going to the movies was out, too. I always claimed I was just too busy to spend any time together. When he wasn't available, I could call on either of two other guys to come over and get the job done. I realized having sex with more than two men in any particular week would make my girlfriends cringe, so I didn't tell them everything. I wasn't hiding my habit. I just didn't feel compelled to set myself up for a lecture from one of my peers.

Although I knew Chee-Chee and Shawn were still kind of prudish because of our upbringing, they weren't damn virgins either, so I was a bit surprised by Shawn's reaction to my latest tryst.

Shawn decided to stay with me at my apartment instead of at home with her parents and siblings so we could have more fun with no curfew. She was, after all, a college junior now. I was a senior. I was working full time and carrying a full-time load at school, which is to say I was very stressed. I had term papers due this week, hadn't had sex in almost two weeks because I had been so busy at work and school. I had a lot of tension needing some release. I was surprised my friend couldn't read the stress on my face when I walked in after work.

She was there with her boyfriend, Mike, and a good-looking friend of his named Teddy. I dropped my briefcase by the door and headed straight for the kitchen to grab a wine cooler.

"Ray-Ray, this is Teddy. Teddy, Ray," she said over the music pumping from my entertainment center.

"Hi. How are you?" I said properly, realizing this brother was from uptown. His tan skin was clear, black hair wavy from plenty of brushing, and his designer jeans and tennis shoes looked fresh. And, whoa! Brother had some big feet, which sent bells off in my bones because the rumor we women laughed about, so far had proven true.

"Fine," he said, confidently, resting back in my old brown, plaid easy-chair leftover from Ron. "Wow! You *are* cute," he said insincerely, glancing over at his friend.

"Ray-Ray, you remember Mike, don't you?" Shawn asked.

How could I forget. She was in love with Mike. Had bought him a bunch of stuff for Christmas and talked about him incessantly the whole spring break. They'd broken up for about a month between then and now, but they were back together and she clearly was thrilled, hugged up under him on the couch.

I cracked a smile at Ted and headed for the kitchen.

"Ya'll excuse me a minute while I get out of these gigs," I said, needing to take off my stockings and step out of my heels.

I grabbed another wine cooler on my way back into the living room, and Shawn decided she and Mike would go to the store and get drinks for everybody. I swear, to this day I don't remember exactly what happened between the time they left and the time they got back. All I remember is Whitney Houston's "I Wanna Dance with Somebody" playing in the background when Shawn and Mike returned from the store and caught me trying to smooth my dress back down.

"Ray-Ray!" Shawn was mortified, embarrassed by her friend the slut.

Ted and I had heard the key in the door, but couldn't jump up out of the easy-chair quick enough. I was pulling down my dress and he was trying to stuff himself back in his pants when they walked in.

"What are you doing!?"

"I was just...dag...ya'll back already?"

I wanna feel the heat with somebody...with somebody who loves me.

What could I say? Sex was just sex. Stress relief. A freedom of sorts. A dance with somebody. It wasn't a big deal like our parents said. It was more like kissing frogs. I thought of the old fairy tale about the princess kissing a hundred frogs before meeting her prince. That's all I was doing—kissing a hundred frogs to get to my prince. All that stuff our mothers and grandmothers taught us about men wanting to marry a virgin, about women guarding their reputation, and saving themselves for marriage, simply meant nothing to me. Marriage was hell. Not just my own. Everybody I knew who was married was struggling to get out, struggling to keep it together, staying in it to save a house or an idyllic family image but feeling miserable. Maybe there were happily married couples, I just didn't see any. A couple of my aunts loved my uncles' dirty drawers, but I knew about my uncle's love for dope or other women, which challenged their wives. I knew my granddads had cheated on my grandmothers. Marriage had no merit in my book. But sex was good.

Chapter Twenty-Five
Do Me Twice

"How could you give it up like that? I told him all this stuff about my friend Ray-Ray. She's so smart. She graduated from high school when she was sixteen. Put herself through college. Yeah, she's working at *The Washington Post* already. How could you disrespect yourself like that?" Shawn was mad as hell, and she was beginning to piss me off with her judgment.

"It just happened," I tried to explain.

"In fifteen minutes, Ray!"

"I was stressed!"

"So much for putting you up on a pedestal."

"I never said I was no saint."

"I'm talking 'bout plain ole decency, Ray. You know I'm right… Damn. That's messed up."

"Okay, okay. Sorry. I'll try to clean it up. I slipped, that's all."

These self-righteous friends of mine had me going back and forth between what we had been trained to believe and the beliefs I was discovering for myself. They believed sex could only be special with one special guy, committed at least to being your boyfriend. I had discovered that my sexual organs were not close to the most valuable parts of me. They could be for my enjoyment and pleasure, but they were not the rarest of jewels we had been trained to believe they were. Nothing that could be taken, by a stranger or by a careless husband, could be valued as much as my untouchables—my heart, mind, and soul. I was discovering this, but in the process, slipping back to my old beliefs—that sex was necessarily serious and the most prized thing a woman could offer or keep, and therefore should be traded diligently.

I called Ted back to the room, motioned for him to sit on the bed, closed the door, and proceeded to explain that I really wasn't like that. I'd been having a hard time at school and work and please don't think of me that way and…I could sense he didn't care one way or the other.

"That just makes you an independent woman who knows what she wants, right?" he said, putting his hand on my knee for reassurance.

"I guess," I said, half-heartedly. Eventually, I would completely own, honor, understand and appreciate my sex drive for what it was— a sex drive, not necessarily a prelude to love, not always a bargaining chip. Eventually I'd freely invite men into my home or my life purely for the pleasure of sex, no pretense about romance necessary. This was only the beginning of my awareness of my sexual needs. Eventually, I'd feel confident about my sexual demands. Do me here, do me now, do it right, get up and do it again. Later, I would learn the joy of toys and do myself twice if that's what I needed— for stress relief. At this time, however, I was learning.

Later, I would learn that the majority of women never reach a climax. This made me further appreciate the fact that I can and I do. Prudes be damned. Of course they'd buy into the male mumbo-jumbo about women needing to guard their chastity. If more women enjoyed sex, no group of men could shut them down. It's no wonder in some African countries women must submit to having their clitoris removed. That's men trying to shut down our pleasure. Ted was opening my eyes. I had so much to learn.

"Yeah. You're a woman who knows what she wants and knows how to get it," he added.

"Let's just try to forget this ever happened, okay?" I asked.

"I'm cool," he said.

"Maybe we can go out some time and get to know each other," I added.

"Sure."

Not only did he not call me the rest of the week, but when I finally got his phone number from Mike and caught up with him Saturday evening, he had the nerve to front.

"Why you been ducking me?" I asked. I was in my bedroom about to get back in bed with my books to take notes for the paper I was working on. Shawn and Mike had just left for the movies.

"Don't act like I owe you something because *you* gave it up on the first date!" he said, cutting clear through to my core. I couldn't believe it. I looked at the phone.

"Huh?"

"You heard me. I know you been calling. It ain't like that between us."

"You faggot!"

"That's not what you was saying the other day..."

I slammed the phone down on him.

"Okay. Allah. I know I messed up. I'll try to be better," I prayed silently.

I was so angry I had to get up and use the bathroom, then pace the floor, then drink a tall cup of iced wine cooler.

Sissy-ass talkin' with a lisp gon' try to carry somebody! I thought.

Chee-Chee called to invite me to her church in the morning.

"I gotta finish this paper," I explained.

"Do it when you get back. I know you'll enjoy it," she insisted.

"Nope. Gotta get focused."

"Your ass need to go to church and stop all that craziness," she snapped.

I'd told her about the incident with Ted.

"Girl, I been in church all my life. I'm overdosed on religion, okay? You just now starting. I already been. Been there, done that."

She'd attended a Catholic church growing up, but her mother was nowhere near as intense about their religion as my mother had been about ours. Muslims were different from other religious folks, especially other Black religious folks. For most, religion was something you did on Sunday mornings, and maybe a couple nights out of the week—choir rehearsal and Bible study, if you were really into it. For Muslims, religion is a way of life governing everything you do from the way you eat to the way you wipe your behind when you go to the bathroom. We were supposed to do everything the way Prophet Muhammad had done right down to eating with the three forefingers on our right hand, wiping our behinds with the left hand. Some of us attended Juma prayer service on Friday afternoons and Talim, study service, on Sunday mornings. All of us had tried to maintain the five prayers a day. Prayers that each required a special ritual cleansing of one's body, and, well, by now I'd had enough religion. So, I told Chee-Chee, emphatically, NO!

"I'll pray for you," she said.

"I got enough prayers in heaven to last a lifetime," I shot back.

"Bye, girl," she finalized.

I hung up and opened my textbook on television production to finish drafting my paper. A couple hours later, I turned my lamp out and scooted under my top sheet for comfort. Didn't bother to take off my shirt or sweat pants. I got up to use the bathroom about six in the morning and noticed Shawn wasn't back. I hoped her mother wouldn't call first thing in the morning, leaving me to cover for her as I had last weekend. I pulled the sheet over my head for added comfort and dozed off again.

Sex became my equalizer. It freed me. With it I discovered my humanity—intense joy and pain, and isn't that what I came to life for? I mean, in heaven we're all obedient, right? Before we come to earth as human beings we're just spirit beings automatically in order with God's master plan, right? We come to earth to experience choices, right? I read so much and contended with so many theories about religion and spirituality, and was so unsure of what was real or right, I could just as easily stick to what was tried and true—sex. I could feel it, touch it, taste it, enjoy it, get lost in it, get found in it.

It wouldn't matter who I did it with. I just wanted to feel free, free from others' expectations of me, free from old traditions, and rules and regulations I had no stake in. Free. I had tried the marriage thing, marrying for all the wrong reasons: to avoid going to hell for fornicating. Well, hell is exactly what I found myself in with a husband. But I was free now, and maybe never again would I sign away the rights to my body and my life.

Grandma would say, "A man's gotta get a license to fish, make him get a license to lay with you," and I would think, "I am not a fish to be caught and consumed. What is wrong with you!" One of my male friends liked to say, "Why buy the cow when you can get the milk free?" and I'd yell, "I'm not a fuckin' piece of meat you can own!" I hated when women talked about "giving him some." I believed good sex was giving and receiving for all involved. If anything, the man is the one giving, he's the one who injects a part of himself to grow in a woman's body. I was finally going to enjoy sex on my own terms.

I was washing my face one night when I looked at the contours around my eyes and mouth and was glad they had not become hardened or permanently sad. I knew young women my age who looked like they'd lived a hard life, and I was glad my stripes weren't showing.

I crawled in bed, turned on the clock radio on the nightstand I'd bought recently, and stirred in my thoughts as I waited for sleep to come. My room smelled like dirty laundry, and Marvin Gaye's

"Sexual Healing" came on, reminding me of what I was missing now. I had been so wrong about sex. I remembered being fifteen years old believing sex must be the sweetest thing God put on earth, based on what I'd heard from my mother and her sister-friends. They laughed and talked about the sensuality and spirituality of sex, but taught us that such pleasures could only be enjoyed between a husband and wife. Sex outside of a sanctified union would lead one to hell as sure as the sun comes up in the mornings. We were taught that fornicators get cast into a fire where their skin burns off, they get more skin and that burns off, too. It didn't occur to me that everybody was sinning and if I did go to hell, all my friends would be there or on their way, too. I simply became afraid of fornication, but I figured maybe I could have it both ways. If I got raped by a good-looking guy, I could enjoy the pleasure without God holding me accountable for the sin, because it wouldn't be my fault that this man grabbed me, right? A cute guy could come along and rape me, as long as he didn't beat me up or anything, I thought. I could tell God, this tall, fine guy with a gorgeous smile made me do it.

Lying still with time to think, I wondered if I had unconsciously set myself up for those marital rapes. It seemed like the sickest thing, and really it was, but maybe I had created those rape experiences in my mind long before they materialized. Maybe I was blaming myself the way a judge in a courtroom blames a rape victim for wearing her clothes too short or tight, or having one too many drinks at a nightclub, then going home with a stranger, but I was beginning to reconcile my considerations. I'd considered the sensation between my legs when I washed to be sinful. I had struggled with my sexuality years before Ron entered my life and helped to dramatize that struggle. Now, I would struggle less. I would own my sexuality, and indulge it on my own terms.

Years later, Chee-Chee and I would laugh about the lessons we'd learned through horrible relationships. God, we laughed hard at our silly selves.

"Mitchell was my 'never' man," she said one of these times. "That's why I say 'never say never,' because the very thing you say you'd never do, you end up doing. I'd always said I'd never get with a man who'd been to jail, but if Mitchell's ass wasn't a criminal—who still needed to be in jail...giiiiirl!" We laughed.

"I still don't know how you hooked up with his funny-looking ass," I said.

"I just thank Jesus for deliverance! Glory! Hallelujah!" She laughed.

"Delivery? You still never told me what happened to break ya'll up. Sometimes when I dropped by, your ass was scared to let me in. I know you wasn't letting that little runt of a man put his hands on you," I said. "You coulda thrown his little ass across the room."

She was about twice his weight and at least an inch taller. And she'd been mean enough to survive the Wylie Street girls before Mitchell came along and clearly toned her down. He even changed her damn name back to what her mama named her. Told us that she was too grown for us to be calling her Chee-Chee. He called her Cynthia, and tried to make us, her friends, do the same. I fussed with him about petty stuff, and he tried to give her stuff to do for him or with him so she'd have less time to hang out with me shopping on Saturday mornings. He had changed her in ways I didn't like, but she never told me what was going on. She seemed more ready to talk about it years later when we could look back and laugh.

"Girl, size ain't got nothin' to do with it. That thing starts with mind control. That whole control thing starts with the mind," she said.

"Well, shit, Chee-Chee. You ain't never let nobody control your mind. Your mama couldn't tell you what to do. You never took my advice about going back to school to get a degree. How you let that little runt get ahold of your mind?"

"Girl, you know niggas that's been in prison know how to get to your mind. Them muthafuckas real manipulative. They start in little ways to see where you are first."

I remembered when I was going through Ron's drawers looking for something and found a to-do list he'd written in jail. I was on his damn to-do list. He'd planned to marry me before he even got me out on a date. He had planned to go to the University of the District of Columbia to major in business management, marry Sonsyrea, buy a car, buy a house, and start a business. In one of my college classes, our professor assigned us to create a visual plan for the future, and I had cut and pasted a magazine picture of a man in a business suit with a briefcase. I laughed when I realized that I'd ended up marrying a man in an illegal business—selling drugs. I was mad when I first saw my name on Ron's to-do list, but years later realized we both were learning to plan and visualize what we wanted in our future. I would learn to plan more carefully, and proceed with those plans more strategically.

In the meantime, I enjoyed chatting with Chee-Chee about the crazy stuff we did in our early twenties. Chee-Chee had wanted a man to be the head of her household ever since she was about six and her father left. Her mother had been their sole provider, and she'd felt like it was just unnatural for a woman to have to be the man and woman in the household. She liked the idea that Mitchell would pay all her bills and let her save the money she made as a teacher's assistant. It didn't matter that Mitchell abused his power, it only mattered that she got a chance to live her childhood fantasy—sort of. We both needed to outgrow our old fantasies. We both had to come to terms with the mess we had made and determine to do better in the future. Laughing about the hard times was a start. Laughing about it took the edge off the shame of it all. Laughing about it together lightened the burden of carrying those memories alone. We had been smart high school girls together, had become foolish young women together, and we could grow wiser, stronger, and better together.

"Girl, I think we both had a sign on our foreheads saying, "Fool. Ripe for the Picking." I laughed. "Haul-assing out of the house, tryin' like hell to get away from our family. Mad at the world. Yeah, we was ripe."

"Fresh meat," she added.

"Shit. They didn't even hafta lead us to the slaughter, our asses went running! Damn. What was it we were tryna prove?"

"Girl, who knows?! I just thank God for deliverance from that foolishness!" she said. She said something else that stuck with me for many years, something she'd heard from an older woman friend she met on her job that impressed her so much she couldn't wait to share it with me. I resented her new, older friend sometimes because she'd drag Chee-Chee off shopping or to church in the evenings, and I had less time with her, but one thing the older woman shared helped shape both our futures.

"Ms. Barbara says our experiences can make us better or bitter, and the difference is I," Chee-Chee said. I never forgot that.

Chapter Twenty-Six
Driven to Succeed

I broke down and cried in the classroom taking my last final exam. For the past four months I had worked full time, and studied a full-time course load, twelve credit hours. Also, I had worked with a youth radio network on weekends, producing radio shows by youth for youth. I was pooped. As the professor collected the final, my body just broke down and the tears streamed. Graduation day was still two weeks away, but I was done. All my financial paperwork had been cleared, all my papers signed off by the dean of the mass media department. I was done. I could begin planning my graduation celebration. My grandparents would want to come, also a few of my siblings, Aunt Nell, and even Ma. I didn't have a boyfriend, but a guy who liked me on the job offered to come and take pictures. Gary worked in the sports department and had a girlfriend, but this was an easy way for him to get some extra female attention and call it innocent.

I didn't have a boyfriend now because I was focused on landing my first job as a news reporter. I applied at newspapers across the country, sending, along with my resume or application for long-term internships, coveted letters of recommendation from two of my editors at the *Post*. Reading their letters about me proved enlightening, as they described me in ways I had not yet focused on.

"Sonsyrea Tate is tough-minded…and would be an asset to any newsroom," wrote one. "Sonsyrea Tate is ripe with potential…," wrote the other. The *Post* was one of the top five newspapers in the country at the time and only hired seasoned reporters who had cut their teeth—and been cut themselves—a few times at smaller newspapers in smaller cities. The *Washington Post* covered the nation's capital, the government of the most powerful country in the world. It rarely hired a full-time reporter fresh out of school, but I was hopeful.

I read the letters about my promise and felt hopeful about starting life anew after graduation.

I graduated on May 8, 1988 and was happy that my family was in the audience, cheering me on. At home that evening, other relatives dropped by my mother's house for cake and punch. They left me envelopes with cards and money, and a guy from my office who liked me came by taking pictures. I was excited about the whole evening, and especially wanted a picture of me and my girl Shawn next to the red Hyundai I had bought myself as a birthday/graduation present. We were set to drive off into new lives.

"Cheese," Gary, the guy from my office, said, backing up to get a full view of both of us and the car.

"Heeeeeey!" was what we said, throwing our hands in the air in high celebration.

He snapped the photo, a memory I would keep forever.

Epilogue
Almost Left Behind

In January 2007, I joined a large group for the first annual Martin Luther King Jr. Peace Walk in a community that had been wracked by black-on-black violence. At the beginning of the walk, right after some rah-rah-we're-gonna-take-back-the-streets speeches, Brother Anthony Muhammad struck up a conversation and struck up a nerve.

"So, sister, what do you think about eating one meal a day," he began. "Think about it. One meal a day. You know some of what you learned in the Nation of Islam had to be good," he added. "What do you think about that?"

I realized I've had this conversation often enough with other men since leaving the Nation of Islam. So, I tried to make light of it this time.

"You crackin' on my weight?" I said, joking.

"No, I read the column you wrote, and I got one question: wasn't there anything good you could say about the Nation? It couldn't have been all bad."

I've had similar conversations with Muslim men who practiced Orthodox Islam. Some of them try to convince me that I've foolishly gone astray and they're sure that I will return to the fold. Some shake their heads and suggest that I've gone astray and I am forever condemnable, damned and bound for eternal hell. A few of the wiser or more compassionate Muslim brothers sought to put into context some of the teachings I had found so befuddling. Brother

Muhammad, before the end of our conversation, would do a little of it all.

We debated the merits of the teachings of the Nation of Islam first.

"Sure there was some good, but the price for it was way too high," I said.

I tried to change the subject, knowing where this discussion was headed.

"Let's talk about the weather or something. Isn't it amazing how the rain held up and the sun shined on this walk?"

In mid-January, we were enjoying temperatures in the fifties and sixties, not fully aware that this was indication of the ominous global warming environmentalists feared. Brother Muhammad wanted to discuss his religion, however. Specifically, he wanted to discuss my public criticism of his religion.

He said he had a copy of my first book, *Little X: Growing Up in the Nation of Islam*. "I haven't finished reading it, but I got it."

"You need to read it," I said. "In fact, you need to get the new edition with the new intro. That's where I began to realize some of the good. Read it. My grandmother's read it at least eight times. She loves it because it takes her back to the day. She said every time she reads it, she gets something different."

Brother Muhammad walked in front of his wife and her girlfriend. One of his granddaughters walked in front of us as the crowd we were in proceeded along the avenue named after the civil rights leader whose mission of peace, justice, and equality we were honoring.

Getting no cooperation from me on honoring the teachings of the Nation of Islam, Brother Muhammad tried to discredit that I had sufficient knowledge of or involvement in the Nation anyhow. Since I was only in the Nation, studying its teachings until I was ten, he said, I couldn't possibly know enough about the Nation of Islam to offer an informed judgment. Never mind that I grew up hearing stories and history about the Nation of Islam from my family members who had been members since my grandparents joined as pioneers.

"But *you* were only in it for ten years," he said. "That's like having an elementary school education and trying to go teach college."

I explained that I studied Islam as a Muslim the first twenty years of my life and had the benefit—or burden depending on which day you ask me—of my family's history as Muslims, as well. That was more than enough information and insight for me, I explained. In fact, that was too much.

"Brother, puh-lease. I wish that ten years had not been too much," I said. "That thing was intense. Do you know how long it takes to get over some of that nonsense? Hell. It took me more than ten years to de-brief and come to my damn senses."

He defended the theories we had learned about a mad scientist creating the Caucasian race as an experiment. We had also bought into Elijah Muhammad's theory that overweight individuals should be taxed a penny for each pound they were overweight because they breathed too much air and put too much burden on the earth's surface due to their gluttony. Walking this walk, listening to his talk reminded me of some of the nonsense I was spoon-fed growing up, nonsense it took me twenty years to shake off.

"Brother, ya'll had me out at a picnic, looking up at something in the sky calling it a damn Mother Ship. What kind of nonsense is that for a kid to have to explain?"

"It's the Mother Plane. Don't get it confused with Parliament's Mothership," he said. "You think the Mother Plane's not real?"

I noticed that the main crowd was getting farther away from us. People waved to Mr. Muhammad from across the street. He was an elected official in this neighborhood and many people liked and respected him. He was short, stocky, and cute in a rugged way. I mean, I could imagine him winning a street fight and he was known to speak his mind. But much of his reasoning sounded like old school rhetoric to me. It could impress some young women who had not already been where I had been. He kept asking how old I was and I insisted I was older and smarter than I looked. Bitterness had not become me. I did not wear life's disappointments as if they had worn me out. In fact, by January 2007, I was quite happy with my life, happy with the way I was raised, happy with the unconventional faith I had learned from my parents, and happy about the traditions handed down by their parents. By now, I was happy that I had enjoyed many men and many jobs and many ups and many downs.

By now I did not need this conversation to blame Nation of Islam officials for screwing up my life, nor did I need to hear their explanations of why things had been the way they were. By now, I felt like it was all good. I mean it had all worked together for good, just like the good book says.

"Brother, why are we even having this conversation? Isn't this your third or fourth marriage anyway? You know ya'll run through women, playing marriage like most folks play girlfriend and boyfriend," I said.

I'd heard too many stories about pious women keeping themselves chaste, hoping to get one of those good Muslim brothers, getting left behind as their men find pleasures elsewhere. I've also heard too many stories of women struggling to raise children after their Muslim husband pronounced three times, "I divorce you," and called it done.

"How many boyfriends have you had, sister?" Brother Muhammad shot back.

"That's different," I said. "We knew we were playing and didn't call it anything but playing." I tried to explain that when a woman accepts and takes control of her sexuality and sensuality, she's as apt to call a brother just for physical pleasure as any man. She won't need to pretend it's love or pretend she wants to marry him to give honor to a physical act that's plain old natural. Owning my sensuality and sexuality was a first step, a baby step. Controlling it more than it controlled me would take many, many years—and by January 2007 I wasn't quite there. But Brother Muhammad couldn't comprehend—or wouldn't concede—that a pretty, smart, spiritually sophisticated woman such as me—could call her own shots, that I wasn't completely yanked around by men pulling on my heart strings or my libido.

"You know you're lying," he said. "You know ya'll want a brother to say he's all in love and promise he's gon' marry you."

"Not when you own your heart and soul and own your sexuality," I said. "But why are we even having this conversation?"

I realized that we had drifted behind the others in the Peace Walk, and I motioned to catch up.

"Step up the pace, brother. You got me lagging behind."

We caught up to the crowd and I enjoyed the rest of the day, sunny, brilliant, and now, more energized than I'd expected.

Blessed Just Because

What I know for sure twenty years after graduating from college is this: God is good, and God is great, and God is in me. I know that God is no mystery up in the sky—neither is hell a mythical pit of fire in our collective imaginations.

After all the drama and trauma; after the nonsense and foolishness, often even in the midst of it all, I know that God is great, and God's love is unconditional. This love cannot be bought, sold, stolen, manipulated or traded, I have learned. God's love, to me, is like the air, it just is, and it sustains us just because. God's love is like the ocean that rushes ashore and refreshes sinners and all the same.

I got married on the beach, December 2006, and the moment crystallized God's grace in my life. In that moment, as white and yellow sunrays streaked the clear blue sky, and the sounds of the ocean washing ashore and people playing happily all around filled the air, I knew I was blessed. In the future I would appreciate blessings big and small. More than thirty-five close friends and family members had managed, with short notice, to book travel packages and take off from work a few days to join this celebration. They had noticed a rainbow in the sky as their airplane approached landing in Jamaica that Thursday. For the next four days we would enjoy more food, fun, and fellowship than any of us had imagined.

I had not done all the right things in life to deserve such a moment. I had not struggled to hold on to a good government job, or a good corporate job, which would afford me such a luxury. Neither had I mustered the faith and fortitude to strike it rich as an independent entrepreneur, but here I was on my third trip to the Caribbean islands in a year, and here I was, surrounded by family and friends enjoying much love and laughter. I had not maintained chastity or even managed a year of celibacy, but here I was marrying a very loving, very supportive, very respectful young man. God's love is unconditional.

I had not prayed five times a day in Arabic, fasted during the month of Ramadan, given to Muslim-sanctioned charities, or traveled to the Middle East to make Hajj, following the dictates of my Muslim upbringing. But here I was enjoying a moment of God's blessings just the same. I was reminded of something I learned in a Christian university when I was working on a master's degree in my thirties. The professors there, at this predominantly white university, taught that God blesses people not because they have been perfect but in order that they can become more perfect. Now that was a novel belief, a belief that liberated me from several points of guilt.

In the twenty years since leaving Islam and inching toward Christianity, I had not gone to church every Sunday, tithed ten percent of all my earnings, or studied the Bible to "show myself approved," but here I stood, blessed just the same.

The man I was marrying had not been raised in a church, did not profess any love of God or religion, but his kindness and compassion far surpassed that of many Bible-toting brothers I'd encountered.

In recent years I enjoyed powerful sermons by Bishop T.D. Jakes, Joel Osteen, and dozens of less-known, but equally powerful ministers—men and women. I enjoyed those who challenged traditions and conventional wisdom because in some ways they were speaking for me—speaking what I knew in my heart to be true—and in other ways they provided a better understanding of issues that confounded and confused me. I enjoyed the final freedom to enjoy and embrace religion at my own pace, according to my own needs and offerings.

Standing on the beach shore, looking out at the ocean stretching as far as I could see, I felt redeemed, refreshed, and ready for whatever the future may hold. The future certainly would bring more fun-filled, sunny days of absolute indulgence, and days where I'd have to run for cover like everyone else out of a storm's path. The future would bring more days of familiar support, but also days of isolation when I might need to reflect or recuperate. Whatever the future had in store, at this moment I felt blessed to be standing at the threshold of a new life.

The past twenty years, I realized, had not been so bad. In fact, T.D. Jakes' sermon, "It's All Good," put it all in perspective better than I could.

"Everything you went through, it's aaaaaalllllll good!" he shouted in his New Year Revival Sermon at the Washington Convention Center. I used to hate to hear Baptist-style preachers whooping and hollering, but Jakes' sermon sounded like singing. "Every heartbreak, every disappointment. Every job you lost, every person that betrayed you. It's aaaaaaaallllllll good!" he continued. All things work together for good for those who know the Lord and are called unto his purpose, he reminded the crowd. "In fact, I want you to go home tonight and call somebody and just say, 'thank you.' Tell them 'thank you for firing me because if you hadn't fired me, I wouldn't be in the position God wants me in today. Thank you!"

I went into the new year feeling thankful for the first twenty years of my life and empowered by the next twenty. But the past twenty years is another story for another day.

Thank you for your time and interest in reading this book.

About the Author

Sonsyrea Tate is the author of the highly acclaimed memoir, *Little X: Growing Up in the Nation of Islam*, and has lectured on Islam in the African American community, women in Islam, and telling stories in the African American tradition at many universities and colleges, drawing from her first-hand experiences and research. She has worked as a news reporter for several newspapers, and appeared as a news commentator on local radio and television stations in Washington, D.C. She is managing editor of *The Washington Informer* newspaper in Washington, D.C., and also an adjunct professor of journalism at the University of Maryland at College Park. She lives in Maryland with her husband. She may be reached at sonsyrea@yahoo.com. Visit www.sonsyrea.com

Questions for Book Clubs/ Class Discussions

1) Did the main character appreciate or regret her Muslim upbringing? Explain.

2) Why was she attracted to Ron?

3) Why was Ron attracted to her?

4) What was the pivotal point in her life, the point when she decided to change?

5) Who/what most influenced her to change?

6) Why was it so difficult to change, break from her Muslim ideas and practices?

7) What impact did the abortion have on her personality?

8) What impact did the marital rape have on her personality?

9) What were some of the life lessons she learned through these years?

10) How did these young adult experiences shape her views of God and religion in the end?